All Work and No Play...
How Educational Reforms Are Harming Our Preschoolers

EDITED BY SHARNA OLFMAN

Childhood in America

PRAEGER

Westport, Connecticut
London

Library of Congress Cataloging-in-Publication Data

All work and no play . . . : how educational reforms are harming our preschoolers /
   edited by Sharna Olfman.
        p. cm. — (Childhood in America)
      Includes bibliographical references and index.
      ISBN 0–275–97768–4 (alk. paper)
        1. Early childhood education—United States—Philosophy.   2. Child development.
   3. Learning.   I. Olfman, Sharna.   II. Series.
   LB1139.25.A44   2003
   372.21—dc21   2003053621

British Library Cataloguing in Publication Data is available.

Library of Congress Catalog Card Number: 2003053621
ISBN: 0–275–97768–4

First published in 2003

Praeger Publishers, 88 Post Road West, Westport, CT 06881
An imprint of Greenwood Publishing Group, Inc.
www.praeger.com

Printed in the United States of America

The paper used in this book complies with the
Permanent Paper Standard issued by the National
Information Standards Organization (Z39.48–1984).

10 9 8 7 6 5 4 3 2 1

For my parents Bess Leve and Mitchell Olfman
with my deepest gratitude and admiration.

Contents

Acknowledgments

I would like first and foremost to thank the contributors to this anthology, all of whom worked diligently to bring this project to fruition. Individually, each has made a substantial contribution to research on childhood, and collectively, their voices are a potent force that cannot be ignored. My acquisitions editor at Greenwood, Debora Carvalko, was very quick to recognize the worth of this project, and has been a supportive presence throughout. Kim Bell, Chair of the Department of Humanities and Human Sciences, made herself readily available to share ideas and lend support. I wish to thank Michele Perel Phillips and Tom Bell for their evocative photographs. Joe Zabka, reference librarian at the Point Park/Carnegie Library Center tirelessly tracked down several obscure references, always with good humor and efficiency. My deepest thanks go to my husband Daniel Burston, whose extraordinary intellect is matched by his generosity of spirit. We began a conversation fourteen years ago that shows no signs of abating, and has had a profound influence on my work. *All Work and No Play . . .* launches a new book series entitled "Childhood in America." I dedicate this series to my dear children Adam and Gavriela, who have made the study of childhood irresistible, and inspire me to work toward the betterment of children's lives.

Introduction

SHARNA OLFMAN

Education in America is undergoing a sweeping reform. Its guiding mantra is "Standards, Accountability, Testing, and Technology" and its effects reverberate from Ivory Towers to Head Start programs. At the preschool and kindergarten level, it translates into early academics, "scripted teaching," desk work, computer-based learning, and a paucity of play. As a result, a rich multidisciplinary literature demonstrating the critical role of play for cognitive, social, emotional, and ethical development—a literature that was decades in the making—is being ignored.

Remarkably, current educational reforms are not driven by the findings and recommendations of educators and child-development experts, but by politicians and policymakers at the federal, state, and local levels, with the express intention of ensuring America's competitive edge in the new information-based economy. This agenda was first articulated in the 1983 Nation at Risk report, issued by President Reagan's National Commission on Excellence:

> If only to keep and improve on the slim competitive edge we still retain in world markets, we must dedicate ourselves to the reform of our educational system . . . Learning is the indispensable investment required for success in the 'information age' we are entering (cited in Kane, 1999, p. 10)

The "high-stakes" testing movement and race to "wire the class-room" were launched by Reagan in 1983, given renewed vigor by Presidents Bush and Clinton, and have now gained further momentum with George W. Bush's 2001 No Child Left Behind Act, which received overwhelming bipartisan support. On January 16, 2003, the current administration announced that it is implementing a standardized assessment of all four-year-olds in Head Start programs nationwide to assess reading readiness, thus officially delivering "high-stakes" testing to preschoolers. In addition, the Early Care and Education Act, now before Congress, will give bonuses to states that demonstrate that their preschool programs are successfully teaching early literacy skills, necessitating even more academic pressure and wide-scale testing of preschoolers.

TESTING AND TECHNOLOGY: A FAILING GRADE

Given that education reform is now spearheaded by politicians and the corporate elite rather than by experts in childhood, it comes as no surprise that the "accountability" movement, now in its twentieth year, and its handmaiden, "the wired classroom," has not only failed to improve education, but indeed, has also undermined it. Recent results of the congressionally mandated National Assessment of Educational Progress (NAEP), commonly referred to as the Nation's Report Card, which has been assessing school performance for almost thirty years, reveal that states with the *highest* stakes attached to standardized testing are more likely to perform below average on the NAEP, whereas states that give minimum import to standardized tests are more likely to perform above the average. Furthermore, in 1998, the highly acclaimed Third International Math and Science Study (TIMSS), which compared a half-million students from forty-one countries, revealed that U.S. high school seniors were tied for last place in math among developed nations (Sacks, 1999).

"Teaching to the Test": Narrower and Shallower

The impact of tying teachers' and administrators' bonuses, salaries, and job security; state and federal funding of schools; and students' graduation to standardized tests is that teachers are compelled to "teach to the tests." The tests, which are usually multiple-choice, merely sample the curriculum and do not assess depth of understanding, meaningful application of knowledge, or original thinking. Consequently, the curriculum becomes narrower and shallower, and drills, rote learning, and practice tests increasingly dominate the teaching methods. James Stigler and his colleagues from UCLA demonstrated this by analyzing videotapes of Japanese, American, and German high school math classes as part of the TIMSS assessment: "[R]ote, mechanical, and superficial teaching was far more evident in the American classrooms than in Japan" (cited in Sacks, 1999, p. 133). The Japanese lessons covered much less content in any given class as compared to the American lessons, but did so for the purposes of achieving depth of understanding, and meaningful and creative application of the concepts.

In the race for high test scores, kindergarten students and even preschoolers are now subjected to a similar barrage of academic drill work at an age when they are meant to learn through play and hands-on experience. If the NAEP and TIMSS results are any indication, these teaching methods are unsuccessful; yet, they are being introduced at increasingly younger ages, in the vain hope that they'll somehow "take," if we start young enough.

Screens in Preschool: "Failure to Connect"

A very similar scenario prevails with respect to computer use in the classroom. As Jane Healy (1998) documents in *Failure to Connect: How Computers Affect Our Children's Minds and What We Can Do about It*, children with specific handicaps and older children benefit from thoughtful applications of computer and Internet technologies. But their use with preschoolers and children in the early grades actually undermines the very skills that they are intended to support: literacy, higher-order thinking, problem solving, and creativity. Even when young children learn to decode the words on the page with the aid of reading software, they are often unable to understand what they have read, let alone apply the knowledge meaningfully; a trait that Healy terms "alliteracy." And certainly, the pervasive presence of screens in our culture undermines the desire to read. As Barry Sanders (1995) argues in *A Is for Ox*, the proliferation of screen technologies actually threatens to eradicate literacy.

TESTING AND TECHNOLOGY: THE KEY TO THEIR POPULARITY

And yet, despite these dismal prognoses, the titans of testing and technology remain popular among policymakers and the general public. Given the appalling results of these reforms so far, their appeal is remarkably robust. Why? Perhaps the rhetoric surrounding them contains a piece of the puzzle. Standardized testing and access to the Internet are nowadays touted as the great levelers in society which will ensure quality education for all. "No Excuses" is the motto of the No Child Left Behind Act. Parents are told that all children and schools will be held to a uniform standard of excellence and given access to the same vast store of information through the Internet. And so, whether a child becomes a president or a street person depends exclusively on her own effort and resolve.

These rhetorical strategies are irresistible on two counts. First, any thoughtful and ethical individual supports, indeed *demands*, high standards and accountability from the public school system. With the co-optation of the language of "standards," it becomes difficult to stand in opposition. Unfortunately, the critical debate about what these standards should be and how they should be measured is not taking place. Second, the rhetoric of "standards" embodies the quintessential American Dream: "Hard work and fair play will liberate us from the bondage of blood lines, social class, and racism."

The reality, however, is that the "accountability" movement is profoundly deepening class and race divisions. As Peter Sacks (1999) noted in *Standardized Minds*:

> [I]f social engineers had set out to invent a virtually perfect inequality machine, designed to perpetuate class and race divisions, and that appeared to abide by all requisite state and federal laws and regulations, those engineers could do no better than the present-day accountability systems already put to use in American schools. (p. 158)

Standardized Testing: Rooted in Racism

The use of standardized intelligence tests as tools of racist policies has a long and inglorious history in the United States. Terman and Brigham, the American Fathers of standardized testing, were overtly racist in their attitudes and agenda (cited in Sacks, 1999). Today, the rhetoric of testing is more politically correct, but the overall effects are the same; the measurements we are using to assess children are culturally loaded in favor of white middle- and upper-middle-class children (Biddle, cited in Sacks, 1999). The race to "wire" the classroom often intensifies these problems. When poor school districts feel compelled to overcrowd their classrooms; strip their libraries; and eliminate music, art, physical education, and playtime in order to pay for computer and Internet access—so that their students can take "field trips" on-line—quality of education is tragically diminished (Cordes & Miller, 2000). As a result, across the nation, poor and minority children in dramatically disproportionate numbers are failing, and are made to feel like failures.

Egalitarianism versus Genetic Determinism

This sad state of affairs reflects a curious paradox at the heart of American culture. On the one hand, we embrace ideals of egalitarianism and self-determination. On the other, we are captivated by the deterministic notion that all of our traits, including personality, intelligence, creativity, and mental health, are chiefly determined by our genes. Genes do contribute significantly to our physical and psychological makeup, but their effects are exquisitely sensitive to environmental input. Nevertheless, the media feeds our insatiable appetite for stories about the genome project, cloning, or the latest claim that gene A is the "depression" gene and gene B dictates our preference for Pepsi over Coca-Cola. And in this climate of striking cultural contradictions, we allow intelligence and achievement scores, which allegedly disclose children's true abilities, to determine their future, regardless of their abilities in the real world. Similarly, we seek to enhance our genetically programmed brains, which we liken to organic computers. If a child is struggling in the classroom, we are more likely to tinker with their "hardware" by using drugs that increase attention or lessen anxiety than to address underlying psychological or socioeconomic issues that give rise to their symptoms. Environment has very little role in our gene-driven discourse on learning nowadays, so we have no qualms about holding different children or different school districts to the same standard, despite dramatically diverse circumstances. As a result, the following scenarios become increasingly common.

Mary attends a school that is rich in resources, with small classes, state-of-the-art science labs, yearly textbook upgrades, a beautiful library, weekly field trips, well-paid and well-educated teachers, and an abundance of parent volunteers. She lives in a safe neighborhood with lawns that beckon her to play, and has access to the finest medical care. Conversely, Susan dodges bullets and drug dealers on her walk home from school. Her school is drafty, overcrowded, and has a high turnover rate of underpaid teachers struggling with dated textbooks. She had to enter the hospital as an emergency case before receiving treatment for a recent infection, and her devoted mother, a single parent, works two full-time, minimum-wage jobs to make ends meet. At 10 P.M., Susan still waits anxiously for her mother to return home from work, with the noise of the television to bolster her courage and keep her "company." Before her mother returns, she warms a can of soup for herself and her little brother. She struggles to make sense of her homework, but fear and loneliness overwhelm her.

Mary and her school district performed well above average on the mandatory state end-of-year assessment. Her parents are proud of her test scores, and district teachers received handsome bonuses. But Susan missed the cutoff score by a few points and has to repeat her year. Her school district is in desperate need of resources and teachers, but was denied both state and federal aid and placed on notice. Susan feels demoralized; her self-esteem is shaken. Her mother tries to enroll her in a neighboring school district with better resources, but is told that they have a waiting list.

Meanwhile, Susan's brother, Joseph, is four years old. He is enrolled in a Head Start program. His class is large, and support staff has been downsized because a portion of the budget went to the purchase of new computers and reading software. Play has been eliminated from the curriculum to give children like Joseph a "leg-up" in the academic race. Joseph is small for his age, slightly malnourished, chronically asthmatic, and longs for affection and the opportunity to run freely and play, unfettered by concerns for safety. He struggles to sit still in front of the computer terminal. On the recommendation of his teacher, Joseph is sent to a local clinic where he receives a diagnosis of Attention Deficit Hyperactivity Disorder (ADHD) and a prescription for Ritalin. He no longer disrupts the class. However, by the time Joseph is in middle school, he has been held back twice and has been taking Ritalin for a decade. Lacking hope and incentive to do better, he now hoards and sells Ritalin on the street to buy clothes, CDs, or drugs that are more to his liking.

By the logic of "accountability," Mary and Susan were measured by the same yardstick. So either Susan didn't try hard enough or she is simply less capable than Mary. Clearly, though, the root cause of Susan and Joseph's classroom struggles are not genetics or the absence of standards, but poverty, a two-tiered school system, and the absence of essential family services such as subsidized and regulated day care and after-school programs, a living wage, and humane medical coverage. Thus, under the guise of equality, the system privileges wealthy families and the corporations who manufacture the testing and computer technologies. Admittedly, the story of Susan and Joseph might have turned out differently. They might have beaten the odds, succeeded academically and gone on to successful careers; many such children do just that. However, the issue is not whether it is *possible* to do so, but whether it is morally defensible to require some children to leap over so many additional hurdles along the way.

THE "INFORMATION-PROCESSING" APPROACH TO EDUCATION

Although the current educational climate creates unequal conditions for poor and minority children, it is important to emphasize that it is actually less than optimal for *any and all* children. As explained below, the proliferation of computer and Internet technologies has altered how we conceptualize learning, and the educational goals we establish for our children are to their detriment.

In the 1960s, inspired by breakthroughs in the computer field, psychologists created the "information-processing" model of cognition, which likens the mind to a computer. Information-processing research analyzes how children manipulate information in order to solve problems, and has generated beneficial learning strategies in circumscribed situations, such as approaching a particular content area more efficiently or supporting children with learning disabilities. Beyond that, however, information-processing research has had a profound influence on curriculum development in the average American classroom, eclipsing other approaches to cognition that were once more influential in the field of education, including Piaget's (1950) stage theory and Vygotsky's (1978) sociocultural theory. Piaget's work underscored the value of experiential/discovery learning, and the need to be aware of developmental time lines and individual differences. Vygotsky emphasized that learning is a culturally embedded activity that requires sensitive mentoring.

However, the presence of computers in the classroom and the pressure to prepare children for standardized tests mesh well with the information-processing approach. The Piagetian revolution that transformed the classroom in the '60s and '70s from a place of passive learning to an experiential workshop, and the opportunities for one-on-one mentoring afforded by small class size, are rapidly receding into the background and being replaced by "scripted teaching" and computer programs that prepare children for multiple-choice tests.

There is a potent synergy between mechanistic models of the mind and the current technological revolution that numbs our hearts and dulls our minds, so we become increasingly comfortable with the idea that children are information processors, or that the mind is an organic computer, and that education should have the explicit goal of preparing our children to serve technology-based industries. In the current climate, which is rife with contradictions and an overweening technocratic agenda that blinds us to our children's real needs, it becomes easy, indeed expedient, to overlook the glaring limitations of a mind-as-machine metaphor.

So, let us be clear. In sharp contrast to a computer, a child possesses a *self*, which imbues her with the desire to give her life meaning, purpose, and a moral compass. A child is motivated to learn by the desire to be grounded in her family, in her community, and the natural order, and yet at the same time to express herself and place her own personal stamp on the world. Her thinking is infused with emotion, sensory and bodily kinesthetic experience, artistry, imagination, and soulfulness. It is through this uniquely *human* prism, in the service of uniquely *human* needs, that she processes information. Thus, it is a tragic irony that we idealize the disembodied, emotionless computer and try to teach our children to think according to its operating principles. Unfortunately, however, when mere information is what we seek to instill or elicit from our students, the content and context of the information at issue becomes completely secondary to one's ability to access and manipulate it. Real psychological growth ceases, and the educational system encourages a growing cynicism and despair, evidenced in a recent upsurge in adolescent homicide and suicide attempts.

Developmental Stages—The Missing Link

A significant flaw in the information-processing model is that (1) it does not recognize the role of (biologically influenced) stages of development, and (2) it artificially separates cognitive processes from other lines of development. Piaget (1950) taught us that development unfolds over time in recognizable stages that nonetheless allow for considerable individual variation. In each of these stages, a child's understanding of her world is *qualitatively* different, and in the preschool and kindergarten years, children learn optimally through play, hands-on experience, artistic expression, and sensitive mentoring. In addition, it is now apparent that all modes of development, including the intellectual, social, emotional, ethical, personality, and physical, are inextricably linked (Greenspan, 1997). We embrace stage theories that pertain to our children's physical development: they must be able to sit before they can stand, stand before they can walk,

and so on. We understand that the child who enters puberty at sixteen as opposed to eleven is nonetheless normal, and may tower over
us five years hence. However, we have no such patience for cognitive abilities. Woe to the child who, for example, comes late to her
handedness, and consequently reads and writes at seven, rather than
five!

In the absence of sound guidelines to inform curriculum development, we have no qualms about taking a curriculum designed for students in grade one and forcing it on preschoolers to boost their
achievement. At the same time, we demote play, artistic expression,
and experiential learning to the status of mere diversions (in between
the "real" work contained in worksheets) and substitute face time
with computers for human mentoring. Then, when students struggle
with the content or format of the curriculum, we bristle with an impressive array of psychiatric labels and a powerful pharmacopoeia
of psychiatric drugs, when often what is needed is the patience and
sensitivity to allow their development to unfold, and humane teaching methods that do not compartmentalize thought, feeling, and
social development, as we typically insist on doing.

RECLAIMING THE LANGUAGE OF STANDARDS
AND ACCOUNTABILITY

The goal of this anthology is to reclaim the language of *standards* and
accountability, and ground them in principles of child development and
humane pedagogy in the service of educating children to be caring,
ethical, creative human beings, who prize humanity and nature, and
who will be masters rather than servants of the technologies they help
to create. This anthology represents the work of educators and academics from the disciplines of neurology, educational philosophy, and psychology, who are concerned about recent trends in education and
technology, having dedicated years of their professional lives to studying the nature of learning, the vital role of play, and the impact of computer technologies on children's lives.

ORGANIZATION OF THE ANTHOLOGY

Each of the chapters can be read independently. A brief biography
of the contributor is located at the end of each chapter. The volume is
divided thematically into four parts:

Part I: The Power of Play in Early Childhood Education

The first section examines the current climate of early childhood education in the United States and Europe in relation to wider cultural trends. The authors reflect on the nature of a developmentally appropriate preschool curriculum, with an emphasis on the role of play.

In Chapter 1, Joan Almon, a renowned Waldorf kindergarten consultant and coordinator of the U.S. branch of the Alliance for Childhood, brings three decades of experience to her observations on the vital role of play in child development. Using vivid case examples, she elucidates the nature of play and reviews its benefits for social, emotional, and intellectual development. Almon ties the demise of play in the classroom and on the playground to the influence of screen entertainments, and to federal legislation that has been a catalyst for early academics and "scripted teaching." Almon also explores the relationship between play and health in childhood. The chapter concludes with recommendations on how to foster healthy play in the classroom, and how to advocate for change at the policy level.

Dorothy G. Singer, senior research scientist in the Department of Psychology at Yale University, and Jerome L. Singer, professor of psychology at Yale University, have made a prolific contribution to the literature on play, including *The House of Make-Believe: Children's Play and the Developing Imagination* and *Make-Believe: Games and Activities for Imaginative Play*. In Chapter 2, together with research assistants Sharon L. Plaskon and Amanda E. Schweder, the Singers present their innovative "Learning through Play" research, in which teachers and parents of preschoolers were given the tools and training to stimulate healthy symbolic play. The project was developed as a corrective to the dearth of play in preschool curricula, and the abysmal level of school readiness among preschool children. The play intervention resulted in significantly higher test scores of school readiness. The authors include an overview of new federal and state guidelines that promote early formal academic curricula and compare them with the results of a survey of what teachers and parents regard as essential criteria for preschool programs. They also describe settings in which preschool children are typically spending time; while some settings are exemplary, in a majority of cases, play is viewed as a form of relaxation or entertainment and is not meaningfully incorporated into the curriculum.

In Chapter 3, Christopher Clouder, director of the European Council for Steiner Waldorf Education and cofounder of the Alliance for Childhood, presents illuminating research on European trends in early childhood education. In striking contrast to the United States, where formal academics now begin in preschool, several European countries are in the process of *raising* the age at which they begin formal schooling to six or seven in light of research that demonstrates that children have greater academic success when they begin their studies later. While American federal policy emphasizes that education is a tool for economic success, many European policymakers start from the assumption that "the interests of young children are the interests of the whole of society" (Clouder, p. 72). Recent policy statements emphasize that education and care are conjoined, and must be flexible and developmentally appropriate.

Part II: Wired Classrooms/Wired Brains

The next section examines the direct and indirect impact of the computer on child development and pedagogy. Increasingly, the computer is used as a classroom tool, or even as a surrogate teacher, but it has also shaped how we *define* intelligence and our educational goals. In addition, the computer may also be "hard-wiring" children's brains.

Educational psychologist Jane M. Healy is an internationally renowned educational consultant and the author of several books on children's brain development. In Chapter 4, she describes the impact of computer use on brain development and on every facet of psychological functioning, including motor coordination, perception, attention, memory, self-concept, imagination, language, and thought in early childhood. She underscores the importance of respecting developmental imperatives and the critical role of play, physical activity, hands-on learning, the arts, and mentoring as key ingredients for healthy learning environments and healthy brain development.

In Chapter 5, Frank R. Wilson, a clinical professor of neurology at Stanford University, and author of the Pulitzer Prize–nominated book *The Hand: How Its Use Shapes the Brain, Language, and Human Culture*, argues that the computer is at the center of our current educational crisis. He takes us on a twenty-five-million-year evolutionary journey to demonstrate that the evolving hand provided the stimulus for changes in brain function, and that the human brain and hand have become an integrated system for perception and action. The hand is a catalyst and an experiential focal point for the organization of the young child's perceptual, motor, cognitive, and creative world, which passive, screen-based learning is threatening to undermine.

Part III: Building Blocks of Intellectual Development: Emotion and Imagination

In this section, we see that contemporary theories of intelligence are the direct heirs of the Enlightenment philosophy of Rene Descartes, who privileged abstract thought that was devoid of emotion and direct experience. It is this disembodied ideal that is at the root of a system of education built around computerized learning and standardized testing.

In Chapter 6, Jeffrey Kane, an educational philosopher and vice president for academic affairs at Long Island University, and his research assistant, Heather Carpenter, present biographical sketches of Nobel Prize–winning geneticist Barbara McClintock, Albert Einstein, and renowned architect Frank Lloyd Wright. We learn that the intellectual depth and originality of their thought was dependent on their imaginative capacity, which they developed through *creative play as children*. Kane and Carpenter demonstrate not only that child's play does not detract from intellectual development, but also that when children are obligated to work precociously at formal academic lessons before the imagination has become a "vital, fluid foundation for knowledge," their future ability for original scientific or artistic discovery is compromised.

Stuart Shanker is a professor of philosophy and psychology at York University, Canada, a prolific author, and codirector (with Stanley Greenspan) of the Council of Human Development. In Chapter 7, he presents Greenspan's path-finding research, which demonstrates that emotions create, organize, and orchestrate many of the mind's most important functions, including intelligence and emotional health. He locates the difficulties we are experiencing in education today in Descartes's rationalist philosophy that reason must govern the "base emotions." To this day, cognitive scientists continue to study child development as if a child's emotional growth had no intrinsic bearing on cognitive development. "The analogy here to our attitudes towards education is disturbingly apposite. For the fact is that the rationalist model of education is so entrenched in our thinking, that, despite the legion of problems that we are witnessing today, which get worse every year, we cannot conceive of any alternative to the current course we are on, except to pursue it even more aggressively" (Shanker, p. 152).

Part IV: A Mental Health Crisis among Our Children: The Rise of Technologies and Demise of Play

In this section, the authors examine the impact of increasingly stressful and developmentally inappropriate learning environments on children's mental health.

In Chapter 8, Thomas Armstrong, educational psychologist and award-winning author, presents compelling evidence that current approaches to education that promote screen time and minimize opportunity for play are exacerbating the Attention Deficit Hyperactivity Disorder epidemic. The "rapid-fire" stimulation that children are exposed to increasingly on television and computers requires the brain to adapt information-processing strategies that become dysfunctional in contexts such as the classroom, in which—at increasingly younger ages—sustained attention is required. Armstrong also presents research that links physical play to frontal lobe development, which supports the capacities for organization, classification, synthesis, reflection, and cooperation. Diminished opportunities for rough-and-tumble play may thus be compromising frontal lobe development and exacerbating symptoms of hyperactivity, distractibility, and impulsivity.

Eva-Maria Simms, director of the developmental psychology graduate program at Duquesne University, presents a play therapy case in Chapter 9, which illustrates the power of play as a tool for psychological healing. This case study also elucidates the central role of play for emotional, social, intellectual, and ethical development, and for the development of selfhood.

As a clinical psychologist and associate professor of psychology at Point Park College, I consider in Chapter 10 how the current climate in early childhood education and wider social trends have fostered the recent upsurge in rates of child psychopathology across a wide range of diagnostic categories. We create educational environments that do not respect children's individuality, introduce concepts before they are ready to master them, deny their need for play, subject them to uniform curricula and assessment, and transform their three-dimensional and vividly experiential world into one dominated by two-dimensional "virtual reality." Then we label and drug the children who do not fit in. Our preoccupation with the genetic and neurological explanations of mental disorder and our corresponding indifference to the impact of the environment speak to our increasingly mechanized conceptualization of human nature. I conclude that we must humanize our classrooms and curricula, and stop diagnosing and drugging children whose creativity, energy, and budding intellect render them incapable of adjusting well to the narrow constraints of a technological society.

REFERENCES

Cordes, C., & Miller, E. (Eds.). (2000). *Fool's gold: A critical look at computers in childhood.* College Park, MD: Alliance for Childhood.

Greenspan, S.I. (1997). *The growth of the mind and the endangered origins of intelligence.* Cambridge, MA: Perseus Books.

Healy, J.M. (1998). *Failure to connect: How computers affect our children's minds and what we can do about it.* New York: Simon & Schuster.

Kane, J. (1999). On education with meaning. In J. Kane (Ed.), *Education, information, and transformation: Essays on learning and thinking* (pp. 1–21). Upper Saddle River, NJ: Prentice-Hall.

Piaget, J. (1950). *The psychology of intelligence.* New York: International Universities Press.

Sacks, P. (1999). *Standardized minds: The high price of America's testing culture and what we can do to change it.* Cambridge, MA: Perseus Books.

Sanders, B. (1995). *A is for Ox.* New York: Vintage Books.

Singer, D.G., & Singer, J.L. (1990). *The house of make-believe: Children's play and the developing imagination.* Cambridge, MA: Harvard University Press.

Singer, D.G., & Singer, J.L. (2001). *Make-believe: Games and activities for imaginative play.* Washington, DC: Imagination Press.

Vygotsky, L.S. (1978). *Mind in society: The development of higher psychological processes.* Cambridge, MA: Harvard University Press. (Original works published 1930, 1933, and 1935.)

Wilson, F.R. (1998). *The hand: How its use shapes the brain, language, and human culture.* New York: Vintage Books.

Part I

The Power of Play in Early Childhood Education

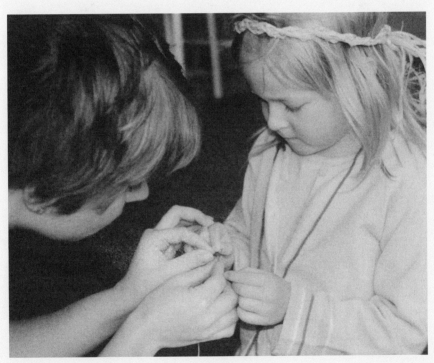

Photo courtesy of Michele Perel Phillips.

1

The Vital Role of Play in Early Childhood Education

Joan Almon

> The ability to play is one of the principal criteria of mental health.
> —Montagu, *Growing Young*

In more than thirty years of working with children, families, and teachers in Waldorf kindergartens all over the world, I have observed one consistent feature of childhood: *Creative play is a central activity in the lives of healthy children.* Play helps children weave together all the elements of life as they experience it. It allows them to digest life and make it their own. It is an outlet for the fullness of their creativity, and it is an absolutely critical part of their childhood. With creative play, children blossom and flourish; without it, they suffer a serious decline. I am hardly the first to note this fact; the central importance of creative play in children's healthy development is well supported by decades of research. And yet, children's play, in the creative, open-ended sense in which I use the term, is now seriously endangered. The demise of play will certainly have serious consequences for children and for the future of childhood itself.

Parents, teachers, and mental health professionals alike are expressing concern about children who do not play. Some seem blocked and unable to play; others long to play, but policies and practices at home and in school have driven open-ended, self-directed play out of their lives. Children no longer have the freedom to explore woods and fields and find their own special places. Informal neighborhood ball games are a thing of the past, as children are herded into athletic leagues at increasingly younger ages. Add to this mixture the hours spent sitting still in front of screens—television, video game, and computer— absorbing other people's stories and imaginations, and the result is a steady decline in children's play.

Increasingly, preschool and kindergarten children find themselves in school settings that feature scripted teaching, computerized learning, and standardized assessment. Physical education and recess are being eliminated; new schools are built without playgrounds. While allegedly these approaches are providing "quality education," they trivialize and undermine children's natural capacities for meaningful and focused life lessons through creative play, and this leaves many children profoundly alienated from their school experiences.

Although I have observed the steady decline of play over the past thirty years, even I was astonished by a recent call from a counselor in an elementary school in Virginia. She had been talking with a first-grade class and used the word "imagination." When they stared blankly at her, she explained its meaning, but the children continued to look puzzled. "You know," she said, "it's when you pretend to be someone you're not," and she gave an example from her own childhood when she loved to play Wonder Woman. She would put on a cape and fly down the hill near her house with arms outstretched, pretending to be aloft. "That's imagination," she explained. "But we don't know how to do that," said one child, and all the others nodded their heads in agreement. Not one child in that first grade seemed to know what imaginative play was.

THE NATURE OF PLAY

If we are to save play, we must first understand its nature. Creative play is like a spring that bubbles up from deep within a child. It is refreshing and enlivening. It is a *natural part of the makeup of every healthy child*. The child's love of learning is intimately linked with a zest for play. Whether children are working on new physical skills, social relations, or cognitive content, they approach life with a playful spirit. As a friend said of her eight-month-old recently, "It just seems that she's working all the time." But is it work or play? In childhood, there is no distinction.

Adults are convinced that we need to "teach" young children. It is certainly true that we need to set an example in all kinds of activities. We also need to create appropriate spaces where children can play and learn, we need to lend a helping hand—and, at times, even intervene when things are going wrong. But mostly we need to honor the innate capacity for learning that moves the limbs and fills the souls of every healthy young child.

One-year-old Nathan came with his parents to the house we share as a family each summer. He was delighted to find several staircases in this house, for there was only one step in his own home, which he had already mastered. Now he gave full vent to his wish to climb stairs. Over and over he would climb up and down. We took turns standing guard, but he rarely needed our help. He was focused and concentrated, and did not like to be taken away from this activity. He gave every sign of being a happy, playful child while climbing, yet he was also clearly exploring and mastering a new skill that was important for his long-term development. Most important, it was a task he set for himself. No one could have told this one-year-old to devote hours to climbing. He did it himself, as will every healthy child whose sense of movement has not been disturbed.

In another example of child-initiated play that is also learning, four-year-old Ivana came to kindergarten one Monday morning and proudly announced that she could tie her shoes. I must have looked skeptical, because it is beyond the skill level of most children her age. Ivana—determined to demonstrate her new prowess—promptly sat down on the floor and untied and then retied her shoes into perfect bows, looked at my astonished face, and beamed. Later in the day, I asked her mother how Ivana had learned to do this. Her mother laughed and described how over the weekend Ivana had pretended that she was going to a birthday party. She folded scraps of paper into little birthday packages. She then raided her mother's yarn basket and used pieces of yarn to tie the packages with bows. She probably tied sixty or seventy packages until she had at last mastered the art of tying bows. She clearly felt ready, and she did her work in the spirit of play. If, instead, someone had required Ivana to learn to tie her shoes before she signaled her readiness and interest, and proceeded to give her formal instruction, learning would have been transformed into a tedious and stressful task.

The simple truth is that young children are born with a most wonderful urge to grow and learn. They continually develop new skills and capacities, and if they are allowed to set the pace with a bit of help from the adult world, they will work at all this in a playful and tireless way. Rather than respecting this innate drive to learn, however, we treat children as if they can learn only what adults can teach them. We strip them of their innate confidence in directing their own learning, hurry them along, and often wear them out. It is no wonder so many teachers complain that by age nine or ten, children seem burned out and un-interested in learning. This is a great tragedy, for the love of learning that Nathan and Ivana displayed can last a lifetime. Furthermore, it is intimately bound to our capacity to be creative and purposeful.

Psychologist Mihaly Csikszentmihalyi identified a creative state that he termed "flow," and which I believe is comparable to the state that children enter when deeply engaged in play. In their book, *The Creative Spirit,* Goleman, Kaufman, and Ray (1992) describe the state of flow as the time "when people are at their peak. Flow can happen in any domain or activity—while painting, playing chess, making love, any-thing. The one requirement is that your skills so perfectly match the demands of the moment that all self-consciousness disappears" (p. 46). Csikszentmihalyi (in Goleman et al., 1992) recounted the following vignette to illustrate the nature of flow: "A neurosurgeon was deeply engrossed in a difficult operation. When the procedure was finished, he inquired about a pile of debris in the corner of the operating room. He was informed that part of the ceiling had caved in during the op-eration. The surgeon had been so engaged in the flow of his work that he had not heard a thing!"

Children engaged in healthy play display a depth of concentration that can also be characterized by flow. I think of five-year-old Peter watching intently as two girls in the kindergarten were creating an especially beautiful play scene on a tabletop. They were deeply en-grossed, and so was he. It happened that on that day the Fire Depart-ment descended on us because one of the teachers had called them after noticing an electrical odor in her room. Three fire engines roared up the driveway. Peter's friend, Benjamin, ran up to him, crying, "Peter, Peter, the fire engines are here!" But Peter was so intent on watching the play scene that he did not respond. Benjamin tried again, with the same result. He shrugged and rushed back to the window to watch the firemen arrive. Finally, Peter emerged from his concentra-tion, saw the fire engines, and hurried to the window.

The state of flow experienced by scientists, physicians, artists, and others can be intimidating. Do we want to enter so wholeheartedly into life and learning? It does not fit the contemporary picture of multi-tasking, where one is doing many things at once, but usually none of them very deeply. Yet it is an important state of being if we want to flex our inner capacities to the fullest and offer our greatest gifts to the world.

THE DEVELOPMENT OF PLAY

The secret to helping young children thrive is to keep the spirit of creativity and playful learning alive and active. An important ingredient in this is our own work as adults, for children naturally imitate grown-ups. This inspires their play. Their learning is a combination of their own deep inner drive to grow and learn, coupled with their imitation of the adults in their environment. These two elements interweave all through early childhood. They provide the underlying basis for play, yet their outer expression changes year by year as children develop.

An important milestone in play—the capacity for make-believe (also known as fantasy play)—occurs at around two-and-a-half or three years of age. Before that, children are more oriented to the real world: their own bodies; simple household objects like pots, pans, and wooden spoons; and simple toys like dolls, trucks, and balls. Toddlers imitate what they see around them; common play themes include cooking, caring for baby, driving cars or trucks, and other everyday events.

These themes continue and expand after age three, but now children are less dependent on real objects and create what they need from anything that is at hand. Their ability to enter into make-believe allows them to transform a simple object into a play prop—a bowl becomes a ship, a stick becomes a fishing pole, a rock becomes a baby, and much, much more. The three-year-old becomes so engaged in make-believe play that objects seem to be in a constant state of transformation. No play episode is ever finished; it is always in the process of becoming something else. The playful three-year-old often leaves a trail of objects as her play evolves from one theme to the next.

In contrast, four-year-olds are generally more stationary and thematic in their play. They like to have a "house" to play in, which might also be a ship or a shop, and many enter the "pack rat" stage, where they fill their houses with so many objects that it seems they cannot freely move around. This does not bother them at all, however. Like three-year-olds, they are inspired in the moment by the objects before them. They are quite spontaneous in their ideas for play.

The fantasy play of the five-year-old is characterized by the ability to have an idea and then play it out rather than being inspired in the moment by the object at hand, as is the case with three- and four-year-olds. Often, five-year-olds will announce what they want to play as they enter the kindergarten. Their mothers report that the children wake up in the morning with an idea for play in mind. Although they

may play out the same theme for several days or weeks, subtle variations emerge as they gain focus, come in touch with their own ideas,
and acquire the will to carry them out in playful detail.

There is one more important aspect to the development of make-
believe play that usually does not occur until children are six years old.
At this age, they will often play out a situation without the use of
props. They may build a house or castle but leave it unfurnished, then
sit inside it and talk through their play, for now they are able to see
the images clearly in their minds' eyes. This stage can be described as
imaginative play, for the children now have the capacity to form a well-
articulated inner image. It is around this time that a child will say
something like "I can see Grandma whenever I want. I just have to
close my eyes." Or she may set up a play scene with her toys but close
her eyes and play it out "inside" (Jaffke, 1988, pp. 13–15).

In all of these stages of dramatic play, children may play alone or
with others. However, the way they engage in social play with others
changes over the years. The one-year-old tends to play alone, while
social play of two-year-olds is generally called parallel play, for young
children play side by side without fully interacting with each other
(Hyun, 1998). I would characterize the play of three- and four-year-olds
as playmate play. The children enjoy playing with each other (with
occasional squabbles as part of the play experience), but generally they
are not deeply invested in each other. They enjoy playing together
when they are in nursery school, but tend to forget about each other
when they are apart. An exception to this, in my experience, occurs
among children whose families are friends or who carpool together.
In such situations, life thrusts the children together outside the usual
playtimes, and playmates become more like family members who have
an important, abiding role in a child's life. Normally, however, children of this age happily play with their playmates in school and forget about them for the rest of the day.

The social play of five- and six-year-olds is different. The doors to
deeper social relationships are opening for them. They form friend-
ships and talk about their friends at home. They think about their
friends when they are apart. They may want to call them on the phone
or visit in their homes. Mothers laugh over the social calendars they
have to maintain, for suddenly their six-year-olds want to spend much
time outside school with their friends. This may sound like a preview
of adolescence; in fact, this stage is sometimes called "first adolescence." The sociodramatic play of this age group is rich and varied,
and it is a great tragedy that so few children in the United States have
a chance to fully experience it, for their time in kindergarten or first

grade is generally fully devoted to academic subjects with little time left over for play. The absence of play in childhood may have long-lasting repercussions on the child's overall social development.

THE SOCIAL, EMOTIONAL, AND INTELLECTUAL BENEFITS OF PLAY

In the '70s and '80s, Israeli psychologist Sara Smilansky (1990, p. 19) conducted groundbreaking research on the role of *dramatic play* and *sociodramatic play* in cognitive and socioemotional development. She defines dramatic play as having four elements: (1) the child undertakes a make-believe role; (2) the child uses make-believe to transform objects into things necessary for the play; (3) verbal descriptions or exclamations are used at times in place of actions or situations; and (4) the play scenarios last at least ten minutes. In sociodramatic play, these four elements are present plus two more: at least two players interact within the play scene, and there is some verbal communication involved with the play.

Observing three- to six-year-olds, Smilansky developed a method of assessing children's play in preschool settings. Using her assessment tools, she and other researchers observed and assessed children from ages three to six at play in a number of preschool locations in the United States and Israel, from a variety of socioeconomic settings. They also assessed the children's ability to organize and communicate thoughts and to engage in social interactions. In one study, children were followed and tested in second grade in literacy and numeracy. Their ability to engage in dramatic and sociodramatic play was found to be directly linked to a wealth of skills, all of which are essential for academic success. Smilansky's findings (1990, p. 35) are summarized below:

Gains in Cognitive-Creative Activities
Better verbalization
Richer vocabulary
Higher language comprehension
Higher language level
Better problem-solving strategies
More curiosity
Better ability to take on the perspective of another
Higher intellectual competence

Gains in Socioemotional Activities
More playing with peers
More group activity

Better peer cooperation
Reduced aggression
Better ability to take on the perspective of others
More empathy
Better control of impulsive actions
Better prediction of others' preferences and desires
Better emotional and social adjustment
More innovation
More imaginativeness
Longer attention span
Greater attention ability
Performance of more conservation tasks

Smilansky (1990, p. 25) concludes:

Sociodramatic play activates resources that stimulate emotional, social, and intellectual growth in the child, which in turn affects the child's success in school. We saw many similarities between patterns of behavior bringing about successful sociodramatic play experiences and patterns of behavior required for successful integration into the school situation. For example, problem solving in most school subjects requires a great deal of make-believe: visualizing how the Eskimos live, reading stories, imagining a story and writing it down, solving arithmetic problems, and determining what will come next. History, geography, and literature are all make-believe. All of these are conceptual constructions that are never directly experienced by the child.

Smilansky's research points to the fact that imagination is as important a medium for learning in the elementary school years as is make-believe for the preschool child. If a child has been allowed to engage in make-believe play during the nursery school and kindergarten years and to develop inner imagination before entering first grade, she is then ripe and ready to learn. While one or another may have a learning difficulty, their enthusiasm for learning—and for overcoming difficulties—is enormous. By contrast, when a child has not had rich play opportunities, and/or the curriculum fails to engage the imagination, learning is a dull affair. My own experience has also been that the children who were the most active players in the kindergarten were also the most active learners in elementary school.

A study conducted in 1970s Germany, at a time when many kindergartens were being transformed into academic rather than play-oriented environments, bears out the relationship between preschool play and elementary school success. It compared fifty play-oriented kindergartens with fifty academically oriented ones. The children were followed until fourth grade, at which point the children from the play-oriented kindergartens excelled over the others in every area measured—physical, emotional, social, and intellectual development. The results were especially striking among lower-income children, who clearly benefited from the play-oriented approach. The overall results were so compelling that all German kindergartens were switched back to being play-oriented (*Der Spiegel*, 1977). They have continued in this mode until the present time, although during recent visits to Germany I heard more of the rhetoric one hears in this country: that to prepare children for a globalized economy they must get a head start on literacy, numeracy, and other subjects.

The benefits of play-oriented preschool programs were also established in a series of studies that examined early childhood programs in Ypsilanti, Michigan. In one study of low-income children, sixty-nine three- and four-year-olds, who were at high risk for school failure, were randomly assigned to one of three types of programs: High/Scope, traditional nursery school, and direct instruction. Both the High/Scope program and a traditional nursery school encouraged child-initiated play activities, while the direct-instruction approach did not. I.Q. scores rose in all three programs, but various social indicators showed that the children in the programs that encouraged self-initiated activity, including play, were faring significantly better than the children in the more academic, direct-instruction program. At age fifteen, the following results were noted:

> Initially, all three curriculum approaches improved young children's intellectual performance substantially, with the average IQs of children in all three groups rising 27 points. By age 15 however, students in the High/Scope group and the Nursery School group . . . reported only half as much delinquent activity as the students in the Direct Instruction group. (High/Scope Summary, 2002)

Findings at age twenty-three continue to support the conclusion that the High/Scope and nursery school groups are better off than the direct-instruction group in a variety of ways. Either the High/Scope group, the nursery school group, or both, show statistically significant advantages over the direct-instruction group on seventeen variables. Most important, compared with the direct-instruction group, the High/scope and nursery school groups have had significantly fewer felony arrests of various kinds and fewer years of special education for emotional impairment. In addition, compared with the direct-instruction group, the High/Scope group aspires to complete a higher level of schooling. It thus appears that preschool programs that promote child-initiated play activities contribute to the development of an individual's sense of personal and social responsibility.

A recent study by Rebecca Marcon (2002) of the University of North Florida found similar results when children from different preschool programs were followed through fourth grade. Those who had attended play-oriented programs where child-initiated activities predominated did better academically than those who had attended academic-oriented programs.

THE DEMISE OF PLAY IN EARLY CHILDHOOD EDUCATION

Given the compelling evidence for the importance of self-initiated creative play for social, emotional, and intellectual growth, it is alarming that play has lost so much ground in young children's lives during the past thirty years. Since the 1970s, it has become common for public kindergartens in the United States to focus so strongly on academic achievement that there is little or no time devoted to self-directed play.

Kindergarten teachers in Pennsylvania told me that in their school district, the kindergarten curriculum had been prescribed by the state legislature. Every morning, children were to spend twenty minutes each on reading, writing, arithmetic, social studies, science, and so on. One teacher looked nervously over her shoulder and whispered, "I break the law every day and let my children play for fifteen minutes." The other kindergarten teacher sadly admitted that she only managed to bring in play twice a week for short periods.

That was in the mid-1980s. Since then, the situation has become even more grim. The first-grade curriculum has become entrenched in the kindergarten. With standardized testing starting ever earlier—for five-year-olds in some districts—an atmosphere of hurry and pressure pervades the kindergarten. To ease the pressure a bit, many states have raised the entrance age for kindergarten so that the youngest children are usually five when they enter rather than four years and nine months, as was previously the case. On the other hand, there is such concern about five-year-olds learning enough that many school districts are switching to full-day kindergarten. One might hope that half the day would be devoted to play and the arts, but I have not heard any reports of that being the case.

Even when playtime is made available to children in the classroom, chronic media exposure has a direct negative effect on their ability to make use of these opportunities. As a kindergarten teacher, it became easy for me to recognize which children were "television children," that is, children for whom TV was a steady influence in their lives. Such children often had difficulty finding their own ideas in play and were prone to acting out the ideas they had seen on the screen. In severe cases, these media children could *only* play out roles they had seen and became very upset if other children wanted to change the play scenario.

In *What Happened to Recess and Why Are Our Children Struggling in Kindergarten?* Susan Ohanian takes a hard look at what is happening to young children in school today. She refers to New York Public School 9, which is bucking the trend by providing kindergarten children with recess: "In a seven-hour day, they get 25 minutes free from academics" (Ohanian, 2002, p. 11). Anyone who has had experience with five-year-olds will know that twenty-five minutes of free time in a seven-hour day will not suffice.

Ohanian also describes the situation in Chicago's public kindergartens, referring to a report in the *New York Times* by Jacques Steinberg:

> The teacher knows it's the 53d day because "Day: 053" is printed at the top of the recommended lesson plan open on her desk, a thick white binder crammed with goals for each day and step-by-step questions given to her and the city's 26,000 other teachers by the school system's administrators at the start of the school year. The page also identifies the section of the Iowa Test of Basic Skills to which that day's entry corresponds . . . Every teacher in Chicago gets this day-by-day outline of what should be taught in language arts, mathematics, science and social studies. The *New York Times* reporter notes that some see this as the logical outcome of the standards movement, providing "an almost iron-clad guarantee that all students will be exposed to the same material and that all teachers, regardless of qualification, will know exactly how to present it." (Ohanian, 2002, pp. 11–12)

In the face of such demands on five-year-olds and their teachers, to speak of play seems almost frivolous. Yet five-year-olds are young children. Where did we ever get the idea that they should be on the fast track to high scores and global careers? We are on a slippery slope heading downhill, and the pace is accelerating. Must we find our children broken on the rocks of our fears and ambitions before we call a halt?

And we're not at the bottom yet. In the name of early literacy, plans are being developed to refocus nursery school children away from play and toward early reading. There are aspects of early literacy that young children need: a rich experience of language spoken by caring adults, nursery rhymes and verses, storytelling and puppetry, and books read aloud. All these lay a vital foundation for a lifetime love of language and reading. But the term "early literacy" is coming to imply something much narrower than that.

As of this writing in early 2003, Head Start is scheduled for re-authorization by Congress during this year. On January 17, 2003, the *Washington Post* described the president's intention to have all four-year-olds in Head Start assessed as to how much they learned in terms of early literacy and early numeracy. The purpose is to evaluate the success of Head Start programs. As always, there is something positive to be said about assessment, but when the stakes are too high and the means of measuring too narrow, serious abuses enter the system, and it is the children who bear the brunt of the problem. Many Head Start teachers are already feeling considerable pressure to give up playtime and focus on early literacy, and this situation will only grow worse (Strauss, 2003).

Even before the new plan for assessment was announced, Susan Ohanian wrote about the growing stress on early literacy in Head Start:

> With all good intentions the current Bush administration is advocating a rigorous skill model for Head Start preschool programs across the country. Three- and four-year olds are drilled about letters, dividing words into syllables and spelling. The plan is that this will prepare poor children to learn to read when they go to kindergarten. The Department of Health and Human Services, which oversees Head Start, is developing a curriculum that every Head Start teacher will be expected to follow. (Ohanian, 2002, p. 10)

However, it is not just the 900,000 children in Head Start, but all young children in the United States, who are being targeted for early literacy programs. In spring 2002, legislation was introduced by the Senate H.E.L.P. Committee, then chaired by Senator Ted Kennedy, to make more funds available to early education programs in each state. A total of one billion dollars per year was anticipated. The legislation, initially called S.2566, Early Care and Education Act (U.S. Senate, 2002) addresses the importance of physical, social, and emotional development, as well as early literacy.

While in theory this is a positive development, in practice, the legislation calls for bonuses to be given to states that can show gains in children's school preparedness. This will almost certainly result in a sharpened focus on early literacy activities for three- and four-year-olds. Much more time will be spent on learning the alphabet, breaking words into parts, basic reading skills, and the like. We have seen this pattern before in kindergarten: soon there will be no time left for play in preschool literacy.

Children are not machines. You cannot simply add more fuel and speed them up. They are governed by internal processes that are sometimes called "the laws of child development." We cannot ignore these natural developmental timetables without doing serious harm to children that touches many areas of their lives—physical, emotional, social, and intellectual.

The Alliance for Childhood, of which I am the U.S. coordinator, submitted a position statement to the Senate committee that was drafting the Early Care and Education Act. The statement was endorsed by some of the leading experts on child development in the United States, including T. Berry Brazelton, David Elkind, Jane Healy, Stanley Greenspan, and Alvin Poussaint. It read, in part:

> The key to developing literacy—and all other skills—is to pace the learning so that it is consistent with the child's development, enabling him or her to succeed at the early stages. Ensure this initial success and the child's natural love of learning blooms. Doom him to failure in the beginning by making inappropriate demands and he may well be unable to overcome the resulting sense of inadequacy. This is especially true of children whose families are already under social and economic stress. (Alliance for Childhood, 2002)

There are many individuals and organizations committed to restoring play to young children's lives. One reason it is difficult to make progress, however, is that many parents misguidedly prefer that their young children focus on academics. Their concern about their children's future easily turns to fear, and they then place considerable pressure on nursery and kindergarten teachers. An October 1995 report by the National Center for Education Statistics (NCES) entitled *Readiness for Kindergarten: Parent and Teacher Beliefs* found that

> Parents of a majority of preschoolers believe that knowing the letters of the alphabet, being able to count to 20 or more, and using pencils and paint brushes are very important or essential for a child to be ready for kindergarten, while few kindergarten teachers share these beliefs . . . [C]ompared with teachers, parents place greater importance on academic skills (e.g., counting, writing, and reading) and prefer classroom practices that are more academically oriented. One reason for this may be that parents perceive that there are specific activities they can do to teach their children school-related basic skills, whereas ways of changing the social

maturity or temperamental characteristics of their children are less
apparent. (National Center for Education Statistics, 1995)

If I could offer parents one piece of advice regarding play and early
academics, it would be to relax and stop hurrying their children. Children have such deep resources for growth and learning that with good
nurturing and reasonable help, most will succeed wonderfully. Some,
of course, will need special help and can be given it. This is a hard message to convey, however, especially in America, where we are committed to growing our children faster and better than anyone else. There
is a story that Piaget, the great Swiss psychologist, did not like to speak
to American audiences because after he had described the natural pattern of children's development, Americans would invariably ask, "Yes,
but how can we get them to do things faster?" Compared to the young
of other mammals, our children take much longer to mature. They
deserve the right to grow and ripen at a human pace. A major part of
this is allowing time for play.

THE DEMISE OF PLAY AND CHILDREN'S HEALTH

The absence of play is generally a sign of illness in children. Parents,
for instance, will often describe the severity of a child's illness in terms
of whether or not he or she continued to play. "He had chicken pox,"
a parent might report, "but it wasn't too serious. He was playing the
whole time." Or another mother might say of her child, "She was really sick. She didn't want to play at all."

Stuart Brown (1999), a retired psychiatrist who founded the Institute for Play in Carmel, California, confirmed the instinctive wisdom
of these parents in linking play and health. As a young doctor in Texas
he worked with very ill children, some of whom did not recover. Over
time, Brown began to notice a pattern. Occasionally, a very sick child
would develop a playful gleam in his eyes. He would check the charts
and find that although the child's fever was still high, or the blood tests
still worrisome, usually within a day's time the outlook would
brighten. He came to realize that the return of a playful spirit was an
excellent predictor of recovery in his young charges.

Given the relationship between health and play, what then are the
implications of the demise of play for children's mental and physical
health? Are there accompanying signs of illness in children today?
Research does, in fact, indicate that this is the case. The growing number of suicides among children and youth is a powerful and tragic in-
dictment of contemporary trends in childhood. Between 1952 and 1996,

rates of suicide among adolescents tripled. Suicide is currently the fourth leading cause of death among children between the ages of ten and fourteen (Surgeon General, 1999).

In recent years, former Surgeon General David Satcher sounded the alarm about children's physical and mental health. In 2001, he issued a "Call to Action to Prevent and Decrease Overweight and Obesity," which stated that in 1999 about 13 percent of children and adolescents were overweight and that since 1980, this number had doubled for children and tripled for adolescents (Surgeon General, 2001a, p. xiii). Type 2 diabetes, previously considered an adult disease, and closely linked to overweight and obesity, has increased dramatically in children and adolescents.

In 2000, Satcher organized a conference to address the growing crisis in children's mental health. A report on his Web site states the following:

> The nation is facing a public crisis in mental healthcare for infants, children and adolescents. Many children have mental health problems that interfere with normal development and functioning. In the United States, one in 10 children and adolescents suffer from mental illness severe enough to cause some level of impairment. Recent evidence compiled by the World Health Organization indicates that by the year 2020, childhood neuropsychiatric disorders will rise proportionately by over 50 percent, internationally, to become one of the five most common causes of morbidity, mortality, and disability among children. (Surgeon General, 2001b)

In the past decade, growing numbers of children have been diagnosed with Attention Deficit Hyperactivity Disorder (ADHD) and several million receive potent stimulant medication such as Ritalin each year. The Centers for Disease Control reports that the American Psychiatric Association estimates 3 to 7 percent of children suffer from ADHD and that some studies show an even higher percentage (Centers for Disease Control, 2002).

Diagnoses of Autistic Spectrum Disorders in children (Asperger's Disorder, in particular) have also increased dramatically. In the state of California, for example, cases of autism grew from 3,864 to 11,995 between 1987 and 1998, an increase of 210 percent, and the median age of the patients dropped from fifteen to nine years of age (California Department of Developmental Services, 1999, pp. 7, 10).

A striking feature of these health trends is that, unlike the traditional illnesses of childhood that are especially prevalent among poor children in developing nations, they are affecting children across the socioeconomic spectrum in technologically advanced nations, often beginning in the United States, and then slowly spreading to other technologically advanced nations.

It is crucial that we ask ourselves the difficult question, what is it about our contemporary lifestyle that is causing or contributing to so much illness in children? I wish I could report on one single cause that we could turn our full attention to and eradicate the source, as we have done with smallpox and other illnesses. Rather, children's lives have changed significantly in myriad ways during the past fifty years, and many of these changes are stressful. Healthy children can cope with one or two stressors—and it can even be argued that they grow stronger through some adversity. Yet few children can cope well with five or six unhealthy factors that are constant and permeate their lives.

This is especially true when the most basic of all human needs is not being met—the need for consistent love and care of devoted parents and other adults. Thus, when the home life is stressed or too hurried; when child care is of mediocre quality with little possibility for lasting bonds with loving caregivers; when preschool demands "too much too soon" in the areas of literacy and numeracy; when hours are spent each day sitting still in front of screens; and when the diet is frequently filled with too much sugar, fat, and food additives, we have a situation that is bound to wreak havoc on a young child's health. Stressors affect each of us differently depending on our underlying temperament and constitution, and so we see a range of stress-related illnesses in our children. This is a health picture in urgent need of further investigation, and it would be excellent if the Surgeon General and national health organizations could work together to define the scope of the problem and the contributing factors. We may not like their conclusions, however, for it is a hard truth to swallow that our current lifestyle is harming our children, even as it is harming our environment and our global relations with others. The decline in play appears not only to be a serious problem in itself, but it may also be the canary in the mineshaft that is pointing us toward much more serious, lasting problems in children's lives.

FOSTERING HEALTHY PLAY IN THE PRESCHOOL AND KINDERGARTEN CLASSROOM

The Physical Environment

In order to foster healthy play in the classroom, it is important to create an optimal environment. To a large extent, any space will do if the right mood and orientation for play exists. I once taught in a summer program for young children that took place on a large college campus. There was no fenced area for the children or other obvious safe space for their play. There were, however, two mounds of earth left from a construction project. Knowing that young children love to play on hills, we adopted these mounds as our playground. My co-teacher would seat herself on the grass between the mounds and weave wonderful grass nests or make other simple toys from the grass. The children happily played on the mounds for at least an hour a day for the three weeks of the program. They also went for walks across the campus, but were always very content to come back to their small and simple play area. This was an unusual situation and certainly not one to normally recommend, but it was a wonderful lesson in how little space and equipment children actually need to be engaged players. It also echoes the experience of children in poor countries playing on the garbage heaps that litter their landscape. Their toys are the objects of the trash heap, such as tin cans. Their surroundings may be unhygienic and even dangerous, but in many cases, their lives are rich in play.

By contrast, many children today are bombarded with an over-abundance of toys and other play objects, as well as by an overload of sense impressions. These can actually interfere with their play. The newborn's cradle, for instance, is often so festooned with patterns and prints, mobiles, and toys that one wonders how the poor baby will find peace for sleeping. An infant's cradle used to be protected by draped cloths that kept the world a bit away and created a sense of peace. This is no longer the case. By the time a child is in nursery school or kinder-garten, he is surrounded on every side by walls covered with pictures and charts with bright colors, words, and numbers. There is often not a square foot of peaceful wall space where a child can safely rest his gaze and daydream. Everything is designed to wake the child up. Stimulation is the call of the day, but in truth it amounts to massive overstimulation of the young child's nervous system. Few adults would choose to work in such an environment, for they would find it impossible to concentrate; yet we subject children to it daily.

It is also true that you can create environments that are under-stimulating for children, and I have been in such surroundings in some of the township Educare programs in South Africa, where the rooms are bleak and there is nothing adorning the walls. There are also few toys or other play materials. I have seen fifty or more children in such a room and, to keep order, the teachers insist that the children stay in their chairs most of the time. That is clearly an unhealthy situation, with far too little activity or sense stimulation of any kind for the children. But we need to realize that overstimulation can be just as much of a problem as understimulation and pay more attention to our excesses.

In my early years of teaching, I experimented with different play environments. I gradually found that the children were most relaxed and played best if the space was fairly simple but pleasing to the senses. It should be calming and lovely, but not so beautiful and complete that the children hesitate to move anything or disturb the order. Play is a messy business in the best sense of the word, for it is hard to create without making a mess. A good play environment invites you to come in and change it—but it is orderly enough that it is easy to clean it up again. There's a place for everything and it becomes fun for the children to know where each object lives and put it back at the end of playtime. When cleanup is handled through imitation of adults who enjoy it and do it in a cheerful mood, most of the children participate as wholeheartedly as they do in play itself.

For preschool children, the simpler the play materials, the more effective they are for stimulating creative play. A variety of plain cloths, for instance, can be used in dozens of ways—from capes and gowns to the roofs and walls of houses. Simple logs and stumps serve as building materials. For a few years, I had both wooden "unit" blocks and wooden logs in my kindergarten for building. I observed that with the unit blocks—standard wooden blocks that are cut along mathematical principles to represent one square "unit" or multiples of that—the children tended to use small cars and other man-made materials. With the logs, the children gravitated more to natural materials such as shells and stones and to simple handmade dolls and animals for their play. The children also became more inventive with their play materials, making or finding what they needed to complete their play. Gradually, I disposed of the unit blocks (this is practically a heresy for an American preschool teacher to admit) and just gave the children logs for building. They never complained, and their play grew stronger and more creative.

The presence of natural materials such as wool, cotton and silk, stones, wood, and metals also filled the environment with life. These provide a healthy stimulus for the senses, and the children quickly learn that things feel different and have different aromas and qualities, such as being cool or warm to the touch. Most kindergartens today are filled with plastic that is cool to the touch and does not warm up as children handle it. In addition, everything ends up feeling much the same, whether it is a truck or a doll.

Boys, in particular, are strongly drawn to wheeled vehicles and will often play with nothing else if a car is at hand. I wanted the children in my kindergarten to explore the full range of play materials, and after a while, I eliminated all wheeled vehicles from my kindergarten. The children created their own cars from logs and boards, if they so desired. A side blessing was that with the absence of cars, most of the machine noises that the children made to accompany their car play also disappeared. Eventually, the only wheels we had were on our carpet sweeper, which may account for why the boys especially loved to clean the carpet.

Generally, within fifteen minutes of the children's arrival, the kindergarten would be completely transformed with almost everything in use. A group of twenty children could easily create six or seven play areas for themselves. There was a fair amount of negotiation that took place as they sorted out who was going to use what and in which area. Occasionally they needed help with this process, especially in the beginning of the school year, but they soon developed their own techniques for dividing up the materials. Adjustments were sometimes made as the playtime progressed, especially if one group had clearly taken more than they needed while others were undersupplied.

The Role of the Adult in a Play-Oriented Classroom

The role of the adult in a play-oriented preschool or kindergarten is critical but subtle. A teacher can easily dominate the play situation, overriding the children's own initiative, or, through frequent questions and conversation, force children to become too conscious and purposeful in their play. The latter is a common situation in play programs today.

Offering Children Suggestions.   Sara Smilansky (1990) researched the impact of adult intervention on children's play and demonstrated that when adults encouraged children to role-play, enact fairy tales, and so forth, there were significant gains in the children's ability to play. Yet, through questionnaires given to 120 preschool teachers, half in the United States and half in Israel, she found the following:

- All reported that there was a playhouse corner in their room and that children could play in it for at least 30 minutes each day, however, most thought play was only good for developing personality and furthering social and emotional development. 90% said they did not feel it prepared children for future success in school.
- They assumed children would learn to play by watching other children and that they did not need to do very much to help children play.
- None of the teachers had been trained in the use of play. They did not remember a university course on the importance of play or on how to help facilitate play. (Smilansky, 1990, pp. 36–40)

Smilansky concludes that, "Basic attitudes clearly need changing . . . It is clear that play expresses the child's ongoing intellectual, social and emotional development and growth. This growth, like any other, can be aided by teachers with sensitivity to the child's needs, wishes, and current status" (1990, p. 40).

Modeling Healthy Work.   Decades of classroom experience and observation of Waldorf kindergarten teachers both in the United States and Europe have convinced me of the central importance of imitation for stimulating healthy play. Young children are physically active and have a strong but usually unfocused will, which contributes to the turbulence of their behavior. Young children are inspired by the sense of purpose that adults bring to their work. Therefore, when the teacher spends time each day engaged in the practical household work of the kindergarten such as cooking, sewing, gardening, and woodworking, the children use this as a model for their own focused play, and the more deeply focused the teacher is in her work, the more focused the children are in their play. In addition, young children have a strong desire to imitate the teacher and will work alongside her for a period of time, which draws the children into a closer relationship with her, while acquiring new skills.

A recent experience in Tanzania helps illustrate the relationship between adult work and children's play. During a visit to a Waldorf school in Dar es Salaam, I was scheduled to spend a couple of hours with a new kindergarten teacher who had been specially trained to work creatively with small groups of children. It was a wonderful experience to watch her playfully interact with one or two children, but a class of twenty-five active children was rather overwhelming for her. Each time I passed her kindergarten I could hear the sounds of chaos. I felt great sympathy for her because it reminded me of my own early kindergartens, but I was perplexed as to how I could best help her in such a short period of time. On the morning of my visit to her kindergarten, I arrived early and asked the teacher if there was some work I could do. She looked rather blank and said she did all her work for the kindergarten at home in the evenings and there was no work to be done. "No, no," I declared without much tact, "in the kindergarten we do the work in front of the children. That inspires their play." I looked around her rather sparse kindergarten for some sort of work materials such as sandpaper or furniture polish. Any meaningful work would do, but all I could find was a basket of yarn scraps from a project that was under way. The tangle of yarn pieces, each perhaps 18 inches long, was not too inspiring, but better than nothing. As the children entered, they found me at a table untangling the yarn and winding tiny balls of yarn while singing a little song. The children were fascinated, and soon all twenty-five were gathered around the table watching intently. When the last little ball was rolled, the whole class turned, like a flock of birds, and spread into every corner of the room, rearranging the furniture and props into play structures, including houses, shops, a bus made of chairs, and a plane made of a table. For the next hour they played with all the focus and vigor one could ever hope for from a group of three- to six-year-olds.

The Art of Intervention. It is critical that the teacher has her ears wide open to all the sounds of the kindergarten so that she knows when intervention is necessary. Some children get overexcited or upset in play but can work this out themselves. In other cases, the teacher needs to intervene quickly before chaos results and a child gets hurt. Gradually, the teacher comes to know the sounds of her kindergarten as a mother knows the sounds of her child's cries. She knows when to help a particular child and when to sit still.

Direct adult intervention is needed if a child is about to hurt himself, another person, or an object. Sometimes it suffices to simply redirect a young child. For children age five and under, one can teach a great deal about appropriate behavior through the "royal *we*," as in, "We don't take other children's toys, hit children, and so forth." By age six, children generally welcome a quiet but more direct "no" and clear indications as to what is possible.

If a child needs to be removed from a turbulent play situation, bringing her to the teacher's work table or providing her with a quiet space and a basket of smaller play things, such as little logs, polished stones, dolls, and animals, helps her to reengage in play, albeit in a more quiet and focused way. After a short while, the child is sufficiently calm and centered to play with others.

Supporting Healthy Play at Home

Parents today feel tremendous pressure from many directions, including from government agencies and corporate advertisers, to stimulate their children and promote their intellectual development at ever-younger ages. While some children do need additional stimulation, there are many who are being overstimulated. It is important that parents seek the right balance for their own children, one that allows for growth and development without stress and provides ample time for play each day.

There are a number of things parents can do at home to support healthy play. One is to develop a deep appreciation of their child's play, and the ways in which he reveals his own unique nature through play.

Through simple observation and quiet appreciation, parents communicate the message that play is good. Giving space and time for play is vital, especially in our overfilled lives, as is offering simple play materials, often drawn from household objects. For example, babies and toddlers love playing with pots and pans, wooden spoons, and other commonly used objects. Children engaged in imaginative play love having a sheet draped over furniture and creating tents, houses, and ships.

Including purposeful, physical work in the daily routine of the home is a great help in inspiring children's play. It is important for parents or caregivers to spend time each day working with their hands at comprehensible tasks in the presence of their child, whether it is raking leaves, baking, or hammering a nail. The old adage of "whistle while you work" has meaning here, for although one does not need to actually whistle, a happy mood while doing work draws children near and motivates them in their play, while a grumbling, unhappy attitude on the part of the adult keeps children away.

A growing problem for young children today is the amount of time they spend in front of screens—television, video, and computer. TV Turn-off Network cites figures from the Nielson Media report of 2000, which indicate that children from two to seventeen spend on average nineteen hours and forty minutes per week (or nearly three hours per day) watching television. Combining videos and computers, children spend a total of nearly five hours per day in front of screens (TV Turn-off Network, 2003).

In addition, many children are profoundly influenced by the often violent, fast-paced, and sexual content of television, films, and computer games to which they are routinely subjected. This precocious exposure to the world around them can engender fear and mistrust, rendering it difficult for them to relax and imitate their caregivers and teachers. In imitation, there is a breathing in and out of one another, which requires a relaxed state and a trustful outlook. In addition, children often observe their parents at home sitting in front of a computer screen and performing an abstract task that does not offer the raw materials and physical gestures necessary to inspire focused, creative play.

The weakening of imitation makes it far more difficult for children to play, but it also makes it hard for them to relate to other human beings in the simple, relaxed way that children normally do. This can have long-lasting implications for their social and psychological development. For all these reasons, it is of the utmost importance that parents both minimize and supervise their children's exposure to screen-based media or, better yet, eliminate it altogether from their children's daily routines. Most children show wonderful signs of recovery within a week or two after the removal of screen time from their lives, especially if there is an increase in human interaction.

As a kindergarten teacher committed to helping children with creative play, I was struck by how quickly one could see the difference in children's play according to whether their media viewing at home was growing or declining. Research could be done on this that could help parents and educators understand the direct negative relationship between media engagement and self-directed, creative play on the part of young children.

LAUNCHING A NATIONAL EFFORT TO RESTORE PLAY

As play disappears from the landscape of childhood, we need to recognize that its demise will have a lasting impact. Decades of compelling research has shown that without play, children's physical, social, emotional, and intellectual development is compromised. They will develop without much imagination and creativity. Their capacity for communication will be diminished and their tendency toward aggressiveness and violence will increase. In short, human nature as we have known it will be profoundly altered, intensifying many of the problems that are already afflicting children and society. If we do not invest in play, we will find ourselves investing much more in prisons and hospitals, as the incidence of physical and mental illness, as well as aggressive and violent behavior, escalates.

It is not too late, however, to commit ourselves to reestablishing play in children's lives. Here are some suggestions:

- *Study the importance of play in children's lives.* Appoint a blue ribbon commission of respected individuals with expertise in child development, play, and education, including those representing national organizations that focus on these areas, to thoroughly investigate the importance of play and its essential nature in early childhood, underscoring, as appropriate, the message that it cannot be displaced without doing serious harm to children.
- *Assess early literacy and numeracy.* An honest assessment is needed of the success or failure of direct instruction and other early academic approaches in kindergartens and nursery programs. We must stop politicizing education and instead focus on the question of what children need for their long-term healthy development.
- *Clarify the health picture of children today, including the increase in mental illnesses.* Appoint a blue ribbon commission with the Surgeon General and

other prominent health-care professionals from the National Institute of Health, the Department of Health and Human Services, and national organizations such as the American Psychological Association, the American Academy of Child and Adolescent Psychiatry, and the American Academy of Pediatrics to elucidate and draw attention to the dramatic increase in psychological disturbance among children.

• *Organize a massive public education campaign about play.* Before it is too late and play has completely slipped out of the lives of young children, we need to organize public awareness campaigns about play's importance, directed at parents, teachers and policymakers. How to fund such a campaign? Perhaps we should imitate California in this regard; through Proposition 10, the state has levied new cigarette taxes, with all the funds raised being earmarked for early childhood programs.

These are major national efforts, and they will take much focus and energy, but the old adage still holds that where there's a will there's a way. If we want to help today's children, we will need to move quickly. It is hard, although not impossible, to reawaken the spirit of play in an adolescent or adult through storytelling, the arts, and other means, if they did not experience play in childhood. It is important that we bring play to those who missed it, but even more important that we protect children's right to play through a concerted effort in homes, schools, and communities. In light of the determined attempts by corporations and government agencies to banish open-ended creative play and replace it with much narrower, defined play or focused learning of letters and numbers at ever-earlier ages, it has become imperative that we band together and create a protective circle around childhood and the child's need and right to play.

REFERENCES

Alliance for Childhood. (2002). *Children from birth to five: A statement of first principles on early education for educators and policymakers* [on-line]. Available: http://www.allianceforchildhood.com/projects/play/index.htm.

Brown, S. (1999). State of the World Forum, Whole Child Roundtable, San Francisco.

California Department of Developmental Services. (1999). *Changes in the population of persons with autism and PDDs in California's developmental services system: 1987, 1998.* A report to the legislature [on-line]. Available: http://www.dds.cahwnet.gov/autism/pdf/autism_report_1999.pdf.

Centers for Disease Control. (2002). *ADHS—A public health perspective* [on-line]. Available: http://www.cdc.gov/ncbddd/adhd/publichealth.htm.

Der Spiegel (German news magazine). (1977). No. 20, 89–90.

Goleman, D., Kaufman, P., & Ray, M. (1992). *The creative spirit.* New York: Dutton Books.

High/Scope Summary. (2002). *Different effects from different preschool models: High/Scope preschool curriculum comparison study.* Drawn from works by L. J. Schweinhart et al. [on-line]. Available: http://www.highscope.org/ Research/curriccomp.htm.

Hyun, E. (1998). *Making sense of developmentally and culturally appropriate practice (DCAP) in early childhood education.* New York: Peter Lang.

Jaffke, F. (1988). *Toymaking with children.* Edinburgh: Floris Books. (Combined with personal experience and conversations with experienced Waldorf kindergarten teachers such as Elisabeth Moore Haas of Switzerland, Freya Jaffke of Germany, Margret Meyerkort of England, and Bronja Zahlingen of Austria.)

Marcon, R.A. (2002, Spring). Moving up the grades: Relationship between pre-school model and later school success. *Early Childhood Research and Practice, 4* (1), [electronic version].

Montagu, A. (1981). *Growing young.* New York: McGraw-Hill.

National Center for Education Statistics (NCES). (1995). *Readiness for kinder-garten: Parent and teacher beliefs* [on-line]. Available: http:// www.educationworld.com/a_curr/curr027.shtml.

Ohanian, S. (2002). *What happened to recess and why are our children struggling in kindergarten?* New York: McGraw-Hill.

Singer, D., & Singer, J. (1990). *The house of make-believe.* Cambridge, MA: Harvard University Press.

Smilansky, S. (1990). Sociodramatic play: Its relevance to behavior and achievement in school. In E. Klugman & S. Smilansky (Eds.), *Children's play and learning.* New York: Teacher's College.

Steinberg, J. (2000, December 22). Student failure causes states to retool testing. *New York Times.*

Strauss, V. (2003, January 17). U.S. to review Head Start program. *Washington Post,* A01.

Surgeon General. (1999). *Call to action to prevent suicide.* Department of Health and Human Services [o-nline]. Available: http://www.surgeongeneral. gov/library/calltoaction/fact3.htm.

Surgeon General. (2001a). *Call to action to prevent and decrease overweight and obesity.* Department of Health and Human Services [on-line]. Available: http://www.surgeongeneral.gov/topics/obesity/calltoaction/ CalltoAction.pdf.

Surgeon General. (2001b). *Summary of conference on children's mental health.* Department of Health and Human Services [on-line]. Available: http: //www.surgeongeneral.gov/topics/cmh/childreport.htm# sum.

TV Turn-off Network. (2003). *Facts and figures about our TV habit* [on-line]. Available: http://www.tvturnoff.org/images/facts&figs/factsheets/ Facts%20and%20Figures.pdf.

U.S. Senate Bill S.2566. (2002). [On-line]. Available: http://thomas.loc.gov/ cgi bin/query.

ABOUT THE CONTRIBUTOR

JOAN ALMON is the coordinator of the U.S. branch of the Alliance for Childhood, and cochair of the Waldorf Early Childhood Association of North America. She is internationally renowned as a consultant to Waldorf educators and training programs and the author of numerous articles on Waldorf education. Ms. Almon was the editor of the *Waldorf Kindergarten Newsletter* and is a board member of the International Waldorf Kindergarten Association.

2

A Role for Play in the Preschool Curriculum

Dorothy G. Singer, Jerome L. Singer, Sharon L. Plaskon, and Amanda E. Schweder

One of the joys of parenthood is observing preschoolers engaged in imaginative play. A table covered with a sheet becomes a tent in the jungle. Stuffed animals and dolls seated at a small table become the guests at a tea party. Blocks piled up high become a tower where a wicked witch holds the princess as a captive. Household items on a shelf become the products to be sold in a game of "store." A child wearing a police officer's or railroad conductor's hat pretends to be doing the job of an adult. As we watch three-, four-, and five-year-olds playing, we see how much they are learning about the world around them.

Children learn to become flexible when they play. If they do not have a toy airplane, a wooden clothespin can easily become one. Controlling impulsive behavior and delaying gratification are still other benefits. One cannot enjoy the tea party until the water is boiled, the cookies are made out of Play-Doh, and the table is set. If a child becomes aggressive and tries to hit another child during play, quickly the other children or a caregiver will remove the obstreperous child from the game. Children learn, therefore, to curb their negative impulses and express their anger through words. It is more exciting to be part of the pretend scenario than to sit on the sidelines.

In compensatory play, children are able to work out their feelings. If the mother has scolded a child, it is not uncommon to see a child scolding her doll. If a child is jealous about the arrival of a new baby, he or she can enact feelings of anger, jealousy, and later acceptance of this rival through puppet play. And finally, it is just plain fun to play. Children who engage in imaginative play tend to smile and laugh more than those who seem to be at odds with themselves—the children who wander aimlessly around the day-care center, play in a perseverative way with blocks, or annoy their classmates by teasing them or interrupting their play.

Children who have developed a rich capacity for imaginative play are not only emotionally and socially advantaged, but they are intellectually advantaged as well. Indeed, decades of compelling research has documented that imaginative play is an essential building block for the academic challenges that lay in wait for the preschool child. And yet, as concern about school readiness mounts, a common but misguided response is to sideline play and introduce formal academic lessons to preschool-aged children, a trend that is promoted by current federal guidelines for preschool readiness skills.

We begin this chapter with a brief review of the literature that demonstrates the power of play for academic success. Next, we present new federal and state guidelines that promote early formal academic curricula and compare them with the results of a survey of what teachers and parents regard as essential criteria for preschool programs. We go on to describe the settings in which preschool children are typically spending time. While some of these settings are exemplary, in a majority of cases, play is viewed as a form of relaxation or entertainment, but it is not meaningfully incorporated into the curriculum—in part, as a result of the shifting emphases of federal and state guidelines. In addition, many preschool settings have unqualified teachers, few resources, and little or no government support. We summarize the illuminating research of Boyer (1991) and West, Denton, and Germino-Hausken (2000), which reveals that preschoolers are intellectually, socially, and emotionally ill prepared for kindergarten. Finally, we present the results of our Learning through Play research project. As a corrective to the dearth of play in preschool curricula, and the abysmal level of school readiness among preschool children, we created the Learning through Play project at the Yale University Family Television Research and Consultation Center, in which teachers and parents of preschoolers were given the tools and training to stimulate healthy symbolic play, resulting in significantly higher test scores of school readiness.

SYMBOLIC PLAY IN EARLY CHILDHOOD AS A PRECURSOR FOR ACADEMIC SUCCESS

Symbolic or imaginative play emerges at around two years of age and reaches its peak between three and five years (Piaget, 1962). Children playing alone or in groups may enact a familiar role or activity using substitute objects for the real items, such as playing house or school with blocks and cloths to furnish the play kitchen or classroom. Or, symbolic play can involve fanciful or illogical characters and scenarios, such as fairy princesses and pirate boats that sink and then sail away.

Decades of empirical research has established that children's imaginative play is a valuable resource for their social, emotional, cognitive, and language development (Belsky & Most, 1981; Christie, 1983, 1991; Fein, 1981; Singer & Singer, 1990, 2001; Singer, 1973; Yawkey & Pellegrini, 1984). In addition, play has been shown to foster an impressive array of skills that are necessary for school success, including taking another's perspective, regulating one's emotions, taking turns with peers, sequencing the order of events, and recognizing one's independence from others (Saarni, 1999; Singer & Singer, 1990; Singer, Singer, & Schweder, 2002). The benefits of play are especially potent when a parent, caregiver, or educator meaningfully facilitates the play experiences (Connecticut Commission on Children, 2001; Gottfried & Brown, 1986; Lindsey & Mize, 2000; Thompson & Nelson, 2001).

Ginsburg, Inoue, and Seo (1999) discovered that preschool children were able to acquire complex mathematical concepts and applications when learning material was incorporated into their free play. As a result, children felt engaged, and mastered complex concepts. Similarly, early literacy programs that incorporate imaginative play with adult involvement have proven to be particularly successful (Christie & Enz, 1992; Stone & Christie, 1996).

A recent study of low-income preschool children (Coolahan, Fantuzzo, Mendez, & McDermott, 2000) revealed that those who play competently with their peers are more actively engaged in classroom learning activities. Conversely, children who are lacking in play skills are inattentive, passive, and lack motivation. Children who are disruptive in their play with peers tend to evidence conduct problems and hyperactivity in the classroom.

FEDERAL AND STATE GUIDELINES FOR PRESCHOOL READINESS SKILLS

Federal Guidelines

Guilding Strong Foundations for Early Learning: The U.S. Department of Education's Guide to High-Quality Early Childhood Education Programs (Dwyer, Chait, & McKee, 2000) lists several outcomes deemed desirable for children who will have completed high-quality preschool programs. Communication skills encompassing both expressive and receptive language are high on the list. Children are expected to learn new vocabulary, as well as basic computer language. There is an emphasis on phonic awareness, including the ability to identify words with the same sounds and to break words into syllables. Thus, there is clearly an emphasis on reading readiness, understanding that print conveys messages, and that there are print conventions (reading left to right). Children are also expected to begin to write the letters in their own names and to recognize additional letters. Comprehension of stories is important, and visits to libraries, interest in reading, and attempts to write are included in the guidelines (Dwyer et al., 2000). Social skills are not prominently featured in the new federal guidelines, and *nowhere* in this document is there any mention of guided imaginative play as a method for teaching readiness skills for school entrance.

In keeping with the current administration's heavy emphasis on early literacy, G. Reid Lyon, the chief of child development and behavior at the National Institute of Child Health and Human Development, wrote a major part of the Early Reading Initiative, a section of a bill signed into law that pledges $75 million a year for promoting reading in preschools (Schemo, 2002).

The new federal guidelines raise the following concerns: First, although these guidelines exist for prekindergarten curricula, *they are not mandated in the country for kindergarten entrance,* and in most cases, the local schools admit children who may be poorly prepared along with those who have come from quality settings and are ready to engage successfully in the kindergarten curriculum. Second, the current guidelines imply that children's social and emotional needs can be addressed separately from their intellectual needs, and therefore are not required as an integral part of a preschool curriculum. Third, the emphasis on early reading acquisition is at variance with the stage of cognitive development of the average preschooler (Singer & Revenson, 1996), potentially stressing many children and setting them up for experiences of failure. Finally, the guidelines do not acknowledge the central role of play in facilitating literacy (and myriad other skills).

Thus, early literacy programs are being emphasized at the expense of children's emotional and social development, with a flagrant disregard for play as an essential feature not only for sheer joy but as a motivator for learning. Play has been recognized as important for learning by the guidelines of the National Association for the Education of Young Children (NAEYC). We can only hope that the administrators of these preschool reading programs will not omit play in favor of a more limited approach to learning. However, in all of the programs we reviewed (see appendix A), little emphasis is placed on play. More and more, we see preschools involved with reading readiness and the elimination of time for free or guided play in keeping with the spirit of the new federal guidelines. We have yet to see positive results of such a shift in curricula.

State Guidelines

After reviewing the federal guidelines for preschool education and kindergarten readiness, we examined what (if any) standards had been established at the state level.

Saluja, Scott-Little, and Clifford (2000) conducted a national survey tapping every early childhood representative from the Departments of Education in all fifty states to determine how states define and measure school readiness. They found that while states specify an age requirement for kindergarten entrance, there are neither formal definitions of school readiness nor uniform assessment measurements being used. According to the authors, only five states have developed frameworks or benchmarks. Another five states reported that local districts may provide definitions of readiness, and six states emphasized the concept that schools should be ready for all children regardless of their skills.

The authors also found great variations in school readiness measurements, such as the use of standardized tests, naturalistic observations by teachers, locally developed assessment tools, and health and development screenings. In addition, some school districts suggest psychometric instruments that individual schools may choose at will. Among the states, twenty-six do not mandate readiness assessments, but the option is left to local districts. Furthermore, in five states, local schools conduct screenings or assessments, sixteen states have plans under development, and thirteen states conduct screenings/assessments. Six states do not assess at all; some even consider assessment to be potentially harmful for children. Of the states that do use some form of measurement, twelve report that they use school readiness data for instructional purposes, seven use the data for school improvement, six for screening purposes (e.g., to identify special needs), and four report that the districts decide how to use the data (Saluja et al., 2000).

According to Schulman, Blank, and Ewen (1999), ten states appear to spend nothing on the care and education of preschool children. Among the other forty, there is considerable variation found in the money being spent. To date, only Georgia has made a sufficient investment in the education of all four-year-olds whose parents wish them to participate. Evidence from the Abcedarian Project, a longitudinal study of the effects of early intervention, demonstrates the importance of these programs for the children as well as for the social and economic development of the state (Campbell, Helms, Sparling, & Ramey, 1998).

To summarize, while some states are becoming more involved in establishing guidelines, current school readiness curricula and assessments are addressed primarily at the local district and individual school levels. More research and monitoring at the state and local levels is clearly indicated.

A SURVEY OF TEACHERS AND PARENTS

Using semistructured questionnaires, we contacted fifty-four day-care providers, home-care providers, Head Start teachers, parents, and kindergarten teachers to determine the skills they considered were important for children upon entering kindergarten (Bellin, Singer, Singer, & Plaskon, 2000). While all participants in the survey seemed to agree that cognitive skills such as learning and recognizing letters and numbers, knowing shapes and colors, and spelling their own names were important, *the need for social skills ranked high*. Teachers and parents all agreed that learning how to get along in groups, dealing with conflict appropriately, and demonstrating good manners were essential. Self-help skills and independence were frequently cited. Such actions, for example, as being responsible for their belongings, dressing themselves, and demonstrating basic hygiene were viewed as necessary skills for preschoolers before entering kindergarten. The survey also indicated that children need to know their own names, parents' names, their addresses, and phone numbers.

We are in agreement that social skills should be stressed in preschool settings in conjunction with the current emphasis on cognitive skills. Current federal guidelines are not in keeping with either the NAEYC's emphasis on play or the concern of caregivers about social skills development.

AMERICAN CHILDREN'S PRESCHOOL EXPERIENCE

In order to see how the new federal guidelines are influencing preschoolers' experiences, we examined what kinds of settings children are spending time in prior to kindergarten, the quality of preschool teacher training, and how preschool programs are utilizing play.

Where Children Are Being Cared for Before Kindergarten Entry

With 64 percent of all mothers of children under six years of age in the workforce, each day thirteen million preschoolers, including six million infants and toddlers, are in child care (Children's Defense Fund, 2000). Approximately "four out of five first-time kindergartners (81%) receive care on a regular basis from someone other than their parents in the year prior to starting kindergarten. This care is most often provided in a center-based setting (69%), followed by care by a relative in a private home (24%), and care by a non-relative in a private home (15%)" (West et al., 2000, p. 57). As such, the quality of home care, day care, and preschool programs plays a central role in our children's intellectual, social, and emotional development and their subsequent ability to cope with the challenges of formal education. This is particularly true given the considerable plasticity and sensitivity of the brain to environmental influence in the first three years of life (Thompson & Nelson, 2001).

Quality of Preschool Teacher Training

In addition to the standards that are created for preschool education, the skills of the teachers and caregivers who implement these standards, and the resources available to them, are critical to the success of the program. Unfortunately, there is tremendous variation in the quality of day care in the United States. According to Young, Marsland, and Zigler (1997, p. 541), there is "quantitative documentation that state child-care regulations continue to allow infants and toddlers to be cared for in environments that do not meet basic standards of practice appropriate to assuring the safe and healthy development of very young children." The authors report that 67 percent of the fifty states in their study received overall ratings of Poor or Very Poor and not one received an overall rating of Good or Optimal. Quality child-care components are "characterized by low child-staff ratios, low staff turnover, decent wages, appropriate staff training and relatively small classroom size" (Zigler & Hall, 2000, p. 120).

Maternal employment trends, especially the work requirements imposed on welfare recipients, and the increase of two parents working to insure an adequate income have added to the demand for more day-care facilities. Although there are federal subsidies to help low-income families pay for child care, the numbers of families requesting day care has risen dramatically. Subsidies reach only 12 percent of the fifteen million children estimated to be eligible for assistance (Larner, Behrman, Young, & Reich, 2001).

Faced with the need for both more facilities and more funding, an additional issue is evident, that of raising the quality of personnel in existing centers, and preparing teachers for future positions. According to Honig and Hirallal (1998), teachers who have specific training in child development have better results with children than teachers who are not as well trained.

One of the chief problems facing child-care personnel is the lack of national standards with regard to pay, training, and licensing. Ripple (2000) suggests several reasons for low wages. The great majority of child-care workers are female, and many are from minority groups. Many also are in their childbearing years and therefore, confront the problem of finding affordable care for their own young children. In addition, linguistic, ethnic, and educational backgrounds of child-care workers vary considerably (Whitebook & Phillips, 1999). Furthermore, Ripple (2000) claims that there is a prevailing public perception that caregiving does not require special training and that child care is a private family matter. Welfare reform requirements have brought additional mothers into the workforce, many of whom entered the child-care field with little training, education, or knowledge of child development.

According to the Bureau of Labor Statistics (U.S. Department of Labor, 2000), the median annual earnings of preschool teachers were $17,310 in 1998. The middle 50 percent earned between $13,760 and $22,370. The lowest 10 percent earned less than $12,000, and the highest 10 percent earned more than $30,310. Hourly wages varied from less than $5.49 to more than $9.65. Benefits vary for these workers, but are minimal in most instances. Personnel in child-care settings are highly exposed to illness and physical strain, yet often do not receive medical benefits. In addition, many work without breaks and are asked to work extra hours without compensation (Whitebook & Phillips, 1999).

About 40 percent of preschool teachers and child-care workers are self-employed, with most of these as family child-care providers. It is relatively easy to enter the child-care field because of the low training requirements and high turnover. About one-third of workers leave their jobs each year (Whitebook & Phillips, 1999). At the same time, there is employment growth, as child-care needs are expanding with more mothers entering the workforce. Another reason for employment openings in child care is the fact that many qualified child-care workers are leaving these jobs to take more lucrative positions as elementary schoolteachers due to the shortage of such personnel. For example, many welfare recipients enter the workforce through Head Start opportunities, where they receive child-care training and get health and retirement benefits. Once trained, they often seek better-paying teaching positions (Whitebook & Gaidurjis, 1995, as cited in Whitebook & Phillips, 1999).

Ripple (2000) makes an important point concerning the increase of wages for child-care workers; if wages are increased, this will result in higher fees for parents. Consequently, parents in the lower income bracket will seek out less-expensive alternatives for child care, which may compromise the quality. The author also offers suggestions concerning child-care worker improvement, such as an increase in compensation for child-care personnel through additional public funds; raising the minimum wage; educating the public about the child-care crisis, with an emphasis on targeting older generations with this information (more of the elderly are entering into child-care positions); combining elder-care and child-care quality campaigns to strengthen their causes, as many of the issues regarding quality of care are similar; unionization for child-care workers; and turning child care into a profession that is linked to education.

Preschool Programs That Allow for Play

A survey of preschool programs that do allow for free play during the day revealed that *guided imaginative play* was rarely mentioned in any of these preschool programs as a means of helping children achieve the skills needed to perform well in kindergarten, despite the central role that the NAEYC gives to play (see appendix A for a description of the programs). In addition, when we observed children in a variety of settings during free play periods, we rarely witnessed teachers using this opportunity to focus on kindergarten readiness skills. Children are generally left to make their own play choices with teachers available to keep discipline. As such, many critical opportunities for teachers to use guided play were lost. Strategies such as acknowledging and encouraging children's efforts, modeling and demonstrating, creating challenges, supporting children in extending their capabilities, and providing specific directions or instructions can be used effectively in the "context of play" (Bowman, Donovan, & Burns, 2000).

Thus far, we presented research in support of the critical role of symbolic play in preparation for formal schooling. We then summarized federal and state guidelines, and the nature and quality of preschool care that American children currently have access to. In so doing, we established that preschool guidelines and programs are plagued by (1) a one-sided emphasis on formal academic training with a focus on reading that is insensitive to preschool children's developmental readiness, (2) inadequately trained and stressed caregivers, and (3) a disregard for the importance of play as a learning tool and source of psychological well-being. It comes as no surprise, therefore, that research on kindergarten readiness indicates that preschool children are ill prepared for kindergarten.

KINDERGARTEN READINESS: AN OVERVIEW

Research findings on children's preparedness for kindergarten over the past decade are alarming. A decade ago, Boyer (1991) conducted a pivotal survey that alerted educators, child development specialists, and politicians about the urgent need to improve the quality of preschool care our children receive. According to the more than 7,000 kindergarten teachers who were surveyed, 33 percent of our nation's children were ill prepared upon entrance into kindergarten. Close to 60 percent of children in the inner cities were not ready for school. Poorer children displayed problems in language, emotional maturity, general world knowledge, social confidence, and moral awareness (Boyer, 1991). As a result of these findings, numerous meetings were held around the country and another report was issued, *Years of Promise: A Comprehensive Learning Strategy for America's Children* (Carnegie Task Force on Learning in the Primary Grades, 1996). A White House Conference on Early Childhood Development and Learning (1997) was held, calling for the revamping of existing preschool programs in order to help children achieve the skills necessary for a satisfactory kindergarten experience. As a result of this conference, material was prepared and made available at no charge to parents and educators, such as the *America Reads Challenge: Ready-Set-Read*, and *Early Childhood Development Activity Kits* (Corporation for National Services, 1997).

Ten years after the Boyer report, a larger sample—22,000 children in 1,000 kindergarten programs (West et al., 2000)—was assessed through telephone interviews with their parents/guardians, and with questionnaires completed by their kindergarten teachers. The children were also assessed directly. The findings suggest that not enough was accomplished by child-care personnel over the ten-year span in terms of quality of their curricula. According to West et al., 34 percent of the children had difficulty recognizing letters, and 71 percent had difficulty understanding the beginnings of sounds.

When teacher reports of the children were analyzed, social skills limitations emerged. Of the sample of children reviewed, 25 percent had difficulties with peers in terms of friendship patterns and arguing or fighting; 10 percent were found to be arguing and fighting with others; and 25–33 percent had problems in persistence, paying attention, and their eagerness to learn. Parents also reported difficulties among their children as follows: 15 percent had problems when playing with others, in making friends, and in comforting others; 33 percent were found to engage in arguing with others; and 20 percent were characterized as fighting and getting angry easily. These "at risk children," who experienced difficulties in social relationships and were less eager to learn, were offspring of parents who had less than a high school education and were single parents. In general, older children and children whose mothers had a college education performed at higher levels in reading, mathematics, and general knowledge than younger children whose mothers had a lower level of education.

Given that so many preschoolers are still ill prepared for the classroom ten years after Boyer's seminal report, it appears that the efforts at intervention have been ineffective. Improving early childhood care and education must take into consideration (1) the working conditions and training of the caregivers, (2) access of poor and struggling families whose children are most at risk to excellent quality day care and preschool, (3) a greater sensitivity regarding children's developmental needs, and (4) an appreciation of the intimate interconnection of social, emotional, and intellectual development. In light of our concerns about the current quality of early childhood education and the pivotal role that play could serve, we created the Learning through Play research project.[1]

LEARNING THROUGH PLAY: A RESEARCH PROJECT

Given that children's capacity for pretend play is so ripe during the preschool years, it should be viewed as a competency that can be capitalized upon to maximize children's likelihood for success in school, particularly for low socioeconomic status (SES) children. The thesis underlying our project is that teachers and parents who enjoy playing make-believe games with children in their care will successfully teach vocabulary, colors, shapes, numbers, manners, and knowledge about everyday events through *play*, rather than through a didactic approach. We have developed a training manual for caregivers and a video for parents, teachers, and children, and found that the children who took part in the play protocol scored significantly higher on tests for kindergarten readiness when compared to children who had not experienced "play training."

Learning through Play: Phase 1

In an effort to demonstrate a technique for enhancing pretend play skills in children, Learning through Play, a short-term early childhood education intervention, was created to improve children's preparation for formal schooling (Singer, Singer, & Bellin, 1998; Singer et al., 2002). In the initial evaluation of this intervention, we trained low SES parents to use pretend games with their preschool children to see if the children's pretend play was enhanced, thereby producing improvements in their readiness for school. Significant improvements in overall scores on a school readiness test were found for children whose parents received play training, in comparison to children whose parents received no training. Modest increases were also found in subcomponents of the overall test, including (a) vocabulary, (b) knowledge about nature, (c) general information knowledge, and (d) knowledge about manners. Qualitative observations of children's play behavior at school, however, revealed that the children were not playing the pretend games during school. Similarly, observations of teachers indicated that they did not encourage the children to play pretend games in their classrooms.

Learning through Play: Phase 2

Because so many children today spend a great deal of time at day care or preschool, in the second phase of the Learning through Play project, both parents and teachers were trained to use pretend play games (Singer et al., 2002). Three groups of four-year-old children's caregivers received training: (a) parents only, (b) teachers only, and (c) parents plus teachers. A fourth group was included as a control group (no training with either parents or teachers occurred). Parents signed a letter of consent granting permission for their children to participate in the project. The Yale Human Subjects Committee approved the entire research protocol.

Caregiver training curricula were developed and adapted into a two-part program, employing a written manual and a video used to demonstrate examples of games for fostering children's pretend play skills (Singer et al., 1998; Singer et al., 2002). A facilitator explained the purpose of the training to the parent and teacher groups and then used the video to illustrate how each game could be played. The video began with an introduction about the value of play for preschool children and included a total of six pretend games narrated and played by adults and preschoolers to provide parents and teachers with concrete ways to initiate pretend play with their children. An example of a game presented in the training video was the "Restaurant Game"; a story about a birthday party at a pretend restaurant designed to enhance skills in sequencing, cooperation, shape recognition, and fine motor skills. Parents and teachers were provided with printed records to keep during each week of the training program and were asked to record the games they played with their child along with the amount of time they spent playing each game each day over the two-week period. The forms also asked for an evaluation of the play.

Trained observers visited the children's classrooms before and after the caregiver training sessions to rate the children's play behavior during free playtimes. Four aspects of children's play behaviors were rated on a scale from one (i.e., very little of the behavior) to five (i.e., very much of the behavior), including: (a) persistence, (b) imaginativeness, (c) positive affect, and (d) cooperation during play.

A school readiness test was created for the Learning through Play intervention to examine the skills that children improved upon following the caregiver training in pretend play (Singer et al., 1998; Singer et al., 2002). These items were selected as per recommendation from the NAEYC based on kindergarten teachers' feedback. The test was administered to each child before and after the training sessions, and included domains such as cognitive, social, and emotional development. Practitioners and researchers alike have identified the concepts assessed by these test items as important skills for preschool children to have when they begin school (see, for example, Peth-Pierce, 2000).

Analyses indicated that among the teachers who played with the children for long periods of time, greater change was found in the preschoolers' persistence during play compared to those children whose teachers played with them for less time. These findings suggest that there may be an important threshold or range of intervention time that needs to be met in order for the techniques to be most effective.

Certain aspects of play behavior rated by observers during free playtime at school (e.g., greater imaginativeness, persistence, and cooperation) were positively associated with higher levels of school readiness. Other findings include increases from pre- to post-training for some of the groups. For instance, knowledge of numbers slightly increased over time for children whose *parents only* were trained and whose *parents plus teachers* were trained. Children's knowledge of forms/shapes and of general information increased over time for children when all adult groups were trained.

It seemed that it might be more effective to deliver the training to parents and teachers in a forum where the children were also present. As a result, our next phase involved the preparation of new games and materials, including a video especially prepared for children to view along with adults and a training manual for the adults. The video consisted of five games that included such skills as cooperation, sharing, numbers, identifying emotions, matching letters with words, and learning concepts such as *near, far, above, below, under,* and *over.* The manual was designed to be a stand alone training tool eliminating the need for training workshops. It also included materials for the children to use in the imaginative games (such as a numbers page for the counting games, an alphabet page, pictures of animals used in a nature game, and play money) and resources for the adults (including titles of books relating to readiness skills, phone numbers to call for materials, and a summary of developmental stages).

The participants, who were nearly equal numbers of teachers, home-care providers and parents (N = 118), filled out a questionnaire yielding background information including whether or not they had taken courses in child development. Participants were asked to keep a record of the games they played, as well as which games they and the children liked best. They also evaluated the video, the manual, and, on a five-point scale, rated the children on variables such as persistence, imagination, self-help/independence, and social skills (cooperation, sharing, taking turns). School readiness skills such as numbers, colors, shapes, and letters were also rated to indicate any improvement on the part of the child after the play training had begun. Children were to play the games guided by the adults over a two-week period with a minimum of ten minutes per day. At the conclusion of these play periods, all participants attended focus groups to share their impressions of the materials and the outcome of their efforts.

Results indicate that parents and especially home-care providers averaged more time using videos with children in the first week than did the teachers. By the second week, teachers played the videos enough times to reduce the earlier significant differences between them and the other adult groups. Basically, the same finding occurred for the number of times the games were played, with parents and home-care providers playing the games more times with children in the first week than did the teachers. By the second week, however, the teachers caught up enough to reduce the significant effect. It may be that there is less time available to teachers due to the more rigid structure of the day-care centers than the home-care or parent settings. Overall time spent in training and playing with the children averaged four hours per week, with no significant differences among the three groups.

Post-training results indicated that children across all three groups showed significant increases in spontaneous imaginativeness, and an increase in pro-social skills such as cooperation, sharing, and taking turns. We also found increases in children's persistence on tasks, concentration, and displays of positive emotions (smiling, laughing, interest/excitement). There was also an increase in the ability of the children to identify letters. There were no significant effects for numbers, colors, or shapes. The reason for this was that by midyear of our project, the children were well along in their ability to count to ten and recognize colors and common shapes such as squares, triangles, and rectangles. The strongest results tended to be for those children who were trained by parents or by home-care providers. It was apparent that parents and home-care providers who had no structured curriculum spent more time playing and encouraging the games with the children.

Qualitative data from the questionnaires and from the focus group sessions suggest that parents, teachers, and home-care providers enjoyed the materials and felt that they were easy to use. The children "loved" the video and wanted to see it over and over. The three groups claimed that they would continue to play these games and were inspired to play other make-believe games with their children. They offered us many suggestions for future videos, such as one on safety, self-help, more on emotions, and social skills.

We then tested our materials again in Connecticut and in sites such as Alabama, California, Maryland, Minnesota, Ohio, Wisconsin, and Wyoming. We incorporated some of the earlier participants' suggestions for new games, and the final video included seven games and a new simplified manual that adults could easily follow before presenting the video to the children. Results of this final phase were gratifying. The children, parents, and teachers enjoyed the games, and played them on an average of thirty minutes per week for two weeks. Parents and teachers then filled out forms commenting on the usefulness of the video and manual. Adults rated the children on pre- and post-test forms on the same variables in the earlier studies. Results indicated that gains were made on most of the variables in all sites.

SUMMARY AND RECOMMENDATIONS

About one-third of America's preschool children and two-thirds of socioeconomically disadvantaged children are still having difficulty upon entry into kindergarten. Unfortunately, the majority of the states have no standardized entrance requirements for kindergarten. Preschool centers vary in their offerings for children, but when we examined the preschool programs of two states that are progressive, plus the recommendations of Jumpstart, Headstart, and the Department of Defense's preschool program, we noted that the curricula of these match the recommendations of the NAEYC (see appendix A). This brief sampling offers hope that other preschools could, with financial and consultant support, upgrade their school readiness requirements to meet accreditation by the NAEYC or by other national preschool associations.

Richard Rothstein, education columnist for the *New York Times*, suggests that more five-year-olds will be better placed for kindergarten if improvements are made regarding access to and quality within the preschools (Rothstein, 2001). He lends support to our thesis that children can learn through play, stating that "guided play teaches social, emotional and academic proficiency" (p. B7). Rothstein's argument corresponds to the philosophy in the research project presented above. Based on parents' and teachers' suggestions for a preschool curriculum and using play as a modality for helping children prepare for kindergarten, results indicated that when children were engaged in imaginative games with teachers and parents that encompassed such things as numbers, shapes, colors, vocabulary, and civility in the play training, they learned significantly more than others who did not have such exposure or modeling.

Regarding child-care issues, Gormley and Lucas (2000) argue that financial incentives to encourage child-care facility accreditation is one way to help improve the quality of child-care centers and family child-care homes. They also state that differential reimbursement is "not a magic bullet, but rather . . . one tool in the tool box of child care quality improvement" (p. 17). One example utilized by several states is differential reimbursement, in which accredited facilities receive increased state subsidies. Connecticut and Massachusetts require prekindergarten programs to apply for NAEYC accreditation in order to receive state dollars. If the facilities do not achieve accreditation within four years, funding may cease. Florida offers a property exempt status and a tax exemption for the purchase of supplies for child-care facilities that achieve high standards ("Golden Seal" centers).

Gormley and Lucas also suggest that there can be more than one accrediting organization to participate in the differential reimbursement process. So far, only the Department of Defense facilities are required by the federal government to have accreditation. There is substantial state variation in the rules that qualify child-care providers for participation in differential reimbursement programs. The list of such accreditation associations is long, such as the National Early Childhood Program Accreditation (NECPA); the National School-Age Care Alliance (NSACA); the Council on Accreditation of Services for Children and Families (COA); and the National Accreditation Commission for Early Care and Education Programs (NACECEP). Montessori schools have their own accrediting bodies, as do Christian facilities.

States can offer financial incentives for child-care personnel to continue their education in child development. Teacher education and compensation are the most difficult problems facing the child-care industry. State agencies and private foundations can help pay for workshops, retreats, and on-site counseling to give their accreditation process a boost. The TEACH program in North Carolina offers financial incentives for child-care development courses at community colleges and other institutions of higher learning (Gormley & Lucas, 2000). Leaders of the Focus on Our Future initiative have been pressuring national and state legislatures to increase public funding for early childhood programs. This has resulted in state funding in Pennsylvania, where the North Carolina program was emulated (Mintron, 2001). We need more studies concerning the state-level efforts that have led to changes in early child education policies. What works at state levels might not work at federal levels, but as Ripple (2000, p. 18) suggests, "federal legislation might provide the framework and the funds to complement state-level approaches, particularly in the areas of education and training and in national performance guidelines for quality programs for children."

The data concerning employment of child-care workers and the difficulties they encounter in terms of education and pay are compelling. If, indeed, thirteen million preschoolers and six million infants are in child care each day (Children's Defense Fund, 2000), this nation must become more active in upgrading child-care centers through better curricula and better pay and training of the workers themselves.

We also need to expand the population of workers who are entering child care by seeking such people as older citizens, more male teachers, and more college graduates, and to differentiate among those who choose elder care vs. child care as a profession. Research would be helpful in determining the factors that underlie such choices. We need to consider the effect of unionizing child-care workers. Furthermore, there is a need to develop and disseminate outcome measures that are associated with high-quality care. Demonstration projects of successful preschool programs, such as the ones in Seattle and in Allegheny County, PA need to be reviewed and offered as models for how early child care can be improved (Ripple, 2000).

A major dilemma persists for most parents in choosing suitable child-care placement. There are cost and quality factors that need to be balanced. More aid in terms of both state and federal funds, as well as national standards for accreditation, would help alleviate the problems immeasurably. We owe it to our children, who are the future keepers of our nation, to help them prepare for a successful kindergarten entry, the first step toward success in later school achievement. We can do this if our preschool facilities are updated with better-trained personnel, more stringent curriculum requirements, and accreditation. We were able to demonstrate the ease of relatively short-time training of child-care workers and parents of preschoolers in how to use imaginative games to help their children learn particular skills. Research data strongly suggest that integrating the motivating features of guided imaginative play with cognitive and social components can make a productive contribution to readying children for school entry.

NOTE

1. Copies of the video and manual are available from the Media Group of Connecticut, 7 Maple Street, Weston, CT 08883.

REFERENCES

Bellin, H.F., Singer, J.L., Singer, D.G., & Plaskon, S.L. (2000). *Circle of make-believe.* Prepared for U.S. Department of Education Early Childhood Institute. Unpublished manuscript, Yale University, New Haven, CT.

Belsky, J., & Most, R. (1981). From exploration to play: A cross-sectional study of infant free play behavior. *Developmental Psychology, 17,* 630–639.

Bowman, B., Donovan, M.S., & Burns, M.S. (Eds.). (2000). *Eager to learn: Educating our preschoolers.* Washington, DC: National Academy Press.

Boyer, E.L. (1991). *Ready to learn: A mandate for the nation.* Princeton, NJ: The Carnegie Foundation for the Advancement of Teaching.

Campbell, F.A., Helms, R., Sparling, J.J., & Ramey, T. (1998). Early-childhood programs and success in school: The Abcedarian Study. In W.S. Barnett & S.S. Boocock (Eds.), *Early care and education for children in poverty: Promises, programs, and long term effects* (pp. 145–166). Albany, NY: State University of New York Press.

Carnegie Task Force on Learning in the Primary Grades. (1996). *Years of promise: A comprehensive learning strategy for America's children.* New York: Carnegie Corp.

Child Health and Development Institute of Connecticut. (2001, November). How training of child care professionals improves early care and education for children. *Impact.*

Children's Defense Fund. (2000). *Child care and early education basics* [on-line]. Available: http://www.childrensdefense.org/childcare/cc_facts.html.

Christie, J.F. (1983). The effects of play tutoring on young children's cognitive performance. *Journal of Educational Research, 76,* 326–330.

Christie, J.F. (ed.). (1991). *Play and early literacy development.* Albany, NY: State University of New York Press.

Christie, J.F., & Enz, B. (1992). The effects of literacy play interventions on preschoolers' play patterns and literacy development. *Early Education & Development, 3,* 205–220.

Connecticut Commission on Children. (2001, February). *School Readiness Update.*

Connecticut State Department of Education, Bureau of Early Childhood Education and Social Services. (1999). *Connecticut's preschool curriculum framework and benchmarks for children in preschool programs*: Author.

Coolahan, K., Fantuzzo, J., Mendez, J., & McDermott, P. (2000). Preschool peer interactions and readiness to learn: Relationships between classroom peer play and learning behaviors and conduct. *Journal of Educational Psychology, 92,* 458–465.

Corporation for National Services, U.S. Department of Education, & the U.S. Department of Health and Human Services. (1997). *America reads challenge: Ready-set-read early childhood development activity kit.* Washington, DC: Author.

Department of Defense. (1997). U.S. Military Child Development. *Making a difference in child care: Lessons learned while building the military child development system.* Arlington, VA: Author.

Dwyer, M.C., Chait, R., & McKee, P. (2000). *Building strong foundations for early learning: The U.S. Department of Education's guide to high-quality early childhood education programs.* Washington, DC: U.S. Department of Education.

Federal Interagency Forum on Child and Family Statistics. (2000). *America's children: Key national indicators of well-being, 2000.* Washington, DC: U.S. Government Printing Office.

Fein, G.G. (1981). Pretend play in childhood: An integrative review. *Child Development, 52,* 1095–1118.

Ginsburg, H.P., Inoue, N., & Seo, K.H. (1999). Young children doing math-
    ematics: Observations of everyday activities. In Juanita V. Copley (Ed.),
    Mathematics in the early years (pp. 88–99). Washington, DC: National As-
    sociation for the Education of Young Children.
Gormley, W.T., Jr., & Lucas, J.K. (2000). *Money, accreditation, and child care center
    quality.* Working Paper Series. New York: Foundation for Child Devel-
    opment.
Gottfried, A.W., & Brown, C.C. (Eds.). (1986). *Play interaction: The contributions
    of play materials and parental involvement to children's development.* Lex-
    ington, MA: Lexington Books.
Henderson, L., Basile, K., & Henry, G. (1999). *Prekindergarten longitudinal study:
    1997–1998 school year annual report.* Atlanta, GA: Georgia State Univer-
    sity Applied Research Center.
Honig, A.S., & Hirallal, A. (1998). Which counts more for excellence in
    childcare staff—years in service, education level, or ECE coursework?
    Early Child Development and Care, 145, 31–46 (ERIC Journal No.
    EJ580288).
Jumpstart New Haven, 258 Church St., Ste. 201, New Haven, CT 06510.
Larner, M., Behrman, R.E., Young, M., & Reich, K. (2001). Caring for infants
    and toddlers: Analysis and recommendations. In Richard E. Behrman
    (Ed.), *The Future of Children* (vol. 11, no. 1, pp. 7–19). Los Altos, CA: The
    David and Lucile Packard Foundation.
Lindsey, E.W., & Mize, J. (2000). Parent-child physical and pretense play: Links
    to children's social competence. *Merrill-Palmer Quarterly, 46,* 565–591.
Mintron, M. (2001). *Achieving quality early childhood education for all: Insights
    from the policy innovation diffusion research.* Working Paper Series. New
    York: Foundation for Child Development.
Peth-Pierce, R. (2000). *A good beginning: Sending America's children to school with
    the social and emotional competence they need to succeed.* Report from The
    Child Mental Health Foundations and Agencies Network. Bethesda,
    MD: The National Institute of Mental Health.
Piaget, J. (1962). *Play, dreams and imitation in childhood.* New York: W. W.
    Norton & Company, Inc.
Raden, A. (1999). *Universal prekindergarten in Georgia.* Working Paper Series.
    New York: Foundation for Child Development.
Ripple, C. (2000). *Economics of caring labor: Improving compensation in the early
    childhood workforce.* Summary of meeting convened by the A. L. Mail-
    man Family Foundation and the Foundation for Child Development,
    Working Paper Series. New York: A. L. Mailman Family Foundation
    and the Foundation for Child Development.
Rothstein, R. (2001, March 21). Ambitious but misguided: Kindergarten aca-
    demics. *New York Times,* p. B7.
Saarni, C. (1999). *The development of emotional competence.* The Guilford series
    on social and emotional development. New York: Guilford Press.
Saluja, G., Scott-Little, C., & Clifford, R.M. (2000). Readiness for school: A sur-

vey of the states. *Early Childhood Research & Practice, 12* [on-line]. Available: http://www.ecrp.uiuc.edu.

Schemo, D.J. (2002). How the pressure begins for Bush's reading expert. *New York Times,* January 19, p. A19.

Schulman, K., Blank, H., & Ewen, D. (1999). *Seeds of success: State prekindergarten initiatives 1998–99.* Washington, DC: Children's Defense Fund.

Singer, D.G., & Revenson, T.A. (1996). *A Piaget primer: How a child thinks.* New York: Plume/Penguin.

Singer, D.G., & Singer, J.L. (1990). *The house of make-believe: Children's play and the developing imagination.* Cambridge, MA: Harvard University Press.

Singer, D.G., & Singer, J.L. (2001). *Make-believe: Games and activities for imaginative play.* Washington, DC: Magination Press.

Singer, J.L. (1973). *The child's world of make-believe: Experimental studies in imaginative play.* New York: Academic Press.

Singer, J.L., Singer, D.G., & Bellin, H.F. (1998). *Parenting through play for school readiness: Report, year one.* Prepared for U.S. Department of Education Early Childhood Institute. Unpublished manuscript, Yale University, New Haven, CT.

Singer, J.L., Singer, D.G., Bellin, H.F., & Schweder, A.E. (1999). *Parenting through play for school readiness: Report, year two.* Prepared for U.S. Department of Education Early Childhood Institute. Unpublished manuscript, Yale University, New Haven, CT.

Singer, J.L., Singer, D.G., & Schweder, A.E. (2002). Enhancing preschoolers' school readiness through imaginative play with parents and teachers. In R. Clements & L. Fiorentino (Eds.), *The child's right to play: A global approach.* Westport, CT: Greenwood Publishing.

Stone, S.J., & Christie, J.F. (1996). Collaborative literacy learning during sociodramatic play in a multiage (K–2) primary classroom. *Journal of Research in Childhood Education, 10,* 123–133.

Thompson, R.A., & Nelson, C.A. (2001). Developmental science and the media. *American Psychologist, 56,* 5–15.

U.S. Army Child and Youth Services, Army Child Development Centers. (2000). *Professional development program for entry level staff.* Alexandria, VA: Author.

U.S. Department of Labor, Bureau of Labor Statistics. (2000). *Occupational outlook handbook, 2000–2001 edition* [on-line]. Available: http://www.stats.bls.gov/ocohome.htm.

West, J., Denton, K., & Germino-Hausken, E. (2000). *America's kindergartners: Findings from the early childhood longitudinal study, kindergarten class of 1998–99, fall 1998.* NCES 2000-070 (Revised). Washington, DC: U.S. Department of Education, National Center for Education Statistics.

Westat, Inc., Ellsworth Associates, Inc., Abt Associates, Inc., & The CDM Group, Inc. (1998). *Head Start program performance measures, second progress report.* Washington, DC: U.S. Department of Health and Human Services.

White House Conference on Early Childhood Development and Learning. (1997, April 17). Washington, DC: Author.

Whitebook, M., & Phillips, D. (1999). *Child care employment: Implications for women's self sufficiency and for child development.* Working Paper Series. New York: Foundation for Child Development.

Yawkey, T.D., & Pellegrini, A.D. (1984). *Child's play: Developmental and applied.* Hillsdale, NJ: Lawrence Erlbaum.

Young, K.T., Marsland, K.W., & Zigler, E. (1997). The regulatory status of center-based infant and toddler child care. *American Journal of Orthopsychiatry, 67(4),* 535–544.

Zigler, E.F., & Hall, N.W. (2000). *Child development and social policy.* Boston: McGraw-Hill.

Zigler, E.F., & Lang, M.E. (1991). *Child care choices.* New York: The Free Press.

ABOUT THE CONTRIBUTORS

DOROTHY G. SINGER received her doctorate in school psychology from Teachers College, Columbia University. Her title is senior research scientist, Department of Psychology, Yale University. She is also co-director, with Jerome L. Singer, of the Yale University Family Television Research and Consultation Center, and fellow, Morse College at Yale. In addition, she is a senior research associate, Yale Child Study Center. Formerly, Dr. Singer was the William Benton professor of psychology, University of Bridgeport. She is a fellow of the American Psychology Association. Research interests include early childhood development, television effects on youth, and parent training in imaginative play. Her latest books with Jerome L. Singer are *Handbook of Children and the Media* and *Make-Believe: Games and Activities for Imaginative Play.*

JEROME L. SINGER received his doctorate in clinical psychology from the University of Pennsylvania. He is professor of psychology at Yale University, where he served for many years as director of the graduate program in clinical psychology and also as director of graduate studies in psychology. He is a specialist in research on the psychology of imagination and daydreaming. Dr. Singer has authored more than 270 technical articles on thought processes, imagery, personality, and psychotherapy, as well as on children's play and the effects of television. He is a fellow of the American Psychological Association. Recent books include *The House of Make-Believe* and *Repression and Dissociation.*

SHARON L. PLASKON earned a B.A. in psychology with a concentration in research and theory from Albertus Magnus College in New Haven, Connecticut, where she was the recipient of the Psychology Department Award for Academic Excellence. She went on to receive an M.S. in school psychology from Southern Connecticut State University, where she is currently pursuing school psychology certification. As a research assistant at the Yale University Family Television Research and Consultation Center, she has worked on several projects dealing with the media and with the education of young children. These included the coordination and testing of video-based training programs for parents and teachers to help preschool children increase their school readiness skills.

AMANDA E. SCHWEDER received her Ph.D. in developmental psychology from Yale University. Prior to beginning her studies at Yale, and after graduating from Skidmore College with a B.A. in psychology, she worked at the Manpower Demonstration Research Corporation (MDRC) conducting public policy research. While at Yale, her research activities have focused on evaluating a preschool intervention aimed at instructing teachers and parents to use pretend play as a way of readying preschoolers for school. Currently, her research is focused on examining the correlates of, and individual differences in, aggressive behavior problems in children who have been maltreated and subsequently removed from their homes, as well as in a normative, representative sample of young children. Dr. Schweder is also interested in using her research both to develop and evaluate early childhood intervention and prevention programs, and to shape child welfare policies.

APPENDIX A: A SAMPLE OF PRESCHOOL PROGRAMS THAT MAKE TIME FOR PLAY

Connecticut

Connecticut's Preschool Curriculum Framework and Benchmarks for Children in Preschool Programs (Connecticut State Department of Education, 1999) specifies not only the skills children are expected to demonstrate by the end of preschool, but also the opportunities they are expected to be offered in preschool programs. The goals and standards are organized by four areas of development: personal and social, physical, cognitive, and creative expression/aesthetics.

Children are expected to demonstrate a sense of themselves as learners, have a sense of responsibility, function effectively in a group, and be aware of their own and others' feelings. Physically, they are expected to develop fine and large motor skills, eye-hand coordination, spatial awareness, and to choose nutritious meals and snacks. They are expected to practice basic hygiene and self-help skills. Intellectually, they should be able to think, reason, problem-solve, and use language to communicate, understand directions, and exhibit an interest in reading and writing. Creative expression encompasses an appreciation for the arts, exploration of materials, engagement in pretend play, and an appreciation of music and creative movements.

Connecticut has also been active in training child-care providers with funding from the Children's Fund of Connecticut and the Connecticut Department of Social Services. Wheeler Clinic administers the training in different sites across the state. As of June 2001, 4,156 child-care providers have participated in training, with 20 percent of the training conducted in Spanish (Child Health and Development Institute of Connecticut, 2001).

Georgia

Since Georgia was the first state to offer universal prekindergarten to four-year-olds, we examined this initiative to determine what elements matched our survey and Connecticut's curriculum. Georgia's program, which became statewide in 1995, is funded by a state lottery. This prekindergarten effort served 61,000 students during the 1998–1999 school year with an average yearly cost of $3,516 per child. Children attend school for six and a half hours per day for five days a week. Extended day care is available at the parent's expense. Georgia's universal prekindergarten plan cooperates with existing Head Start facilities in the state (Raden, 1999).

Aides were required to be at least twenty years of age, to have a high school diploma, and to show experience working with children younger than five years of age. Teachers were required to have certification in early childhood education, or a college degree specializing in early education. They could also have certification in elementary education, or a Montessori or vocational childhood education degree.

There are six approved curricula (all reviewed and approved by the state's Education Department) that are used in the Georgia preschools. These include Bank Street, the Creative Curriculum (based on Jean Piaget's theory), High Reach, High/Scope, Montessori, and Scholastic Workshop models. Guidelines suggest that the curriculum chosen by a preschool must be developmentally appropriate and not merely a junior version of a grade school program. Principles established by the National Association for the Education of Young Children (NAEYC) were to be followed, suggesting that children learn best when their physical needs are met and when they feel psychologically secure (Raden, 1999). Active involvement with people and materials is stressed, as well as the recognition of individual variation in learning, and that children's curiosity and interests motivate learning. The NAEYC principles also emphasize that children *learn through play* (Raden, 1999).

Depending on which of the approved models is used, different approaches to learning are emphasized. For example, the Montessori method emphasizes practical life skills and academic skills using specially designed materials to encourage children to learn on their own. The Creative Curriculum proposes the use of ten interest areas to support age-appropriate instructional practice and social competence. The Scholastic Workshop uses theme-based activities and integrated hands-on materials. All programs, regardless of curriculum chosen, stress parental involvement.

There is consensus among kindergarten teachers that children who were in the Georgia prekindergarten programs were performing better in pre-reading, pre-math, and social skills than children who had not participated in these programs (Henderson, Basile, & Henry, 1999). Without consistent follow-through in primary grades, however, many significant gains tended to diminish over time (Raden, 1999).

Jumpstart

Jumpstart is a nonprofit organization that offers a supplemental program for preschool students who are having difficulties learning in their schools. Jumpstart trains college students to tutor children in school readiness skills, which include language and literacy, communication, and social development. The program not only encourages family involvement and school success for preschoolers, but also teaches its "corps members" to become efficient educators. As of 2001, more than 6,000 children across the country have been served by about 1,000 college students representing various participating universities (Jumpstart New Haven).

To establish a baseline performance level for children and to identify their needs, a checklist is used that addresses skills that the program seeks to improve or encourage. This checklist is based upon the High/Scope Educational Research Foundation's Child Observation Record (COR). The COR was developed to assess the performance levels of students in Head Start programs.

Some of the skills that are included in the COR checklist are: receptive and expressive language; knowledge of books (holding a book correctly, turning pages, and following print in the right direction); identifying letters and numbers; copying or writing alphabet letters; problem-solving skills; planning and carrying out activities; negotiating with others to solve conflicts or calling on an adult for assistance; and understanding and expressing feelings and noticing or responding appropriately to the feelings of others.

Head Start

Project Head Start was conceived to give children of low-income families a head start on their education (Zigler & Lang, 1991). Since its inception in 1965, Head Start has grown to the point of serving about 800,000 children and their families a year (Westat, Inc. et al., 1998). According to the *Head Start Program Performance Measures, Second Progress Report*, the ultimate goal of Head Start is to promote social competence in children. The five objectives of the program include: providing healthy growth and development; strengthening families; providing education, health, and nutritional services; linking families to community resources; and involving parents in decision making for the program (Westat, Inc. et al., 1998).

Specifically, understanding and use of language, learning vocabulary, learning letters and colors, learning numbers, and training in fine and gross motor movements are part of the suggested curriculum. However, there is considerable variation in how these components are taught, since there is no national curriculum with specific lesson plans recommended for the various Head Start centers. There is also variation among the centers in provisions made for exceptional children.

In 1998, revised Head Start Program Performance Standards became effective, covering all children from birth through age five who were served by both the Early Start and Head Start preschool programs. The goal to promote children's social competence and the five objectives listed above also apply to Early Start, but specific indicators for this younger age group are currently being developed. At least once every three years, the Head Start programs are monitored for adherence to the standards. Head Start is probably one of the few national educational programs that has had continuous evaluation of its program. The major findings from the Family and Child Experiences Survey (FACES) (Westat, Inc. et al., 1998) indicate that a good deal of variation in the academic performance of the children was due to family background differences as well as to differences across programs in the quality of classroom environment.

Department of Defense Child Development Program

To meet the child-care needs of the children of military personnel, the military offers the following programs: Child Development Centers, Family Child Care (home-based programs, but with the same standards as the Child Development Centers), and School Age Care (ages five through twelve). There are more than 800 centers around the world extending care to more than 200,000 children from ages four weeks through twelve years (Department of Defense, 1997). Some special newborn homes accept babies from birth. About 50 percent of the children in military child-care programs are under age three.

Because of the number of single parents in the military and the active-duty mothers, The Military Child Care Act, enacted in 1989, required numerous changes in the child-care system. Components of the act included training and improved wages for child-care personnel; accreditation (more than 96 percent of eligible Child Development Centers are currently accredited); maintaining standards and safety by measures such as unannounced inspections (minimum of four per year); abuse awareness and training, and a twenty-four-hour hotline for reporting abuse; and parent fees based on income and matched by the government (cost-sharing) (Department of Defense, 1997).

The staff of the centers caring for military family children receive training on such topics as nutrition and modeling of good eating habits; how to assess and improve facets of their program, such as space and furnishings; personal-care routines; language-reasoning skills; and parent and staff interactions. The curriculum includes a creative module that promotes creativity, music, and art. Children with special needs are considered in a training module called "Special Needs Supplement." A module encourages pro-social behavior and the cognitive module focuses on thinking and problem-solving skills. Another module concentrates on literacy and communication skills, and use of books. There is also a module that focuses on using the outdoors, and a physical module that promotes gross and fine motor development (U.S. Army Child & Youth Services, 2000).

The curriculum in the military child-care centers is very similar to the curricula in other centers described above, but with one exception: the military staff is given very thorough training in how to use the materials. There is an emphasis on professionalism for the child-care staff in order to carry through the philosophy that quality care comes from well-qualified people. By linking education, training, advancement, and higher wages, the turnover in staff has been greatly reduced, resulting in higher morale and motivation on the part of staff development (U.S. Army Child & Youth Services, 2000).

3

Early Childhood Education: Lessons from Europe

CHRISTOPHER CLOUDER

"Can you do Addition?" the White Queen asked. "What's one and one and one and one and one and one and one and one and one?"

"I don't know," said Alice. "I lost count."

"She can't do Addition," the Red Queen interrupted. "Can you do subtraction? Take nine from eight."

"Nine from eight I can't, you know," Alice replied readily: "but—

"She can't do Subtraction," said the White Queen.

"Can you do division? Divide a loaf by a knife—what's the answer to that?"

—Carroll, *Through the Looking Glass*

Despite the concern expressed by policymakers and educators about improving the quality of education, the present tendency to promote early formal learning presents dangers that are amusingly encapsulated in this imaginary discourse. The battle over when and how to educate young children that is currently being waged across Europe and the United States is the most recent phase of a struggle that began in the early nineteenth century, and at its heart is our *conception of childhood*. Human cultures vary enormously in their approaches to child care, and one culture cannot claim to be the template of good practice for all. Yet, we are united by our common humanity and must therefore recognize that certain features of childhood are universal. Despite historical and cultural variations, a bedrock assumption is that if children are to thrive, they must be welcomed as valued members of their community. The interests of young children are the interests of the whole of society and their importance should be of primary concern if we are to find solutions to the many social and ethical challenges facing us. The Swedish Family Aid Commission (1981) established basic guidelines for child care and education from which all affluent countries could benefit:

> Basic to a good society is that children are welcome, are given a good environment during childhood and are the concern of the whole society. Children have a right to secure living conditions that enhance their development. Preschool has an important function in children's lives. It offers a comprehensive programme and is the source of stimulation in [their] development. It gives them a chance to meet other children and adults and to be part of an experience of fellowship and friendship. It is a complement to the upbringing a child gets at home.

With these goals in mind, current trends in early childhood education that are taking place in Europe are examined.

EARLY CHILDHOOD EDUCATION: TRENDS IN EUROPE

Starting Formal Academic Studies Later

As was the case in the United States, in recent decades, several European countries instituted early academics and standardized testing, and minimized the role of play. However, there are distinct differences as well. Whereas the United States is now considering universal preschool, the vast majority (nineteen) of countries in Europe begin compulsory education at six or seven years of age. Five additional countries (the Netherlands, Malta, England, Scotland, and Wales) begin schooling at age five, and only Northern Ireland has a school entry age of four years.

In addition, several European nations have recently revised their educational policies in order to *increase* the age at which children begin formal academic subjects, *reemphasize play-based curricula* in the early years, and *de-emphasize standardized testing* in the early grades. The catalyst for these changes is a growing, research-based recognition of the success of developmentally appropriate curricula that do not arbitrarily divide children's cognitive, social, and emotional needs, and a deep concern for children's welfare. In 2002, Jane Davidson, the minister of education for Wales, ended formal educational testing of seven-year-olds in favor of a curriculum that is more child-centered so that Wales can be a place "where our children get the best start in life." Similarly, the Swedish government takes particular pride in its *Early Years Curriculum* because it is the *shortest and least prescriptive* in Europe. And, in December 2000, the British House of Commons Education Select Committee issued a report stating that there was "no conclusive evidence that children gained from being taught the 3Rs before the age of *six*." Furthermore, creative play and small class size were deemed essential in early childhood education. The report expressed the following concerns about early academics:

> The current focus on targets for older children in reading and writing inevitably tends to limit the vision and confidence of early childhood educators. Such downward pressure risks undermining children's motivation and their disposition to learn, thus lowering rather than raising levels of achievement in the long term. . . . Inappropriate formalised assessment of children at an early age currently results in too many children being labelled as failures, when the failure, in fact, lies with the system. (House of Commons, 2000, paragraph 62)

Research submitted to the committee from the British Association for Early Childhood Education underscored this point of view:

> Comparisons with other countries suggest there is no benefit in starting formal instruction before six. The majority of other European countries admit children to school at six or seven following a three year period of pre-school education which focuses on social and physical development. Yet standards in literacy and numeracy are generally higher in those countries than in the UK, despite our earlier starting age. (House of Commons, 2002, paragraph 62)

In a paper entitled *School Starting Age: European Policy and Recent Research*, produced for the National Foundation for Educational Research in 2002, Caroline Sharp points out that early compulsory school age is not typically grounded in pedagogical theory and research, but rather in *pragmatic or political concerns*. For example, the early age for compulsory education in the United Kingdom was enacted into law in 1870, in part to protect young children from exploitation and in part to appease employers by enabling an early school leaving age. In light of this, it should not be surprising that while research supports *short-term advantages* when three- to five-year-olds are given formal instruction, there is also evidence of *noticeable disadvantages in the long term*, as Lillian Katz articulated in her 1999 Royal Academy of Arts lecture: "There are two important points to note here. First, it's only in the long term that you can see the disadvantages of early formal instruction. Second, early formal instruction is particularly damaging to boys. . . . [O]n the whole, early learning damages the disposition to learn."

Along these lines, it is interesting to note that Finland, which begins compulsory education at *seven* years of age, scored significantly better than any other European country in literacy, numeracy, and scientific understanding, in the Organisation of Economic Cooperation and Development's 2001 Programme for International Student Assessment (PISA) study, which assessed a quarter of a million children in thirty-two countries. Similarly, the top-performing countries in the 1998 Third International Maths and Science Study (TIMSS) had a school starting age of six. In addition, in the 1992 International Association for the Evaluation of Educational Achievement (IEA) study of reading literacy in thirty-two countries, the ten top-scoring countries had a *later* starting age of *6.3 years* on average. Furthermore, in all of the countries that require children to begin to read prior to age five, there is a significant gender gap in reading achievement by age nine. The study concluded that "[i]t is clearly a plausible hypothesis that boys are too immature to begin reading formally at the age of five, and that their difficulties are represented in low achievement, relative to girls, at both the age of nine and fourteen" (cited in Mills, 1998).

The Negative Impact of "High-Stakes" Testing

Harlen and Deakin-Crick (in press) of the London University Institute of Education conducted an analysis of available research on the impact of standardized assessments on students between four and eighteen years of age. After reviewing 183 studies, nineteen of which they identified as providing valid empirical evidence, they concluded the following: "What emerges is strong evidence of a negative impact of testing on pupils' motivation, though this varied in degree with the pupils' characteristics and with the conditions of their learning. . . . Lower achieving pupils are doubly disadvantaged by the tests. Being labelled as failures has an impact on how they feel about their ability to learn."

Harlen and Deakin-Crick also concluded that new forms of testing need to be created that will make it possible to assess all valued outcomes of education, including creativity and problem solving, and not just literacy and numeracy. Furthermore, they stated that such assessments should only be one element in a more broadly based judgement. In addition, the researchers found that "high-stakes" testing impacted negatively on the quality of the curriculum: "When passing tests in high-stakes, teachers adopt a teaching style which emphasises transmission teaching of knowledge, thereby favouring those students who prefer to learn in this way and disadvantaging and lowering the self-esteem of those who prefer more active and creative learning experiences."

Although this research is more concerned with older students' reactions, we should not overlook the fact that four-year-olds can feel themselves failures, too, and the sense that they are letting their parents down can be devastating and lasting. Passive, structured learning is not in keeping with young children's need for active and creative learning experiences as expressed in play.

A Call for Developmentally Appropriate Curricula

Holistic Education. In June 2001, the Organisation of Economic Cooperation and Development (OECD) issued its long-anticipated and highly regarded thematic review of Early Childhood Education and Care Policy (ECEC) for twelve countries. It is significant that for the OECD, early childhood extends until the age of *eight* and that education and care are conjoined. In addition, the report emphasizes that flexible curricula, built on the inputs of children, teachers, and parents are more suitable in early childhood than detailed, expert-driven curricula. This was an international call for flexible frameworks that give freedom for adaptation, experimentation and cultural inputs: "Contemporary research suggests . . . that the curricula should be broad and holistic with greater emphasis on developmental outcomes rather than subject outcomes . . . more process-related and co-constructive . . . defined by the vital interests and needs of the children, families and communities . . . and more in tune with socio-cultural contexts" (Organisation of Economic Cooperation and Development, 2001).

But although we see universal patterns to development that must be understood and respected, there is also a significant amount of individual variation as to when and how these stages unfold. József Nagy, an educational sociologist, argues that children must not be penalized as a result of individual variation: "Children with a calendar age of six can demonstrate a biological difference of plus or minus one year, a difference in mental development of plus or minus two and a half years and a difference of plus or minus three years in social development . . . The result is that the school career of those entering is predetermined by their stage of development at entry" (cited in Mills, 1998). As a result, the preschool must be exquisitely sensitive to individual variation in preparedness for academic lessons.

An Emphasis on Play.   Play is vital to human learning in myriad ways. It supports language, cognitive, social, emotional, and motor development. But play needs space and time, which are the very factors the "hurried curriculum" threatens to efface. As Sylvie Hopeland, head teacher of the Norwegian School in London, was quoted in *The Guardian:* "We know that we can teach children to read at four if we wanted to but we wanted them to spend those years playing. Here you teach them to give the right answers. We want them to solve problems, cooperate with others and cope with life" (June 12, 2001).

CONCLUSION

Preschool education in Europe, starting in the nineteenth century, had humanitarian roots in catering to children from working-class families. It was said of Margaret McMillan (1860–1931), a great pioneer in this work, that "[h]er anger burned at the violation of the lives of little children. She fought as one inspired to prevent their misuse" (Lowndes, 1960). Ellen Key, the Swedish educational reformer whose influential book, *The Century of the Child,* was published in 1909, shared a similar romantic notion: "The next century will be the century of the child just as the last century has been the woman's century. When the child gets his rights, morality will be perfect." We do not have to be so romantically inclined or so passionately engaged to notice that children and the quality of childhood face new threats in the twenty-first century.

Perhaps at this point we should turn to the evidence of the poets, who are often able to retain their closeness to the qualities of childhood that the rest of us lose. Miroslav Holub, himself a distinguished biologist, remembers his own Czech childhood and the need to inwardly breathe:

Ten million years
from the Miocene
to the primary school in Jecnà Street.

We know everything
from a to z.

But sometimes the finger stops
in the empty space between a and b,
empty as the prairie at night,

between g and h,
deep as the eyes of the sea,

between m and n,
long as man's birth,

sometimes it stops
in the galactic cold
after the letter z,
at the beginning and the end,

trembling a little
like some strange bird.

Not from despair.
Just like that. (Holub, 1991)

What do we destroy if we fill this vital space in a child's imaginative and emotional life? Our analytical approach has its limitations and because we are working and caring for children, we should allow our feelings to participate in this debate. Children have the gift of "becoming," in the sense used by Walt Whitman:

There was a child went forth every day,
And the first object he looked upon, that object he became
And that object became part of him for the day or a certain part of
the day,
Or for many years or stretching cycles of years. (Whitman, 1959)

In this gift of "becoming," we can find the roots of our humanity, our compassion, empathy, and tolerance. Do we really need to squander these because of short-term goals and a lack of foresight and due attention? Listening to the children themselves would be a good start.

We live in our world,
A world that is too small
For you to enter
Even on hands and knees,
The adult subterfuge.
And though you probe and pry

With analytic eye,
And eavesdrop all our talk
With an amused look,
You cannot find our centre
Where we dance, where we play,
Where life is still asleep
Under the closed flower,
Under the smooth shell
Of eggs in the cupped nest
That mock the faded blue
Of your remoter heaven. (Thomas, 2002)

REFERENCES

BBC News Online, (2001, January 11). http://news.bbc.co.uk.

Carroll, L. (1872). *Through the looking glass*. London: Macmillan.

Davidson, J. (2002, August 30). *The Times Educational Supplement*.

Family Aid Commission. (1981). Sweden.

Harlen, W., & Deakin-Crick, R. (in press). Testing, motivation and learning. *Assessment in education*.

Holub, M. (1991). Alphabet. *Poems, before and after*. London: Bloodaxe books.

Hopeland, S. (2001, June 12). *The Guardian*.

House of Commons (2000, December). *Education Select Committee Report: First report: Early years*. London: Author.

Katz, L. (1999, November 22). *Starting them young*. London: Royal Society of Arts, Lecture 22.

Key, E. (1909). Century of the Child. New York: G. P. Putnam's Sons.

Lowndes, G. (1960). *Margaret McMillan—the children's champion*. London: Museum Press.

Mills, C. (1998). *The early years dispatches*. London: Channel 4 Television Publications.

Organisation of Economic Cooperation and Development. (2001). *Starting strong: Early childhood education and care*.

Sharp, C. (2002). *School starting age: European policy and recent research*. London: National Foundation for Educational Research.

Thomas, R. S. (2002). *Children's song*. In *Collected Poems, 1945–1990*. London: Phoenix Press.

Whitman, W. (1959). Leaves of Grass. In *There was a child went forth*. New York: Viking.

ABOUT THE CONTRIBUTOR

CHRISTOPHER CLOUDER is currently chief executive officer of the Steiner Waldorf Schools Fellowship for the United Kingdom and Ireland, the director of the European Council for Steiner Waldorf Education, and a cofounder and facilitator of the Alliance for Childhood. Previous to this, he taught adolescents for twenty years, both within the state system in the Netherlands and Waldorf schools in England. He lectures widely on educational matters and on cultural evolution, and is a visiting lecturer at Plymouth University and Emerson College, United Kingdom.

Part II

Wired Classrooms/Wired Brains

Photo courtesy of Michele Perel Phillips.

4

Cybertots: Technology and the Preschool Child[1]

JANE M. HEALY

WHAT'S WRONG WITH THIS PICTURE?

Caroline is having separation problems. When her parents decided to include her on their ski vacation in Colorado, they understandably refused to pack up Caroline's personal computer, her mouse, and her collection of thirty CD-ROMs. But Caroline misses her accustomed jolts of electronic pleasure, so I have arranged a "play date" with one of our school computers.

Caroline is four and a half years old. Growing up with technologically inclined parents, she has used the computer since she was very small—sometimes up to four hours a day. Her parents encourage her interest, although they allow her only a half hour of television daily. They purchase mainly software that sounds educational and accelerative, with titles featuring words like "knowledge" and "jump start."

"She could spend the whole day on the computer. Wait till you see how she handles these programs!"

Perched anxiously on the edge of a school library chair, Caroline attacks some game-format software with almost frantic intensity. Her entire body tenses and quivers as she is instantaneously lost in maneuvering her way through mazes and puzzles. I wonder, as I watch, whether Caroline's spatial skills with the mouse might possibly transfer to math and science (unproven by research) or if she will enjoy a career as a fighter pilot. Or would she develop better spatial-relations skills by creating something with a set of wooden unit blocks?

I am also struck by the level of stress in this child's tense body. She knows her parents are proud of her ability, and she doesn't want to disappoint them. I think of the studies showing that the young of any species, if exposed to continued stress during early years, are likely to undergo subtle alterations of neurohormones that will leave them more prone to stress and depression throughout a lifetime (*APA Monitor,* 1996).

"Yes! Level five!" she exclaims through clenched teeth as her parents smile approvingly. Quickly, she switches to another familiar program, in which she "drives" a car through an animated landscape, picking up items as she goes to solve a problem (this type of software is sold as "interactive problem solving"). Caroline races her vehicle around the screen, following the "tricks" she has already learned (e.g., pick up the rope here) and repeatedly bumping into blind alleys. Her hand on the mouse is lightning-quick, and she maneuvers with the expertise of an Indy 500 driver.

"Why did you pick up the rope?" I inquire. Caroline shrugs. Her eyes never leave the screen. "What will you use the rope for?" I gently insist.

"Cause you're s'posed to," she mumbles, navigating another corner.

In fact, it turns out that Caroline doesn't understand either the "mental map" of the space she is speeding through or the cause-effect nature of the problem; rather than problem solving in the cognitive sense, she is simply jumping through alternative hoops as fast as possible.

We race through several more programs. Everyone but Caroline is getting tired, so we adjourn.

I am curious. These bright, concerned folks are adoring parents who have a lovely, intelligent child. Does the amount of time she spends on the computer worry them? How are her social skills developing?

"Well, sometimes we worry a little," her mother admits. "But then we look at all she's learning and how much she loves it. She sees us spending a lot of time on our computers. Yes, she does have some difficulty sharing with other children. You should ask her teacher."

Caroline attends a noted and innovative private school with a top-notch early childhood program. "How does her teacher feel about computers for four-year-olds?" I ask.

"She won't allow them in her classroom!" laughs Caroline's mother. "She doesn't approve of them for preschoolers."

Debate rages among parents and educators as to how computers should be used with young children. Thus far, however, public discussion of technology has skirted important questions of age-appropriate use, with marketers cheering when someone opines: "The earlier the better. Let's prepare these kids for the future!" Yet, preparation for the future involves a far different set of abilities. Time spent with computers in the early years not only subtracts from important developmental tasks, but may also entrench bad learning habits, leading to poor motivation and even symptoms of learning disability. Children in different stages of brain development have different needs. I have recently come to believe that computers—at least as they are currently being used—are not necessary or even desirable in the lives of most children under age seven (with the exception, of course, of children suffering from certain handicaps).

Research supporting preschool computer use is almost nonexistent; what is available has mainly been promulgated by those who stand to gain in some way from their advocacy. And there's plenty to gain. Software for toddlers is a rapidly growing market niche, computer "classes" have parents enrolling their children as young as two and a half—and many arrive already familiar with the machine (*Education Week*, 1996). A favorite cartoon in my file shows a young boy entering his mother's kitchen with a downcast expression. "I got sent home from computer camp because I couldn't button my shirt," he announces. I believe we need a reality check, which this chapter attempts to provide.

A BUSY TIME FOR THE BRAIN

During the early years, the brain has a staggering number of developmental tasks to accomplish, and environments influence its formation. If the environment is a poor one, final sculpting of neuronal connections will bypass or distort important aspects of development. During these critical periods when the brain is changing rapidly, we may see relatively sudden growth (interspersed with needed regressions, or "rest periods") in a child's ability to perform certain types of mental operations (Thatcher, 1994). Since virtually all parts of the brain are active during these years, anything that limits appropriate experiences or sets up undesirable emotional/motivational patterns may have profound and lasting effects.

BIRTH TO TWO YEARS

Networks of connections are forming for social, emotional, and cognitive capabilities—with *emotional and language interaction from human caregivers* the main impetus (Denham, 1993). Eighteen months is an extremely important juncture, when a mental growth spurt opens new windows for conceptual understanding of natural laws governing both human behavior and the physical world. This age is also a turning point in sociability and for organizing the child's senses around movement. Putting normally developing babies on computers for any length of time is so ridiculous that it hardly bears further comment. In fact, animal studies looking at "augmented sensory experience," or abnormal overstimulation of more than one sense too early in life, have shown it has lasting negative effects on attention and learning (Radell & Gottlieb, 1992). Scientists can't ethically do this type of research on humans, but some parents seem to be trying!

AGES TWO TO SEVEN

Profound developmental tasks to be mastered include the following seven types of learning, which may be distorted by too much electronic stimulation:

Learning in a Social Context

Since even older children and adults have trouble sorting out the "humanness" of electronic brains, young children may be profoundly affected by the social and emotional relationship they develop with their machines. Computers must never supplant supportive human environments. In a large study of day care, researchers at fourteen universities found that children's intelligence, academic success, and emotional stability were determined primarily by the personal and language interaction they had with adults (*New York Times*, 1997). Optimally, the brain does its important work in a context of relaxed exploration guided primarily by the child and supported by helpful and emotionally responsive but not overly intrusive adults.

Digi-tykes may be especially at risk if certain types of software induce overactivation of the right hemisphere and concurrent underactivation of the left. In one provocative study, four-year-old children with greater amounts of left frontal activation displayed more social competence, while children who showed more right activation displayed social withdrawal (Fox et al., 1995).

Learning to Use All the Senses

From birth, sensory areas in the back of the brain refine the ability to perform basic functions effortlessly, such as looking, touching, and moving. These systems should become automatic so that around age seven children can integrate them smoothly (e.g., watch a guitarist move to the beat; think about story content while writing words; look at the chalkboard and listen to a teacher). This "intersensory integration" is critical for good learning, and it takes lots of practice.

Open-ended computer use—such as a drawing program—offers some combining of sensory abilities, but differs qualitatively from nature's programming of whole-body, three-dimensional sensory experience. A time may come when specially designed software can "teach" intersensory interaction, but I haven't seen any yet that I would trust to do the job.

Learning to Be a Powerful Learner

Early years are a time for learning one's "stance" toward the world. Children are wrestling with important personal issues: (1) Should I trust or mistrust others—or myself? (2) How does the world really work? (3) How powerful am I as an independent learner?

Autonomous control of play materials by the child (as with nonelectronic toys or materials) is very important because the child is laying the groundwork to be either an internally motivated or a weak learner. Young children naturally tend to disbelieve their own power as compared with a computer, which is "opaque"—that is, one can't really understand or see what makes it work. Even though youngsters become adept at running programs, they can't ultimately control the computer's behavior (with the possible exception of LOGO programming). On the contrary, good play materials (e.g., paints, empty boxes, nonanimated dolls, toy tools, Tinkertoy building blocks, and playing cards) are fully under the child's control and operate in accordance with natural scientific laws, such as gravity. They not only empower the young learner/problem solver, but subtly convey major principles of how the world works. For example, cause and effect—as well as self-control—are easy to learn when you're trying to hammer a nail into a board (if I miss, then I might hurt my finger), but hard to learn when a system crashes for no apparent reason or things jump around the screen without a visible source of propulsion.

As frontal lobe development sets up the basis for executive control systems, the preschooler needs experiences in managing his own mind—not having it distracted or programmed from outside. Among other skills, children of this age should work on developing:

- ability to regulate one's own emotions
- problem-solving skills, flexibility, originality

- motivation and persistence
- attention
- social skills
- body rhythm and coordination of movement
- imagination

If these foundations are neglected during a critical period, they may be difficult—or even impossible—to regain.

Learning to Pay Attention

One of the most important learning skills threatened by electronic stimulation is *selective attention*: the ability to direct one's own attention and focus clearly on what is to be learned without succumbing to distraction. Children who can't resist touching anything that comes into sight or whose mental focus shifts every time something happens are said to be "stimulus bound."

Little children's attention naturally jumps from thing to thing, but some forms of electronic media may prolong this immaturity. Distracting graphics and special effects, coupled with the temptation to click impulsively, encourage stimulus-bound behavior, which, in turn, contributes to attention problems (Mariani & Barkley, 1997).

While most youngsters eventually learn to screen out background noise (an ability called "auditory figure ground perception"), it takes an unconscious toll on a child's resources and may result in subtle overstimulation and accumulating stress. A young child stressed by such sensory overload usually reacts in one of two ways: either he shuts down or he gets hyper—both physically and mentally. A child genetically at risk for learning or attention problems may be particularly affected. Many of today's youngsters have grown up in these taxing environments—television, videos, loud music, and now the beep, beep, beep of computer games—so they almost need stressful background noise to feel normal, but at what cost to developing systems for learning?

Learning Visual Imagery and Memory

Frontal lobe maturation throughout childhood and adolescence gradually enables better "working memory," the ability to juggle a number of ideas or thoughts at one time. Likewise, areas mediating visual imagery develop during the years before age seven. For example, preschoolers naturally have difficulty visualizing a story while paying attention to the plot and the characters' names all at the same time; they are not terribly efficient in their thinking because they can't hold many alternatives in mind. With maturation and practice, the brain learns to visualize and hold alternatives. Children with weak visualization skills may always be plagued by inefficient memory and difficulty with more formal symbol systems (e.g., reading and math).

Research suggests that the way adults help children learn to practice these skills makes a clear difference in their thinking abilities (Bjorklund & Harnishfeger, 1990). For example, suggesting such exercises as "Can you make a movie in your mind of how Cinderella looks in the story?" can aid kids in expanding their abilities. For youngsters on a computer, no such spur is available, as the computer simply makes their pictures for them.

Learning to Think Logically

If-Then (Causal Reasoning).   Children between the ages of three and four years are beginning to make logical inferences with "if-then"— or causal reasoning. It is difficult for adults to understand just how elementary their reasoning really is. For example, when three-year-old Paul sees two balls hitting each other and then one rolling off, he is likely to view these as two unrelated incidents. By age five, Paul will be able to infer that the second ball rolled away as a result of being hit by the first. Very young children like to play around with causality (Paul used to drop cookies off his high-chair tray, and would then look up at his mom with an anticipatory grin: If I drop the cookie, then Mom will . . .), but this form of reasoning takes a significant jump between ages three and four.

How do children learn to reason about these abstract relationships? Psychologists have concluded that, along with requisite brain changes, they need *physical experience of action sequences that they themselves control* (e.g., first I do *x*, then as a result *y* happens—and I can change that if I do *x* differently). Thus, the years between three and four may be a particularly bad time to introduce an opaque and arbitrary electronic toy into the child's world. Better quality children's software tries to address this problem, but there is no evidence it can do the job.

If we confuse children of this age about cause and effect by giving them too many things to select and watch, instead of things to do, will we jeopardize their causal reasoning? Teachers today tell us a surprising number of older children don't seem to understand the realm of "if-then" logic; they struggle with math and science concepts, as well as with social relations, strategy use, and ethical choices.

Social Causal Reasoning.   The ability to infer how someone else might be feeling is also important (e.g., If I don't come when Dad calls me, he might feel worried). Progress requires interaction with human beings and human emotions (for instance, I took Jimmy's toy and [as a result] he got so mad he hit me!). Physical and social experiences are intricately tied to the young child's mental development (Frye et al., 1996).

Barbara Bowman of the Erikson Institute in Chicago worries that too many children learn to use computers without understanding their "social contexts." Three- and four-year-olds cannot fully understand that real people with particular points of view produced what is on the screen, she points out, and they need human mediators to help them make sense of what they see. "Even in the age of technology, it is through relationships with others—through joint activities, language, and shared feelings with other human beings—that children grasp meaning" (Bowman & Beyer, 1993–1994, p. 23).

Fact or Fantasy?   Children under age five have a tendency to confuse appearance with reality. If something moves, for example, they may believe it is really alive. They tend to have difficulty taking another's perspective; they are a bit hazy on "theory of mind," understanding what it means is to have a mind containing thoughts or be a discriminating judge of another person's motives and point of view. This would explain their gullibility to Internet advertising or implicit messages in children's computer games.

By ages five to seven, children start to move outside their own perspectives. They begin to discriminate fact from fiction in television viewing. By age seven, most understand that fictional characters do not retain their roles in real life and that fictional shows are scripted and rehearsed. But this development is *inversely* related to the child's viewing experience—the more TV, the less he tends to understand the difference between fact and fiction (Wright & Shade, 1993–1994). For children unable to discriminate what is real from what is not, electronic playmates may be more confusing than we think. Even older children have trouble deciding whether computers are alive or not, and tend to place too much trust in them.

Learning New Symbol Systems

Between ages four and seven, children begin mastering formal symbols of adult reasoning (written words, numerals), and it's a tempting time to introduce software for phonics or early math skills. Yet, the four-, five-, and even six-year-old brain is not necessarily ready for this disembodied learning. A symbol is not really useful until it has been *internalized*: a young child may be able to count to ten or recognize numerals, but until he really understands what "3" represents in the real world (e.g., he can give you three objects when you show him the numeral, or understand that "3" is less than "4"), he has not connected the real number concept to the symbol.

If you want your child to be good at reading, you should *contextualize* the learning, that is, read with him, talk with him about stories and daily events, expand vocabulary, listen to him, and provide him with open-ended manipulative materials (e.g., aids for pretend play, rocks or button collections, building or sewing materials, puppets, a costume box) to encourage concepts and problem-solving skills. If you want him to be good at math, you should talk about number concepts (e.g., "We need *two more* place settings when your aunt and uncle come to dinner") and play board and card games with him. Such games, by the way, constitute the strongest predictor of math ability that researchers have yet found. Thus far, even well-constructed computer programs can't achieve the same result.

One experiment, cited by psychologist Robbie Case (1996), evaluated young children's math learning from playing board games on computers as compared with playing the same games with an adult. Although the researchers thought they had developed a software package to duplicate the benefits of real-life experience, the one-on-one contact with an adult still produced far greater gains. What was the difference? It was the spontaneous language interaction and mental "scaffolding" provided by the adult.

Another reason young children don't profit as much from computer simulations as from real activities is something developmental psychologist Irving Siegel (Ellsworth and Sindt, 1994) calls "representational distance." Children who understand representational distance do better in school because they can separate themselves from the "here and now." They understand that a thing or name can stand for something else (like a flag representing a country) and that something happening in one place can represent something happening in another (like reading about Alaska when you're sitting in Brussels). Children under age seven are only beginning to learn representational competence; computer simulations may confuse them. Even the physical distance between the mouse and the screen (or the two-dimensional touch screen) makes the simulation less powerful than physically holding and moving a piece on a three-dimensional game board. Siegel also found that a big boost in representational competence comes from close conversations with parents and caregivers ("Let's talk about what we did at the park today").

A Study in Early Learning

Ralph and Marco are enjoying their scheduled time in the prekindergarten computer corner. Flipping through the menus of a math software program, they settle on a game, giggling and gently fighting over the mouse, as colored icons flash onto the screen.

"Be quiet over there, you two." The teacher is helping children paint in the easel corner. With eighteen four-year-olds in the room, she and her assistant have their hands full keeping order and seeing to individual needs.

From a help menu that they can't read, Marco randomly selects a subtraction program. A problem appears on the screen: $8 - 1 = ?$ Now the boys get down to business. Fingers come into play. Ralph assiduously counts eight fingers, and then another one. Nine! Smiling, he presses the key to enter his answer.

"Sorry, try again!" replies the computer. The same problem reappears. Ralph's face falls. Marco loses interest and moves away.

Ralph tries again. "One, two, three, four, five, six, seven, eight." He is counting very carefully, touching each finger in turn. "Now, one more—nine!" He counts them all again and defiantly punches in the answer.

"Sorry, the right answer is seven." The computer is impassive and nonnegotiable.

Ralph looks puzzled. He regards his fingers once more as if mistrusting them, shrugs, sighs, and walks off.

I mention this incident to the teacher. I believe the boys have learned some important lessons. Marco has learned to flip from thing to thing and give up quickly with no consequences. Ralph has learned to mistrust the evidence of his own mind and his own senses, to feel powerless in a relationship with an implacable and incomprehensible authority, to believe that math is, after all, difficult and confusing.

"Why are they doing a subtraction program when they don't know what the signs mean?" I ask his teacher later.

"Oh, I didn't know what was happening. But you surely understand I just can't stand over them every minute—I've got a whole classroom full of kids. We really need someone in the computer corner, but we don't have the staff. As a matter of fact, it was Ralph's grandfather who donated those machines—he was convinced his grandson needed to learn computer as early as possible. The software came in a package with the machine. Frankly, I think the kids are better off without computers, but there's so much pressure from the families these days."

In a classroom next door, almost-five-year-old Sam is preparing to build a sailboat. He got the idea from the shape of a flat piece of wood he found while rummaging in a large box of miscellaneous materials his teacher keeps in the carpentry center.

"This looks like the bottom of a boat," mumbles Sam, eyeing the wood scrap speculatively. He runs his fingers over the smooth surface. "But it needs a stick—here," indicating a mast. He rummages further and comes up with a small length of dowel. He smiles. Sam holds the dowel in place, pushing down hard, with the superb confidence of being almost five that it may somehow magically stick. It doesn't. Sam looks puzzled.

He casts about the carpentry table and finds a hammer. He pounds on the top of the dowel. Again, it falls off. Sam replaces the hammer and thinks for a minute. Now he spies a drill, seizes it eagerly and applies himself to drilling a hole in the wood. This is hard work, because drill and wood keep slipping apart, but Sam is determined, and it certainly appears that his brain is fully engaged. Finally, he succeeds. Now he tries inserting the dowel. Once more, it falls out. Sam looks discouraged.

A teacher passes by. She sizes up the situation and picks up a container of glue.

"Would this help?"

Good teachers are able to achieve what this one just has, deftly reaching Sam's "zone of proximal development"—that exquisitely sensitive gap between actual achievement and potential—where the right question or suggestion from a perceptive adult can help the child solve the problem himself. Although some software marketing has adopted this claim as a gimmick, it is difficult at best to program a computer for this type of sensitivity.

Sam applies some glue, inserts the dowel and now has to wait until the glue dries a bit. He is fidgety, but he manages (the attention and self-control areas of his brain are hard at work). When the boat is completed, the expression on his face is wonderful to behold.

What lessons has Sam's brain learned? Among others, the lessons include a feeling of autonomy and power as a learner and problem solver, systematic planning, creative strategy use, attention, motor coordination, patience, perseverance, and visualization. And Sam has something all his own to be proud of.

Two visitors from the central office enter the room. Ignoring other displays of children's work, they stop to examine some computerized printouts in a wall display. These are "drawings" comprising mostly clip art selected from a menu and "pasted" on with a quick click. They admire these fruits of technology. "Isn't it amazing what today's kids can do?" one comments.

Sam watches them, clutching his boat.

Why Age Seven?

I believe that normally developing children are better off without much, if any, computer use before the age of seven. Starting around age seven, certain carefully designed applications may become of educational value if they are thoughtfully incorporated into a total curriculum with developmentally appropriate goals. Most thoughtful professionals I have interviewed agree on one particular philosophy about computer use: if the computer can accomplish the task better than other materials or experiences, we will use it. If it doesn't clearly do the job better, we will save the money and use methods that have already proven their worth. In the case of the child under seven, there are few things that can be done better on a computer, and many that fail miserably by comparison. Younger children are better off spending this critical period of development in a physically and linguistically enriched environment. Even for children who lack this type of privileged experience, there is no evidence that today's computer applications will make up the inevitable gaps. Spend the money on better early childhood programs.

PHYSICAL DEVELOPMENT AND THE IMPORTANCE OF PLAY

Because of the developing nature of preschoolers' eyes, wrists, hands, and backs, and the suspected sensitivity of fast-growing organisms to electromagnetic radiation, we should be very cautious with our youngest pupils. To fully understand what forms of technology are right and which are wrong for young children, we must delve into the elaborate process by which young children use their bodies to acquire mental habits and skills.

Motor Development: Building Intelligent Muscles

For the young child, movement and physical experience provide the foundation for higher level cognition through integration of the brain's sensory association areas, and educators in many cultures make sure to incorporate physical play with formal instruction (Thelen, 1995). Language, foresight, and other hallmarks of cognitive intelligence are connected in the brain through performing rapid movements in sequence and by developing a bodily sense of "beat." The brain areas responsible for playing the piano, doing needlework or carpentry, forming words into a meaningful sentence, understanding language, or planning a party in advance all require specially ordered sequences of movements and thoughts. These find their roots in early object and social play (Calvin, 1994).

Certain visual-spatial skills that contribute to mathematical and scientific thinking are also learned from using the whole body to navigate through space while running, jumping, climbing, and so on. The child's muscles are "smart instruments" that register the spatial properties of objects in the environment and build a foundation for higher conceptual understandings (e.g., proportion, velocity, engineering, and design) (Turvey, 1996).

Many adult experts in fields such as math, science, technology, and the arts still do much of their reasoning with bodily intelligence. Frank Lloyd Wright remembered all his life the blocks that got him started on his career. At the age of eighty-eight, Wright commented, "The maple wood blocks are in my fingers to this day." Kindergarten experiences where children manipulated sticks, modeling clay, and paper to make geometric forms are also given credit for inspiring the works of painters Braque, Klee, and Mondrian (Brosterman, 1997).

Yet, today's potential creators may never have a chance. Phyllis Weikart (1995), consultant for High/Scope early childhood programs, is concerned that "because of today's fast-changing lifestyle, we may have overlooked development of the kinesthetic intelligence, which is essential from birth to approximately age seven." For example, every year she finds more children who can't keep a beat, signifying that their brain has been shortchanged on experiences that will help it work efficiently.

The "Concrete" Learner: Messing Around with Real-World Materials

At a small conference on computers and young children, I was having breakfast with several scientists and educators, including Douglas Sloan of Teachers College. We were, I must admit, making fun of the current tendency to put tried-and-true childhood activities into computer software. We were particularly taken by the ludicrous quality of an ad for a digital "finger-painting" program.

"Why would anyone want to buy such a thing?" questioned Doug, who understands as well as anyone the value of real finger paints in a young child's life (which require planning to get out materials, arranging the space in an organized way, enjoying the sensory experience, integrating brain and body, helping clean up and put things away, etc.).

"Well, you avoid the messes," responded a couple of veteran moms at the table. Doug considered this for a moment. "Why don't they just throw out the child?" he inquired.

It is no accident that formal schooling in most countries begins at the time when the brain is sufficiently organized to grasp abstract symbols. Prior to that time, young children are primarily "concrete learners": they need to "mess around," experiment, and create meaning with their own symbol systems. Preschoolers don't learn language and concepts from two-dimensional flash cards, but from multidimensional experience.

Some early childhood researchers contend that such experiences as a computerized drawing program, which the child controls and understands, may be considered "concrete" if it is meaningful and personal to the child. One might also argue, however, that computers minimize three-dimensional motor and sensory experiences (including smell, a powerful brain stimulus). Even for older children, a computer simulation of a chemistry experiment is decontextualized: no smells, no broken test tubes, nothing goes wrong, except in a preprogrammed way.

Real-life context, usually developed by the child herself in the course of play, allows her (at her brain's own pace) to derive important cognitive principles, or rules, for the way things work—for example, smaller goes inside bigger (math); liquids are runny and solids are firm (science); "you" means one thing if *I* say it and another if *you* do (reading, writing); if I do this, then that happens (behavioral control, problem solving)—to pave the way for an understanding of more abstract symbolic forms and concepts.

The greater danger, of course, is not that children will occasionally enjoy an interesting software program, but that in spending too much time on two-dimensional computers, the child will adopt an iconic mode of reasoning that bypasses real-world foundations. While the learning gained there (e.g., knowing letters, geometric shapes, reciting the names and characteristics of all the dinosaurs) looks impressive to adults, it may be only superficial mastery. Children playing with unit blocks may not know the name of a rectangle, but they have a gut-level understanding of its properties and how it works. At a later point in childhood, such terms become important, and computerized concept building and even drilling on symbols such as spelling rules or math facts will be useful—but only after the child had understood concepts at a personal and physical level.

Real-World Play: Brain Food for Tots

Another major criticism of media technology—no matter how interactive—is that it subtracts from a child's unprogrammed real-world playtime. Although many adults regard play as "only fun," it is the young brain's primary means of intellectual development and creative expression. Adults who have retained their ability to play (with ideas, inventions, materials) are the most productive and innovative people.

The prevalence of spontaneous play across cultures suggests it has important adaptive value. Even the young of animal species spend a great deal of time and energy on play. Studies show a striking correlation between the period of greatest playfulness and the time when brain connections are most actively made (Angier, 1992).

Not long ago, I accompanied Rene, almost three, and her mother to a children's museum and a special hands-on exhibit she had previously loved. On the way to the exhibit, we passed by some fish swimming in a tank. Rene was enchanted. She displayed absolutely no interest in what we had planned for her, but played for as long as we could let her by the fish, mimicking their movements, dipping her fingers into the water (forbidden, but irresistible), and presumably puzzling deeply about questions that our adult minds were too thick to grasp. We thought the exhibit looked much more interesting, but Rene needed to interact with fish that day. I'm glad we gave her the chance to follow the dictates of her brain. "'Hooking" youngsters to electronic stimulation prevents such serendipity.

Play and spontaneous physical activity have other important functions in early life, including stimulation of the cerebellum, which coordinates motor activity, balance, and higher cognitive functions. In early childhood, the child is naturally impelled to jump, hop, spin, and interact with playmates. (Organized sports do not qualify as play in the same sense because they are structured by adults and lack spontaneity.) Because the cerebellum is integral to many mental skills, restricting physical play may have serious long-term consequences.

Informal play helps children gain social skills and learn to handle aggression appropriately. The more an animal—or a child—plays, the better its chance of becoming a well-adjusted member of the society. "Through play bouts, an animal's aggressive tendencies are socialized and brought under control," states Dr. Stephen J. Suomi (in Angier, 1992) of the National Institute of Child Health and Human Development. "Play seems to make the difference in quality of life, between merely surviving and really thriving" (p. C1).

The level of a child's play correlates with intelligence, language development, general well-being, and the ability to understand others. Play reduces stress. It also enhances latent creativity and original thinking. As children use symbolic objects to pretend, they are broadening mental landscapes and building abstract abilities. It is very troubling to hear from preschool teachers that stimulus-saturated young children are losing the ability to play spontaneously. "It takes me until after Christmas to get them to pretend that a block is a loaf of bread," worried one teacher of four-year-olds. "If they lose their imagination and their spontaneity, what's left of childhood?"

Electronic "Play" and the Overprogrammed Child. Parents tell me their child loves "playing" with the computer. Naturally, such an engaging object may be a source of excited exploration, but not everything that looks like play is necessarily beneficial. Hundreds of volumes have been published on the value of natural, unprogrammed play (e.g., Bornstein & O'Reilley, 1993; Bergen, 1988), but children oversaturated with other people's scenarios may lose the ability to create their own. In natural situations, children tend to model or copy what they see and repeat it (sometimes endlessly, it seems) in play; such pretend play prepares children for adult roles as they observe and practice many of the adult functions of their society. Meanwhile, they also master language in spontaneous interactions with peers or adults. They invent stories, fantasies, and adventures. They learn to give and take, and to regulate their emotions (e.g., pretend fighting vs. real fighting).

Parents should know that the greatest stimulation to a child's natural play is seeing adults engaged in constructive real-world work they enjoy. It is doubtless beneficial for today's children to incorporate pretend technology into their play (imaginary phones, cars, computers), yet many of today's children spend playtime at school only mimicking electronic program plots. Is this because screen life is replacing real life for all of us?

"Dramatic (pretend) play is the most important thing a child can do at this age, but my students have already had so much television and computer at home that it takes them awhile to learn to play imaginatively," sighs preschool teacher Marie Randazzo. She compares children creating a pretend play scene with clay to children working on a computer. The children working with the clay are deciding what figures to construct and how to do it, and they are using their bodies to mold them, place them, and move them about. They make up and dramatize the action and the dialogue. In contrast, those using the computer are selecting and "placing" icons in a similar, but vastly impoverished, scene as far as sensory experience, intelligence, or imagination are concerned.

Comments this veteran teacher, "The clay is so open-ended, and it generates much more interaction and dialogue as the children negotiate decisions and enter into fantasy play. With the computer, it really dictates and limits everything. Besides, I like to see children's bodies move in my class; when they're pounding clay or molding it, there's so much imagination and creativity wrapped up in that physical movement."

After viewing a popular software program in which children "play" at creating a story by placing clip art on a landscape, physicist Fritjof Capra (1995) deemed it "a teaching tool for reductionist thinking par excellence. A landscape is composed of items. There are no relationships between the components; you can change them around and replace them. Things aren't connected; it doesn't matter what you do with them; there are no natural consequences."

Electronic landscapes reduce reality in many ways. Less than 10 percent of children in the United States now learn about nature from the outdoors, about one-third from school, and more than half learn about it from some sort of electronic device (e.g., television, nature shows, CD-ROMs). Yet, remarks Clifford Stoll (1995, pp. 224–225), "no computer can teach what a walk through a pine forest feels like. Sensation has no substitute."

IMAGINATION AND CREATIVITY

In *The Road Ahead* (1995), software baron Bill Gates rhapsodizes as he watches a three-year-old play with an animated book program. "Her ability to influence what she sees on the screen—to answer the question 'What happens if I click here?'—keeps her curiosity high" (p. 191). Sorry Bill, but wondering "What happens if I click here?" and watching some flashy canned effects is a pretty low-level definition of curiosity, the cornerstone of creativity. With unconscious irony, this same gentleman goes on to say that his own creativity stems in great part from being lucky enough to be raised in a family that encouraged him to ask questions—real, live, open-ended questions, not programmed ones with programmed answers.

In two other areas, early computer use may block development. The first skill in question is *mental imagery*. A computerized, animated storybook is just one controversial item that might contribute to its decline. Imagery is closely related to imagination and the second skill, the child's level of *creative fantasy play*.

Children's creative play has a clear developmental trajectory. Around two or three, a child who spends a great deal of time pretending is demonstrating maturity and cognitive competence. From ages four to six, children who share their pretend world with peers and play out original scenarios together tend to be more socially and cognitively skilled. From about age six on, pretense diminishes in favor of rule-based games. For good emotional and mental adjustment, children should have their fill of pretend play in early years (Bergen, 1988).

In their book, *The Development of Imagination*, David Cohen and Stephen MacKeith (1992) examine the imaginary worlds, or "paracosms," that have been the childhood realms of many creative adults. Many children have imaginary playmates at some point in their lives, but some youngsters create whole fantasy worlds. Vast differences exist, however, between electronic fantasy worlds in which older youngsters sometimes spend a lot of time—often to parents' concern—and the uses of a young child's imagination.

It is interesting to note that much of the software your children are playing with was developed by a company founded by two brothers who, as children, created their own secret world in an alcove under the stairs, based on their reading of the Hardy Boys adventure series. Although their software is among the better products, I am quite sure its manufactured delights don't hold a candle to that wonderful secret kingdom that occupied so many of their hours—and later enabled them to make a fortune from parents who feared their own children might have too much unscheduled time.

Pretend play is also correlated with intellectual abilities. Dorothy and Jerome Singer (1977) at Yale University have shown that children who are good at imagining (i.e., creating scenarios from their own mind, not from a menu of possibilities) have superior concentration, less aggression, more sensitivity to others, and the ability to take more pleasure in what they do. Researchers now suggest that parents play fantasy games with their children to encourage their imagination and divergent thinking.

Young Children and the Arts

There is sharp disagreement about whether computers enhance or limit artistic tendencies in such forms as dance, painting, poetry, sculpture, drama, and music. Alan Kay is only one expert who thinks computerized drawing is dreadful because it reduces the dimensions of a child's experience and makes it overly formulaic. One popular software program enables children to design birthday cards and invitations by choosing among 1,000 different card elements—click and paste. They can "create" a picture by dragging and dropping characters from a popular TV series, or they can "create" a banner welcoming Mom home from the hospital with a new baby. Unless a child is physically handicapped, one can hardly come up with a justification for such activities. Surely, adults haven't lost so much sense that they would value such products over a smudged, laboriously hand-lettered greeting card or banner, or an original drawing—however primitive it might look.

On the other hand, computer enthusiasts like software reviewer Warren Buckleitner believe that the home computer, used correctly, can be a constructive addition to artistic development. He claims good drawing programs that enable the child to reverse an action with an "Oops" button cause youngsters to become less inhibited in their creativity. Still, he hopes that computer software and good color printers—which can be expensive as well as time-consuming—will never take the place of the joy of a fresh box of sixty-four crayons. He suggests combining computer-aided productions with tried-and-true art materials (Buckleitner, 1996).

Early experiences in the arts are important because they produce intellectual as well as aesthetic gains. In the best-researched example, participation in music seems to do mysterious but wonderful things for the human brain. Music educators have recently become so concerned about parents and educators sending kids off to computer camp instead of music lessons that they have begun funding expert studies on music and intelligence. Although one might wish for a more objective funding source, the results have been provocative. In one example, piano lessons, but not a comparable amount of computer training, had remarkable carryover value to academic skills. Researchers from the University of California, Irvine, compared the two forms of experience in their effects on children's spatial-temporal skills—their ability to form mental images from physical objects or to see patterns in space and time. Such skills are key to understanding proportion, geometry, and other mathematical and scientific concepts. They will also be requisite for the select group who eventually become creators of new technologies. After six months, the piano-taught children had dramatically improved their scores on a spatial-temporal task that involved putting a puzzle together, whereas the computer training had shown little effect. "Obviously, there's more work to be done," commented one of the researchers, "but if I were a parent or an educator, I'd want to take these findings into consideration" (*Education Week*, 1997).

Young children can now presumably "compose" music with a special computer program. We do not know what effects this may have on their eventual abilities, but we should bear in mind that unless preschoolers have significant motor and rhythmic (kinesthetic) experience connected to the music, they may not derive much benefit from the time spent. One noted music instructor told me, "I have no use for those programs at the elementary level. The experience of what it means to be a composer must come first—with the body, as in getting the feel of playing an instrument or moving to music. The things that are on the software we need to unfold with children, not have the computer do for them" (Gilpatrick, 1997).

LANGUAGE DEVELOPMENT AND LITERACY

Language Development in a Visual World

Language development is one of the most obvious victims of too much visual experience. Even in the adult brain, visual, spatial, and verbal (semantic) attention are handled by different systems that compete for circuitry (Petry, 1996). Since there are a limited number of circuits, it is hard to pay attention to both pictures and language at the same time. For children, the pictures usually win, as any parent can attest after trying to get a child to *listen* to her while he was *looking* at the TV or a computer game.

A critical period for language development occurs during preschool years. At about age two, language systems in the left hemisphere start rapid development. During the next few years, groundwork for the adult language system is laid—if the child both hears and uses the grammar and vocabulary of the language(s) in his environment. Most children have almost fully developed oral grammar by the time they enter school. Unlike natural languages, computer languages have no critical period and can be learned at any age. It makes sense to concentrate on the natural language while the brain is most open to this important form of stimulation.

Cybertots with too much screen time and too little talk time may have difficulty listening accurately or expressing themselves well. They may have good thoughts and even a decent vocabulary, but they lack practice in formulating ideas into succinct and meaningful sentences. Language problems extend into social relationships, reading, and writing; they also limit the child's inner voice—called "inner speech" or "self-talk"—by which the brain regulates behavior, attention, meta-cognition, and understanding.

Orality, the cornerstone of language, must be practiced with human companions, both adults and peers. In studies of the way literacy skills are developed, we find that children who talk to each other while playing, and particularly those who play together with language (e.g., silly rhymes, riddles, and tongue twisters, as well as discussions, arguments, and negotiations), will tend to become earlier and better readers (Pellegrini & Galda, 1993). Talk bridges the gap between a child's concrete, sensorial world and the world of images and abstract concepts; thus, it teaches "representational distance," which is so important for learning to think about symbols and things that aren't immediately present (as in math concepts or reading comprehension). To expect children to become literate before they have a base of language understanding is an exercise in futility. They may learn to sound out words, but that's where the story ends.

Adults reach a child's "zone of proximal development," where learning is primed to happen, by constantly challenging her to understand and express herself in more mature ways:

FATHER: "What was Peter Rabbit doing?"
CHILD (*pointing*): "Lettuce! He eated lettuce."
FATHER: "You bet! He was hungry and he ate lettuce."

One ideal time for this type of interaction is when you are reading aloud to your child. In fact, training mothers in dialogic reading of picture books—that is, learning to ask meaningful questions and encourage the child to discuss the material as you go along—had powerful effects on children's language and reading skills in several studies. In one case, the computer was used effectively *to train the mothers* to do a better job when reading to their children. There is no way it could do this job for the children (Arnold, 1994).

Developing an Inner Voice. Nature has given young children the delightful assignment of telling themselves stories. In fact, their planning abilities develop from personal narratives, which also become a foundation for ethical choices. Talking—either out loud or, by around age seven, in one's own head—helps them pay attention, imagine a course of action, predict its effects on others, and decide whether or not to do it.

This inner speech originates from talking with adult caregivers—and then having enough time and quiet space to practice it alone. Children vary dramatically both in the amount of and in the timetable for inner speech, which is also related to parenting style and socio-economic group. Normally, it should become well-developed between four and six years of age in children from middle-class homes, where parents have traditionally had the time to talk and interact closely with their children. For children from less verbal environments, including middle- and upper-income homes where screen time substitutes for family conversations, this development may be delayed.

Inner speech is important to academic as well as personal development (e.g., Diaz & Berk, 1992). From ages six to nine, gains in math achievement as well as in other subjects are related to the use of self-talk ("How should I do this problem—oh, I think I'll try . . ."). Delays in acquiring and using self-talk may interfere with attention and behavior, as well as effective performance in sports.

"When a child tries new tasks, he or she needs communicative support from an adult who is patient and encouraging and who offers the correct amount of assistance. . . . Gradually, adults can withdraw this support as children begin to guide their own initiative," states language specialist Laura Berk (1994, pp. 78–83). Can a computer offer similar experiences? Not yet—if ever. Even if software were sufficiently advanced, the emotional importance of human interaction is too important a part of the package.

Early Literacy

One of the most promising uses of computer technology with children age five to seven is as a supplement to a well-planned literacy program. My classroom visits have included some large urban classes of six-year-olds, where one or two computers really helped the teacher in motivating children to practice talking together, writing, and reading, as they collaborated in creating, printing, and rereading their own stories. Moreover, computer word processing with large, clear fonts is useful to a parent or teacher who wants to write down a child's dictated story and give him an easy-to-read printout to illustrate. (Of course, the same effect can be achieved with pencil and paper if you don't have a computer.) As computers gain more real-sounding voices, "learn" to read back a child's written words, or someday even write down his spoken ones, they may yet find a place as language and reading tutors. The jury is still out, however, on other popular "literacy" applications—despite the elaborate claims of enthusiasts and hucksters. As Gavriel Salomon's (1979) studies have demonstrated, children who learn in one medium (screen vs. page) will always be inclined to prefer the one in which they learned. So, if you think books are important, you should probably start there. We all have plenty of screens in our lives; it's books that are in jeopardy.

As I have explained in *Your Child's Growing Mind* (1994), reading consists at least as much of a person's "habits of mind"—e.g., sustained concentration, language, imagery, questioning strategies—than it does of reciting words or alphabet sounds. Computers most readily lend themselves to drill-and-practice software (electronic workbooks), which may do more harm than good if used too soon and too extensively. Generally speaking, the better programs do build certain skills (and thus may be useful at the right ages), and they tend to raise older children's scores if the tests focus more on mechanics of reading than on deeper comprehension skills. But drill-and-practice may have subtle negative outcomes, especially for very young children. In one study, children using very popular reading software drill-and-practice (disguised as games with reward screens) demonstrated *a 50 percent drop in their creativity scores*. This decline was not found for either children who did not use computers or those using open-ended (e.g., writing, drawing) programs. The researcher who conducted this study is editor of a computer journal and one of the major boosters of "developmentally appropriate" use of computers in preschool. She concludes that if computers are used, they should be integrated with a regular curriculum and complemented with hands-on activities to reinforce the major objectives of the software (Haughland, 1992).

One school I visited used an elementary-level reading package in kindergarten—which necessitated keeping the classroom unnaturally quiet all day because a small group was always working on the computers. ("They have to be able to hear through those earphones," explained the aide.) Although some of the exercises were useful, the dictum of a silent classroom for five- and six-year-olds runs counter to every recommendation by early childhood experts, not the least of which is the limitations it places on oral language and self-talk. Unfortunately, the school was unable to purchase new materials or upgrade software because of the considerable expense (their grant money was gone), so children in all grades used the same stories and exercises year after year. In short, there are better, less-expensive, and more interesting ways to teach most children beginning reading skills. If the aide were trained in teaching reading instead of teaching computer, for example, she could use the same exercises in a much richer educational context and achieve equal or better results with small groups of children.

Symbol Use in "Screenland"

Among the few who have looked closely at "developmentally appropriate" computer use is Linda Labbo of the University of Georgia, who observed five- and six-year-old children exploring a multimedia program she termed "screenland." Labbo was interested in finding out how youngsters in the early stages of reading would interact with multimedia symbols. This classroom, contrary to the norm, had eighteen children and two experienced teachers (described as "exemplary"), with two computers and a printer. Under Labbo's supervision, the youngsters, most of whom were still nonreaders, used the computers to create pictures that would tell stories, with the occasional addition of alphabet letters (e.g., typing their names or random letter combinations).

Labbo observed that the children enjoyed the experience, and she felt it also enhanced cognitive and social skills as the youngsters explored the computer environment with classmates. Engaging in "dramatic symbolism," they invented characters and dialogue to supplement role playing. The freedom to erase work quickly and try again, she believes, encouraged them to take risks and be more imaginative. On the other hand, they tended to lean heavily on prepackaged clip art. Even more troubling is her observation of relatively sparse use of language, as the children were deeply engaged in the visual aspects of the experience.

Labbo's aim was to watch how children would "create meaning" from the unstructured use of multiple symbol systems. She believes they did, but no assessment of the children's progress in standard prereading skills is presented. In fact, Labbo's main recommendation is that we broaden our definitions of literacy beyond "verbocentrism." How can we conceptualize literacy if our notion of print-based literacy is no longer adequate?" she asks (Labbo, 1996, pp. 356–385).

Did the children gain anything unique from this experience compared with a noncomputerized setting? Would adventures in screenland be either practical or productive in a more standard classroom setting? Most important, did the children learn to read? No evidence of this outcome is provided. Clearly, multimedia influences the types of symbols young children generate. The unanswered question is whether these new forms will positively supplement or negatively detract from print literacy. Because of the compelling nature of the visual display, I am skeptical that it will aid literacy. Lacking more definitive research, I would advocate a consciously balanced curriculum, reserving such classroom computer use until at least first or even second grade, when children have the skills to add written stories into the multimedia mix. We must not underestimate the unique qualities of young children's language in shaping and expanding thought.

CONCLUSION

The immature human brain neither needs nor profits from attempts to "jump start" it. The fact that this phrase is being successfully used to sell technology for toddlers illustrates our ignorance of early childhood development. Our wish to rush young children willy-nilly into the electronic grip of an unproven medium also reflects a belief that learning is something the young must be enticed into, whereas it is, in fact, the driving force of their existence. Unfortunately, many adults don't recognize real learning when they see it—as with Sam and his toy boat.

The brain tends to seek what it needs at each stage of development, and it doesn't need the blandishments of software programmers to distract it. Why, after all, are we so unwilling to trust the wisdom of the young child's brain to seek out the stimulation it needs from a naturally enriched environment? The minute we introduce an artificially engaging stimulus with fast-paced visuals, startling noises, silly scenarios, and easy excitement, the brain is diverted away from its natural developmental tasks. Kids will be enthusiastic about any novelty, but their enthusiasm is uncritical. It's up to the mature minds in the situation to discriminate and select what is truly valuable.

"Yes, we get a lot of pressure from parents, but we believe the gains from working with computers do not outweigh the losses for four- and five-year-olds,' states Mary Ucci of the Wellesley Child Study Center. "At this age they need to be pushing Play-Doh, not buttons" (Personal Communication, 1997).

David Elkind (1994), child development authority, laments our failure to respect the unique qualities of childhood learning. It has become fashionable to try to bring children into many aspects of the adult world too soon, he points out, "collapsing" the stages of childhood and thus depriving youngsters—and their brains—of the opportunity to complete necessary developmental tasks. To enter school successfully, Elkind suggests, children don't need technological expertise. Instead, they should be able to

- express themselves, listen, and follow directions.
- start a task and bring it to completion themselves before jumping off to another project.
- cooperate with other children.

As we have seen, all of these qualities may be eroded by the wrong kind of computer exposure.

Joseph Weizenbaum (1995) of the Massachusetts Institute of Technology was once a booster for everything digital, but now offers articulate warnings about its use. Do we want, he asks, to expose our young children to artificial minds that possess no human values or even common sense? The physical world, not the two-dimensional screen, is where they will learn the real skills for the future and become complex "systems thinkers"—able to relate things to each other, to see real-life connections, patterns, and context.

One preschool teacher says it eloquently: "Let us not let our adult excitement with what computers can do in the adult workplace deter us from offering to children the squishiness of making mud pies, the scent of peppermint extract when making cookies, and the feel of balancing a block at the top of a tower . . . The adult world of the plastic workplace comes all too soon" (in Wright & Shade, 1993–1994).

NOTE

1. Excerpted and updated by permission of Simon & Schuster Adult Publishing Group from *Failure to Connect: How Computers Affect Our Children's Minds—for Better and Worse* by Jane M. Healy, Ph.D. Copyright 1998 by Jane M. Healy.

REFERENCES

Angier, N. (1992, October 20). The purpose of playful frolics: Training for adulthood. *New York Times*, C1, C8.

APA Monitor (1996, June). Stress, depression, and hormones are linked, p. 6.

Arnold, D. H. (1994). Accelerating language development through picture book reading. *Journal of Educational Psychology, 86(2)*, 235–243.

Bergen, D. (Ed.). (1988). *Play as a medium for learning and development*. Portsmouth, NH: Heinemann.

Berk, L. E. (1996, November). Why children talk to themselves. *Scientific American*, 78–83.

Bjorklund, D. F., & Harnishfeger, K. K. (1990). The resources construct in cognitive development. *Developmental Review, 10*, 48–71.

Bornstein, M. H., & O'Reilley, A. W. (Eds.). (1993). *The role of play in the development of thought*. San Francisco: Jossey-Bass.

Bowman, B. T., & Beyer, E. R. (1993–1994). Thoughts on technology and early childhood education. In J. L. Wright & D. D. Shade (Eds.), *Young children: Active learners in a technological age*. Washington, DC: NAEYC.

Brosterman, N. (1997). *Inventing kindergarten*. New York: Abrams.

Buckleitner, W. (1996, spring). Behind the scenes. *Scholastic Parent and Child*, 29–30.

Calvin, W. H. (1994, October). The emergence of intelligence. *Scientific American*, 101–107.

Capra, F. (1995, June). *Computers in education: A critical look*. Invitational Symposium, conducted at University of California, Berkeley.

Case, R. (1996, November). Some thoughts about cognitive development. *Computers and Cognitive Development*. Invitational Symposium, conducted at University of California, Berkeley.

Clements, D. (1993, January). Young children and computers. *Young Children*, 56–64.

Cohen, D., & MacKeith, S. (1992). *The development of imagination*. London: Routledge.

Denham, S. (1993). Maternal emotional responsiveness and toddlers' social-emotional competence. *Journal of Child Psychology and Psychiatry and Allied Disciplines, 34(5)*, 715–728.

Diaz, R. M., & Berk, L. E. (1992, November). Why children talk to themselves. *Scientific American*, 78–83.

Education Week (1994 January 12), p. 33.

Education Week (1996 December 11), p. 5.

Education Week (1997 March 12), p. 6.

Elkind, D. (1994, February). *Education for the 21st century: Toward the renewal of thinking*. Paper presented at an Invitational Symposium at Teachers College, Columbia University.

Ellsworth, C. D. & Sindt, V. G. (1994, February). Helping "Aha" to happen. *Educational Leadership*, 40–44.

Fox, N., et al. (1995). Frontal activation asymmetry and social competence at four years of age. *Child Development, 66(6)*, 1770–1784.

Frye, D., et al. (1996). Inference and action in early causal reasoning. *Developmental Psychology, 32(1)*, 120–131.

Gates, B. (1995). *The road ahead*. New York: Penguin Books.

Gilpatrick, L. (1997, August). Personal Communication.

Haughland, S. W. (1992). The effect of computer software on preschool children's developmental gains. *Journal of Computing in Childhood Education, 3(1)*, 15–30.

Healy, J. (1994). *Your child's growing mind*. New York: Doubleday.

Labbo, L. D. (1996). A semiotic analysis of young children's symbol making in a classroom computer center. *Reading Research Quarterly, 31(4)*, 356–385.

Mariani, M., & Barkley, R. A. (1997). Neuropsychological and academic function in preschool boys with Attention Deficit Hyperactivity Disorder. *Developmental Neuropsychology, 13(1)*, 111–119.

New York Times (1997, April 5), p. 10.

Pellegrini, A. D., & Galda, L. (1993). Ten years after: A reexamination of symbolic play and literacy research. *Reading Research Quarterly, 28(2)*, 163–175.

Petry, M. et al. (1996, February). *The effect of language on visual spatial atten-*

tion. Paper presented at Annual Meeting of the International Neuro-psychological Society.

Radell, P. L., & Gottlieb, G. (1992). Developmental intersensory interference. *Developmental Psychology, 28(5),* 794–803.

Salomon, G. (1979). *Interaction of media, cognition, and learning.* San Francisco: Jossey-Bass.

Singer, D. J., & Singer, J. L. (1977). *Partners in play.* New York: Harper & Row.

Stoll, C. (1995). *Silicon snake oil.* New York: Doubleday.

Thatcher, R. W. (1994). Psychopathology of early frontal lobe damage. In D. Cicchetti (Ed.), *Development and psychopathology* (pp. 565–596).

Thelen, E. (1995, February). Motor development. *American Psychologist, 79–95.*

Turvey, M. T. (1996). Dynamic touch. *American Psychologist, 51(11),* 1134–1152.

Ucci, M. (1997, April). Personal Communication.

Weikart, P. S. (1995, fall). Purposeful movement: Have we overlooked the base? *Early Childhood Today,* 6–15.

Weizenbaum, J. (1995, June). *Computers in education: A critical look.* Paper presented at an Invitational Symposium at the University of California, Berkeley.

Wright, J. C., et al. (1994). Young children's perceptions of television reality. *Developmental Psychology, 3(2),* 229–239.

Wright, J. L., & Shade, D. D. (Eds.). (1993–1994). *Young children: Active learners in a technological age.* Washington, DC: NAEYC.

ABOUT THE CONTRIBUTOR

JANE M. HEALY holds a Ph.D. in educational psychology from Case Western Reserve University and has done postdoctoral work in developmental neuropsychology. Formerly on the faculties of Cleveland State University and John Carroll University, she is internationally recognized as a lecturer and consultant with many years of experience as a classroom teacher, reading/learning specialist, and elementary administrator. She is the author of numerous articles and the books *Your Child's Growing Mind: A Guide to Learning and Brain Development from Birth to Adolescence* (Doubleday, 1994), *Endangered Minds: Why Our Children Don't Think and What We Can Do about It* (Touchstone/Simon & Schuster, 1999), *How to Have Intelligent and Creative Conversations with Your Kids* (Doubleday, 1994), and *Failure to Connect: How Computers Affect Our Children's Minds and What We Can Do about It*. Ms. Healy has appeared on most of the major media in the United States, and lectured for schools worldwide. She is frequently consulted with questions regarding the effects of new technologies on the developing brain.

5

Handmade Minds
in the Digital Age[1]

FRANK R. WILSON

Today's educational world has been thrown into chaos by a sudden loss of the fundamental consensus that usually protects established institutions from all but the worst societal storms and upheavals. The economic, technological, political, and social foundations that support the teaching of young children today have become so entangled, contentious, and volatile that I believe no one can possibly pretend to know in any straightforward way what is best for children at this moment in time, or how best to teach them.

One might well object to this claim—after all, education has been in a state of chaos since the time of Plato. But I would argue that the cultural underpinnings of education have never been so unstable as they are now. As a consequence, the whole enterprise of education seems to have fallen into a state of agitated confusion. And it is not just teachers and parents who seem to have lost their bearings. Even the leaders of educational institutions have begun to question basic assumptions and to doubt their own ability to plan and to act. It is possible that the elegant French term "anomie" best describes this new psychological atmosphere. However bad all this sounds, I doubt that the schools will be abandoned or that the teaching profession will become obsolete. Yes, there is a crisis, but crisis is good for us. After all, human intelligence evolved as a response not only to danger, but also to the absolute certainty of uncertainty. Those who are vigilant and calm will find a way to thrive in the new environment.

CRISIS IN EDUCATION: COMPUTER AS CATALYST

From my perspective, the single most important actor in this crisis is the computer. Please note that I refer to the computer not as a culprit or the enemy, but as an actor. The distinction is important because it is absolutely critical that we realize the computer is a force whose real nature and potential (both good and bad) we simply do not understand very well yet.

Since actors appear in plays, perhaps we should let our imaginations take to a drama—or perhaps a comedy—in which a rich and overbearing cousin (about whom we know very little) suddenly arrives uninvited. Like Sheridan Whiteside, the infamous *Man Who Came to Dinner* in the classic American comedy by George S. Kaufman and Moss Hart (1941), Mr. Computer is a loud, disruptive, and costly problem from the moment he walks through the door. What should we do about him? Obviously we cannot ignore him. Do we throw ourselves out the back window to get away? Should we take him hunting or riding and stage a fatal accident and then send him back home in a wooden box? Or do we stand our ground and use our wits to turn the situation around? Before taking action, I think we have to decide what this play is about. Are we in a play about an alien intruder (the computer), or is it really a play about ourselves?

THE RISE AND FALL OF THE AGE OF ENLIGHTENMENT

Two books that have helped me to remain calm as I watch education's great battle with the computer are: *Artful Science: Enlightenment Entertainment and the Eclipse of Visual Education* (1996) by Barbara Maria Stafford, professor of art history at the University of Chicago, and *In the Age of the Smart Machine: The Future of Work and Power* (2000) by Shoshana Zuboff, professor of business administration at Harvard. Stafford and Zuboff tell us that the rather strange play we find ourselves in is a dramatic fantasy about the end of the European Age of Enlightenment. Here I must borrow from the philosopher Michel Foucault, who thought of enlightenment as a particular kind of personal self-awareness that became a defining theme of European thought over the past five hundred years. Foucault accepted Emmanuel Kant's prediction that the Age of Enlightenment would be the moment when humanity is going to put its own reason to use, without subjecting itself to any authority. For the poet Charles Baudelaire, the enlightened individual is not the man who goes off to *discover* himself, his secrets, and his hidden truth, but the man who tries to *invent* himself. This modernity does not *liberate man in his own being*; it compels him to face the task of *producing himself*.

Education in the Age of the Enlightenment: Constructing the Self

This is the kernel of the idea I want to explore. For at least five hundred years it has increasingly been the highest intention of education not merely to equip but to compel the individual to *produce* himself or herself. The consequence of this process is that the individual becomes the authority behind his or her own actions. I hope to convince you that the hand has had, and almost certainly will continue to have, a central role in the implementation of this grand educational project of Western civilization.

Just a little over five hundred years ago, Europeans were in the early stages of a revolution that was every bit as unexpected and as destabilizing as the present computer and Internet revolution has proven to be. The printing press had been invented with the hope that books would become more widely available. But when Martin Luther's list of questions about papal indulgences was printed and circulated, the world suddenly became a place where "a cat could not only look at a king, but could take his head off with a rhetorical question and a distribution list." The Protestant Reformation was, among other things, the grand opening of the Information Age, and Martin Luther was the world's first media celebrity.

Another milestone from the same period also bears a resemblance to an event of our own time. After overcoming the intense skepticism of the Spanish court's mathematicians and astronomers, the forty-year-old son of a Genoese weaver persuaded Queen Isabella of Spain to make a highly risky investment in a maritime expedition into completely uncharted waters. Few people believed the trip could be safely made, and fewer still believed there was any chance of Columbus and his men returning safely, with or without riches from the East.

A third pivotal event took place when a young Belgian named Andreas Vesalius ended a nearly two-thousand-year-old taboo on human dissection when (in 1543) he published the world's first comprehensive textbook of human anatomy. His book is widely credited as having started the conversion of medicine from a loose collection of folk remedies and magic to a profession founded on scientific observation and analysis.

This trio of transforming events helped us to articulate that what sets humans apart from all other creatures on Earth is our ability to define ourselves through the exercise of our bodies, minds, and spirits and through each other. Our vitality and curiosity are the gifts of our genes; our autonomy and, in Kant's terms, our *authority*, are the fruits of our labor.

Post-Enlightenment: The Age of Human Obsolescence?

So here we are in the year 2003, and we have for all practical purposes the same genes our earliest human ancestors had 200,000 years ago. And we are in a state of confused exhilaration and shock because suddenly life is being transformed too rapidly for us to adapt, so fast that we are unsure of how to educate our children. Five hundred years ago, European civilization was thrown into chaos by the printing press, a sailor who ventured across an uncharted ocean, and a physician who needed to see more. In our time, we are beholden to the Internet, we have been to the Moon and back, and we have machines that can look into the body of a living person. Doesn't it sound oddly familiar? Haven't we already, to use a popular phrase, *been there* and *done that?* What are we worried about?

I think we are worried because we have allowed ourselves to believe that we owe our success to the human brain, and we have been told that our brains are becoming obsolete—an artifact of predigital human civilization. That is why this play we are watching about the computer doesn't feel much like a comedy. But it is not a horror show either, because humans are, in fact, so much more than "brains with storage capacity." Without exception, every child comes with quite a pedigree: he or she is no less than the present incarnation of millions of years of unbroken, field-tested, continually evaluated and updated strategies for adaptation to an environment that has a consistent record of hostility to the incompetent.

HOMO SAPIENS—THIRTY MILLION YEARS IN THE MAKING

A recognizable human prehistory began when advanced tree-dwelling primates evolved into the anthropoid suborder. Five or six million years ago, after living in the trees for twenty to twenty-five million years, climate changes encouraged some of these animals to leave the trees. These were the hominids, the first anthropoids to stand upright and walk on their feet.

These first bipeds no longer needed upper limbs to support their body weight in order to forage in the trees. Evolution might have recognized this reduced functional demand in a number of ways. For example, reduced need for hand and arm skill could have led to a much smaller arm, perhaps something like the kangaroo. Alternatively, if the hominids could have survived on the ground by gathering fruits, nuts, and insects, our ancestors might have kept the arm as it was anatomically, but surrendered the neurologic capacity for aerial gymnastics. That is approximately what happened to the gorillas, which have magnificent arms and hands that nevertheless are never used to manufacture or manipulate tools of any kind.

That the hominids did *not* become land-bound animals with withered arms or indolent lifestyles is almost certainly because they were small animals, and the habitat they entered was no balmy, fragrant Eden: it was a dangerous, sudden-death battleground dominated by powerful and hungry predators. In other words, our ancestors established a place for themselves because they found not less, but *more* for the arm, hand, and brain to do. Indeed, based on what we now know of our own early history and the way that history is written into the human brain, our ancestors staked everything on skilled use of the arm and hand (Wilson, 1998).

The commitment to that specific strategy, the reinvention of the arm and hand, probably began between three and four million years ago among families of small apes living in southern and eastern Africa. We know about the existence of these hominids because of the work of anthropologists who began searching for the fossil remains of early human ancestors in Africa's Great Rift Valley more than fifty years ago. The most important of these fossils was the nearly complete skeleton of a female member of the species, now known as *Australopithecus Afarensis*. Nicknamed Lucy, this animal lived about 3.25 million years ago. She was about the size of the chimpanzee, with a brain volume of 400 cc (approximately one-third the size of the human brain), she walked upright, and her wrist and hand were structurally unique (L. Leaky & M. Leaky, in Morell, 1995).

What we have learned about Lucy's hand, largely through the remarkable studies of the American anthropologist Mary Marzke (1996), is that a few small anatomic modifications had a dramatic impact on its functional capacity. The thumb was longer in relation to the fingers, and the index and middle fingers could rotate at the knuckle joint. This change gave Lucy a new grip, referred to as the three-jaw chuck—this is the same basic grip used by baseball pitchers. So Lucy would have been able to hold larger stones between the thumb and index and middle fingers, and could have thrown them overhand, just as a modern baseball pitcher can. She could also swivel her hips to accelerate the speed of a thrown projectile. What she probably lacked was a computational system to turn that entire novel manipulative potential into a ballistic system. As far as we can tell, she did not have the brain that would have transformed her hand and arm from a feeding and locomotor system to a weapons platform. But that is exactly what her descendants, over the next two million years or so, managed to develop.

The Hand-Brain Complex

One of the most interesting aspects of the hand story has to do with the remarkable tendency of biologic systems to continually modify and adapt whatever is already in place when it is beneficial to do so—small changes can lead to unintended and sometimes monumental innovations. For the hominids, the small changes in wrist and hand structure led to significantly improved throwing, and eventually to a *complete reorganization of the brain*. Being able to hit a target with a stone depends most of all upon the timing of its release. Whenever it was that Lucy or her descendants began to rely upon this new hand to launch rocks at prey or at other predators, they also started building a supremely precise clock to control the activity of muscles in the arm and hand. And once the hominids began to be sharpshooters, evolution started to play with hemispheric specialization in the brain. We can now say with considerable confidence that almost the entire set of distinctive human motor and cognitive skills, including language and our remarkable ability to design and use tools, began as nothing more than an enhanced capacity to control the timing of sequential arm and hand movements used in throwing (Wilson, 1998).

Based on the archeological and anthropologic record and on the way the human brain is now configured, the australopithecines and their descendants came to depend increasingly on manual skills in their daily lives, and inevitably, those who excelled increased their own chances of survival. Somewhere between 100,000 and 200,000 years ago, the hand reached its present anatomic configuration, the brain tripled in size, tools were more elaborate, there was a complex society based on the organization of relationships, alliances, ideas, and work, and we became *Homo sapiens* (Wilson, 1998).

Handwork and Community Life

Anthropologists remind us that the social structure of the hominids was profoundly influenced by the manufacture and use of tools. The hand had long been an instrument for social interaction among primates through ritual grooming, and with the advent of cooperative tool manufacture and use, skilled hand use became associated with an open-ended mix of diversity *and* specialization of skill. This strengthened greatly over time, enlarging the social foundations of human survival, as well as creating a need for greatly expanded and refined methods of communication. What evolved in hominid life, in other words, was not simply a new and clever use of the hand, but a life of shared trust and commitment based on a realization that life for the individual takes its course and acquires its meaning from and within the community.

To summarize so far: human skill and intelligence derive from a history that reaches back into the deep hominid and primate past. Skill is based on far more than muscles, nerves, joints, reflexes, and brain circuits; intelligence cannot be explained by quantifying synapses, or weight, or any other physical attribute of the brain alone. These human potentials are a species adaptation that belongs to the (almost indescribably) long story of hominid and human evolution, and they are manifested in diverse forms in human individuals in specific cultural settings. In this evolutionary process, tool making, innovation, and increasingly sophisticated strategies for environmental mastery gradually transformed the brain, rendering our two hands a cooperative pair, permitting them to signal, teach, and even tell stories through mime and gesture, becoming an integral part of the astonishing success story of the hominids with their new hand and expanding brain.

THE HAND: A FOCAL POINT OF COGNITIVE DEVELOPMENT

As interesting as that story is, its importance extends well beyond the domain of historical and evolutionary conjecture. In fact, it has enormous implications for those of us who inherit the *Homo sapiens* hand-brain complex. The most important of these is that the hand is also a focal point of *individual* motor and cognitive development.

Each of us begins life primed to perceive the world, to learn from it, and to forge our own personal strategies for living. The human genome dictates that at the species level we are all the same, while at the individual level we are all different. How does this work? The British psychologist Henry Plotkin (1993) says it is done with what he calls "heuristics"—meaning inherent, individually specific physical and mental capacities by which we tune into and react to important conditions or events in the environment. Plotkin uses the term "heuristic"—a word from classical Greek, meaning a teaching device or strategy—because he wants us to understand that we are not only equipped to survive physiologically, but also to *learn* how to survive behaviorally in the face of both certain and uncertain dangers. Our personal genetic heritage predisposes each of us to excel in the mastery of certain kinds of survival skills more than we do at others, with the resulting diversity adding strength to organized human communities. From the time we are born, we explore the world, we pay attention to our own reactions to it, and we make our natural affinities a guide to our efforts at improvement.

Children are naturally motivated to learn through modeling and mentoring by adults and children in their family and the wider community, and from the behavior of an infinite variety of objects grasped and manipulated in their hands. When personal discovery and desire prompt anyone to learn to do something well with the hands, an extremely complicated process is initiated that endows work with a powerful emotional charge. People are changed, significantly and irreversibly it seems, when movement, thought, and feeling fuse during the active, long-term pursuit of personal goals. In other words, if the hand and brain learn to speak to each other intimately and harmoniously, something that humans seem to prize greatly, which we call autonomy, begins to take shape.

By the time children reach school age, they already understand how to learn from others and how to teach themselves. But schools can change the learning process for children in profound ways. Most of these are positive, but there are dangers as well; for example, the process can easily become divorced from family and community life, or the school can substitute an approved list of adult career goals for the child's native curiosity as a prime mover behind his or her personal search for skill mastery and understanding.

EDUCATION IN THE DIGITAL AGE

Questioning an Unquestioned Assumption

I now return to the computer, and its increasingly central role in American education. A decade ago, the Clinton administration decided that every child in school should have access to a computer and that every classroom should be "wired" to the Internet. So far, well over $50 billion has been spent to meet this goal, and when we include the cost of teacher training, computer maintenance, and software upgrades, experts estimate that at a minimum, an additional $15 billion will be spent every year for the foreseeable future to meet the national goals for technology in education (Cordes & Miller, 2000).

There is a virtually unchallenged assumption on the part of educators, politicians, and parents that computers and the Internet play an *unconditionally positive* role in education. In addition, in light of the increasingly computerized workplace, it is widely assumed that computer literacy—the ability to understand and use computer software—must be acquired at an early age. Parents, in particular, fear that the child who is unable to use computers will fall behind in school, and will be unemployable. These beliefs are now so deeply entrenched in American thinking that anyone who questions it publicly is considered a fool.

Most Americans are amazed that anyone could doubt the need to bring schools into the computerized, digitized, and Internet-dependent twenty-first century as quickly as possible. But there *are* doubters, and some of them are people who have spent their entire careers in computer science and information technology. In an interview published in July 1999 in the *New York Times,* Professor Mike Dertouzos at the Massachusetts Institute of Technology recalled a conversation on this subject that he had in 1998 with the former prime minister of Israel, Benjamin Netanyahu, who said, "I want to connect all toddlers in my country. I have 300,000 toddlers under the age of 5 and I want to connect them, but I'm having trouble finding the money."

Dertouzos, who is not a politician but a pioneer in computers and Internet technology, said to the prime minister, "Mr. Netanyahu, why do you want to do that?"

The reply from the prime minister, simply reflected what everyone assumed to be true at that time: "Isn't it obvious?"

While it might surprise some people, Professor Dertouzos said, "No, it's not" (Dreifus, 1999, p. F3).

What *is* obvious is that computer and communications technology are entering the schools and *will* play a role in education. This does not guarantee that the transformation will be managed intelligently, economically, or with the children's interests and needs in mind.

Intelligence: So Much More Than Storage Capacity

At least some cognitive scientists—and, I'm afraid, some educators—now wonder out loud if children can ever become as smart as computers. The flaw in this scare story is the same one made by anthropologists in the early part of this century, who thought that intelligence is simply a matter of the size of the "hardware" (this is literally true: until the middle of this century, it was widely held that the only difference between the earliest *Homo* brain and its predecessors was size, the dividing line between the australopithecines and *Homo* being drawn at 750 cc). No wonder some people believe that the optimal strategy for education is to seat one computer ready for data transfer—the child, that is—in front of another computer and to execute the download command.

Of course, there is nothing new about the educational fantasy behind our headlong rush to "wire" the classroom in order to intensify the child's exposure to whatever information is available on the Internet. Paulo Friere (1993), in *Pedagogy of the Oppressed*, cut straight through to the heart of this idea when he said,

> The teacher's task is to organize a process which already occurs spontaneously, to 'fill' the student by making deposits of information which he or she considers to constitute true knowledge. . . . The banking concept of education is based on a mechanistic, static, spatialized view of consciousness and it transforms students into receiving objects. (pp. 57–58)

And, just as with *real* banking, computers and the Internet are an ideal way to get around the inherent expense, messiness, and unpredictability of face-to-face, live, human interaction. This technology affords the opportunity to realize a level of control over the process entirely unimagined just a few years ago. Although the "banking" theory of education is not new, the delivery system now available to transform that theory into a prophecy *is* new and represents an experiment utterly without precedent in the history of education.

HEAD, HAND, AND HEART: INDISPENSABLE AND INSEPARABLE

The former editor of the *Harvard Education Newsletter*, Ed Miller, summarized the proceedings of a recent Teacher's College symposium on technology and education:

> A broad consensus emerged from this meeting of psychologists, physicists, historians, philosophers, and computer scientists—that we need to learn much more about technology's potential for impeding the healthy development of children, especially young children, before we plunge headlong into further investment in computers. Teachers are often seen as the stumbling block in efforts to digitize education. They are ridiculed as "technophobes" who resist progress and innovation. In fact, teachers know more about technology and its limitations than they are generally given credit for. Many of our most effective and knowledgeable teachers are skeptical about the usefulness of computers in schools, and with good

reason. But they have learned that speaking out against the technofaith has become a kind of heresy. Here's my hope for the future: that good teachers and their allies will find their voices. Already there are a few signs. The research community and some thoughtful journalists are beginning to take seriously what teachers have known for a long time: that they can never replace the 'human dimension'—the teacher's voice telling stories that feed the child's imagination; the teacher's helping hand helping the child's to grasp the butterfly net; the teacher's eye and heart that see, as no machine will ever see, the spark of recognition in the child's face.

I cannot say how much of Miller's cautious optimism I share, but I have my own hope: that more teachers will credit the authority of biology in the design of formal learning situations provided to children. It seems abundantly clear to me that, because of the process of co-evolution, the hand enjoys a privileged status in the learning process, being not only a catalyst but also an experiential focal point for the organization of the young child's perceptual, motor, cognitive, and creative world. It seems equally clear that as the child comes to the end of the preadolescent stage of development, the hand readily becomes a connecting link between self and community and a powerful enabler of the growing child's determination to acquire adult skill, responsibility, and recognition. This happens because of the hand's unique contribution to experiences that associate personal effort with skill mastery and the achievement of difficult and valued outcomes.

And I have one additional hope. Working teachers are our society's richest repository of experience and understanding about the needs and the potentials of children as learners. I hope they will credit their own authority and will make themselves heard in the ongoing debate about technology in education—if they do not, we and our children are in unprecedented danger.

NOTE

1. Copyright: Frank R. Wilson, 2001. An earlier version of this paper was delivered at the 24th International Montessori Congress, *Education as an Aid to Life*, Paris, 2001.

REFERENCES

Cordes, C., & Miller, E. (Eds.). (2000). *Fool's gold: A critical look at computers in childhood*. College Park, MD: Alliance for Childhood.

Dreifus, C. (1999, July 6). A conversation with Michael L. Dertouzos: A pragmatist on what computers can do. *New York Times*, F3.

Friere, P. (1993). *Pedagogy of the oppressed*. New York: Continuum.

Kaufman, G., & Hart, M. (1941). *The man who came to dinner*. New York: Dramatist Play Service, Inc.

Marzke, M. (1996). Evolution of the hand and bipedality. In A. Lock & C. R. Peters (Eds.), *Handbook of human symbolic evolution*. Oxford: Clarendon Press.

Morell, V. (1995). *Ancestral passions: The Leakey family and the quest for humankind's beginnings*. New York: Simon and Schuster.

Plotkin, H. (1993). *Darwin machines and the nature of knowledge*. Cambridge, MA: Harvard University Press.

Stafford, B.M. (1996). *Artful science: Enlightenment entertainment and the eclipse of visual education*. Cambridge, MA: MIT Press.

Wilson, F.R. (1998). *The hand: How its use shapes the brain, language, and human culture*. New York: Vintage Books.

Zuboff, S. (2000). *In the age of the smart machine: The future of work and power*. New York: Basic Books.

ABOUT THE CONTRIBUTOR

FRANK R. WILSON, M.D., is clinical professor of neurology at Stanford University School of Medicine and former medical director of the Health Program for Performing Artists at the University of California School of Medicine, San Francisco. Since the publication of his book, *The Hand: How Its Use Shapes the Brain, Language, and Human Culture* (New York: Pantheon Books, 1998) he has participated in a variety of forums where educational policy concerning young children has been discussed. He has presented seminars on educational strategy at the Harvard Graduate School of Education, Columbia University Teachers College, the Massachusetts Institute of Technology, and Stanford University, and has been a recent keynote speaker at several prominent educational conferences. His primary research interests concern the neurologic and anthropologic foundations of hand movement, with a particular emphasis on developmental and educational influences on skill learning, and on the role of computers in early childhood education.

Part III

Building Blocks
of Intellectual Development:
Emotion and Imagination

Photo courtesy of Michele Perel Phillips.

6

Imagination and the Growth
of the Human Mind

Jeffrey Kane and Heather Carpenter

American educational policy and practice are driven by the unstated, unquestioned assumption that the human mind develops through a linear accumulation of information and processing skills of one sort or another. As a consequence, education (although rarely stated in such a direct, declarative form) is intended to provide children with sequenced, factual information and processing rules—whether in the form of phonetics or place values in arithmetic. In this context, it is always better to learn sooner than later, and more instruction is always better than less. As comfortable and reasonable as these ideas may seem—in a time when artificial intelligence is being conflated with the genuine article, human intelligence—it is easy to lose sight of the foundations of the mind that transcend the limits of multiple-choice tests. These foundations do not express themselves in explicit concepts but, when permitted to grow through simple, childhood activities such as unstructured play, create the possibility that ideas may have meaning and creative force in forging understanding beyond the accumulation of factual information. It is to these foundations that we turn our attention.

THE HARD WORK OF GETTING BEYOND ABSTRACTION

This chapter explores the importance of the imagination in the development of the human mind. Discussions about the nature of

knowledge often seem highly abstract and removed both from immediate experience or the practicalities that parents and teachers face in
assuming their educational responsibilities. It is true that exploring the
nature of our own thinking is a daunting intellectual challenge. However, in an ironic twist, the subject itself—our *thinking* and the way we
think about thinking—is anything but abstract.

The cognitive frameworks we use to make sense of everything in
the world and within ourselves is, in large measure, the product of
deep and unconscious cultural assumptions. These assumptions are
not abstract at all. Nor can they be abstracted so that we may study
them as we might an object in nature. They shape what we experience
and understand; they are not the product of critical reflection. They are
embedded in our language, in our social structures, in our homes, in
our schools, and in all that we provide children to guide them in developing knowledge of the world and of themselves.

The thesis of this chapter is that the cultural assumptions that shape
the process of knowing, although very powerful, have run their course
and are now more intellectual impediments than sources of insight and
understanding. Our plan is to reflect upon these assumptions in some
of the key works of a few leading thinkers of the modern Western
world and to imagine an alternative generative framework for thinking that utilizes a radically different model. At the core of the alternative is the role of imagination in creating knowledge.

NOT STARTING WITH THE FACTS

For many of us, it may seem virtually self-evident that knowledge
is composed of discrete facts and information embedded in a set of cognitive skills that an individual needs in order to make judgments and
continue learning. However, all is not as it seems.

When Sir Isaac Newton discovered the law of universal gravitation
and created his model of the physical universe, he began with the assumption that everything was composed of discrete particles interacting in lawful ways. He never considered the possibility that the
particles themselves might be a product of the weaving of patterns of
energy or that the laws he discovered were subject to the effects of
matter. His insights were powerful enough to undergird the development of technologies capable of taking us to the Moon, but the simple
fact remains that his basic assumptions were fundamentally wrong.
There is no such thing as immutable building blocks of matter; matter itself is in constant flux with subatomic particles coming into and
passing out of existence. There is no such thing as "pure space" that

objects may or may not occupy; space is always shaped by gravitational fields that make straight lines curve while yet remaining straight. Time is not fixed, but is always wedded to the speed at which an object travels; time slows as speed increases. In other words, the universe is more fluid and dynamic than Newton could have ever imagined. As much as he has contributed to our understanding of the universe, it was necessary for us to reject his seemingly self-evident assumptions in order to develop greater knowledge.

With respect to our current conception of human knowledge, we are the intellectual heirs of the great seventeenth-century philosopher, Rene Descartes. He created the model of knowledge that has guided the study of human thinking for the last four hundred years in the Western world. His ideas constitute the generative center of what we assume about the functioning of our own minds in the pursuit of knowledge.

Not coincidentally, Descartes's image of the mind—what we may call the "cognitive universe"—mirrors Newton's view of the physical universe. The cognitive universe is composed of unquestionable bits of information, absolute and fixed, that are tied together by strict and logical laws. It did not occur to Descartes that what we think of as absolute object information is, in part, a function of the manner in which we think or the manner in which we are taught to think. The information we use to make sense of the world is greatly influenced by what we learn to look for, by our beliefs about how the world is put together, and by the values we hold. In the West, we believe the world can be fragmented into pieces without affecting what we see. We value logical connections and have little regard for what anthropologist and philosopher Gregory Bateson might call the aesthetic patterns that give shape and form to all that we see—from the spiraling of sea shells to the formation of waves in the oceans (Bateson, 1979). As we shall see, the content of our thinking is intimately connected to how we think and vice versa.

In physics, we have made the transition from Newton's to Einstein's universe. We no longer think of static particles within the absolutes of space and time. Unfortunately, in understanding our own minds as we search for knowledge, we have not made this transition to a fluid and dynamic cognitive universe.

Our educational systems, with their renewed emphasis on short-answer accountability (tests) and their goal of productive intellectual labor for the Information Age, are based on a model of thinking that is fundamentally wrong. Our schools could be successful in a mechanical, seventeenth-century universe populated by mechanical thinkers.

At least there would be a correspondence between our view of the world and our view of the way we think. As rational and practical as such schools may seem to be, they could be based on outdated and disproven assumptions.

Newton's universe never existed; it was a function of the limitations of our capacity to envision all things in connection and flux. We are nonetheless profoundly indebted to Newton for his remarkable insights. Einstein once remarked that he, himself, could see so far only because he stood on Newton's shoulders. We live in an expanding physical universe, one that can be understood in motion, in dynamic relativity. Similarly, there is a corresponding "relativity of the cognitive universe," where perceptions and ideas and the process that interweaves them into understanding continually shape and reshape one another.

The constant interplay and mutual transformation of what and how we think does not come into play only in the rarefied intellectual contexts of scientific research. It is also present in the sandbox. The dynamic flux has always been there, but our models of thinking and knowledge have been too crude to reveal them. Again, what we see is connected to how we think. Although we may draw images from science to provide a clear context (and explicit examples) for illuminating possible conceptions of knowledge, scientific thinking and knowledge are themselves only the tip of the iceberg. From the preschool child scribbling pictures of horses, to the adolescent struggling for identity, to the musician, the architect, the carpenter, and the teacher in the classroom, knowing is a process of continuous cognitive flow, where individual objects and events are shaped and given meaning in their relations.

Nothing is fixed, even as one abstracts things to study them. However, the very process of abstraction, the removing of something from its context, necessarily tears it away from the forces that generate its particular form and substance. When we define knowledge in terms of discrete information and the power to reconstruct the world according to rule, we undermine the unique influences specific objects of thought may exert on the way we think. The objects and events we choose to draw out, as well as the methods and the rules we use to reconstruct reality—whether in a lab, studio, or a local park—are a function of the generative assumptions we have deeply embedded in our thinking. The fact that we have set rules in science does not preclude the possibility that the assumptions underlying those rules, like Newton's, are extraordinarily valuable but *wrong*.

The world is not in pieces, but our thinking is. This is because our culture values the capacities to abstract and to reconstruct. Focusing on these capacities, we de-emphasize other cognitive facilities to the point where we believe they have no place in the generation of knowledge or in the definition of knowledge itself. One such human cognitive facility is imagination.

THE VITAL ROLE OF IMAGINATION IN THE DEVELOPMENT OF KNOWLEDGE

Imagination is at the heart of all knowledge, whether it is tightly bound into specific protocols and processes (as in many physical sciences) or constantly challenging boundaries (as in many of the arts). Generally, imagination is placed in a category along with childhood itself, as something removed from the real world, something more properly associated with Walt Disney or the adventures of Harry Potter than with knowledge. Imagination may seem to be synonymous with *fantasy*, a creative departure from the world rather than a source of insight into it. But again, all is not as it seems. When we overemphasize the explicit aspects of knowledge, we underestimate the importance of the implicit, *the imaginative*, components of human knowing that provide the context rendering meaning and understanding rather than information alone.

Imagination in "Midrash"

The role of the imagination in the process of knowing—that is, the possession of knowledge—is clearly illustrated in the unique Jewish literary tradition known as "Midrash." A form of commentary on Jewish religious scripture, Midrash attempts to unfold an understanding of the meaning of what is written through contemplating the spaces between the Hebrew letters and words rather than attending only to letters and words themselves. Instead of looking at a letter, let us say, "S," as a symmetrically shaped line in an otherwise blank field of white, the Midrash commentator focuses on the white background as foreground with the line giving shape to the space. The letter is not the object of study; the context of the surrounding space, that which shapes the letter and gives it place, is at the center of his interest. Space is not simply a location; it is an active force in creating what we see. What we see in a written letter is not a distinct object that may be abstracted from a given space, but only the visible expression of a context that lies beyond it. So it is with the world according to Midrash.

All that we see, even as our seeing is extending with technology, is only a physical manifestation of interweaving creative forces transcending specific objects. These generative forces, whether we think of them in terms of what physicist David Bohm (1980) calls the "implicate order" of subatomic energies that defy explication, or of the divine as it continuously recreates all that is, are the determinants of what we see. It is only by making our way into the flow of these creative forces that we can understand why that which we see exists just as it does. We can generate enormous control in the natural world by isolating objects and reconstructing them according to set rules (as in the case of laboratory science), but we cannot achieve an understanding without the imagination to enter the flows of energy shaping and transcending the objects themselves. Understanding requires that we, with our imaginations, mirror in terms of our own activity, the creative forces at work in the world. The dynamic and flowing forces in the world demand that we be dynamic and flowing in our minds. Midrash does not deny the value of explicit text or rational commentary, but begins with the idea that deeper understanding demands that we move beyond the letters and words, to the meaning that gave rise to their first being uttered.

Imagining into the World

Although it may seem like a daunting task to use one's imagination to see the formative forces at work in the objects and events we may encounter, it is, quite literally, child's play. The origins of the creative impulses of the artist working through and with varied media to shape a work of art, or the vision of the scientist in complex interplay with empirical evidence to discover the laws at work in shaping phenomena, are rooted in the imaginative activity of childhood. The difficulty here is that so few of us were encouraged to be alone with nature or to play freely (without products that were designed to imagine for us, lest we face the possibility of boredom), that we do not understand what is happening (and unfolding) cognitively when children play. Many of us who were not fortunate enough to have been permitted to be children developed a concept of knowledge that has no place for the imagination. Through atrophy, and the premature formation of concepts and abstract skills, many of us have simply forgotten what we knew when we were children. Also, we have forgotten *how* we knew things when we were children. We are at a loss to understand how children explore the world and themselves, seamlessly, in feeding their dolls, dressing as kings or queens, or in crawling about as cats in search of a mouse. We are at a loss to understand their fascination with, or lessons learned from, splashing water, worms and bugs found in the soil, and the free movement of their own bodies twirling in every direction at once.

Through imaginative play with dolls and dress-up, children can explore the roles of those around them, and even elements in themselves as expressed in the characters they create. They learn the operational values and rules of social life not by examining the behavior of others, but by extending themselves into the place of *the other* to explore how they might understand and respond to the world. Children, imaginatively dwelling in the bodies of animals, feel their way into the physical qualities of their own bodies, and test the possibilities of their varied senses. They extend the contexts for the development of their understanding of the world. They act like physicists working in imaginary *frames* where space and time may reveal properties possible only in environments we can neither create nor find. When children are given the undirected opportunity to interact with nature, its laws—in physics and biology—can be woven into patterns that respond to their own activity like colors blending on the canvas of a painter. They can, when given the opportunity, experience directly, as Midrash, themselves and the world around them. They can build the cognitive foundations of their minds through experience of the flow of forces—the meanings that give rise to social patterns of action, the laws of nature at work in creating what we see. In time, with these fluid understandings as dynamic context, they can articulate specific ideas and test them in the light of experiment and reason.

LESSONS FROM CHILDHOOD

A few fortunate individuals recall the flow of their imaginations into the world and the lessons they learned; lessons that evolved into the scientific and artistic achievements that, at least publicly, have defined their lives.

Barbara McClintock (1902–1992) was a Nobel Prize–winning geneticist, who is most well known for her work with maize. She discovered that certain genes, called transposable genetic elements, could change their position on the chromosomes of cells (Hartl, 2002). McClintock suggested, in contrast to the prevailing genetic theories of her time, that the instructions for genes to move in cells come from the cell, the organism, and perhaps the environment (Keller, 1983). A revolutionary thinker, she fiercely held tight to her beliefs and trusted her imaginative vision, although in consequence she was often ostracized by her peers.

McClintock's insight into the genetic structure of corn was based upon her ability to imagine herself within the cells themselves. She was not on the outside looking in, but on the inside looking out; she was not working from bits of data to governing laws, but from a dynamic, integrated sense of the unity underlying and giving shape to particular phenomena. McClintock wrote,

> I found that the more I worked with them (the chromosomes) the bigger [they] got, and when I was really working with them I wasn't outside, I was down there. I was part of the system. I was right down there with them, and everything got big. I even was able to see the internal parts of the chromosomes—actually everything was there. (Keller, 1983, p. 117)

Her capacity to imagine the patterns of natural law flowing through the genetic structure of corn began with her unstructured play, both inside her house and outside, surrounded by nature. She spent endless hours absorbed in play trying to be, as she put it, "free of the body" (Keller, 1983). This desire for freedom was not so much relative to the physical constraints of her body, but to the desire to break through the boundaries that separated her from the world she encountered. She quite literally spent her time absorbed *in* things. "My mother," McClintock recounted, "used to put a pillow on the floor and give me a toy and just leave me there. She said I didn't cry, didn't call for anything" (p. 20). When asked how she could see "further and deeper into the mysteries of genetics than her colleagues," she echoed her experiences as a child. "One must have the time to look, the patience to 'hear what the material has to say to you,' the openness to 'let it come to you.' Above all, one must have 'a feeling for the organism'" (Keller, 1983).

Albert Einstein (1879–1955), the most celebrated scientist of the twentieth century, is revered for his development of the general and special theories of relativity that transformed our fundamental understanding of the physical laws of the universe. By common intellectual standards, Einstein was brilliant, but when matched against his contemporaries in physics, his mathematical or technical skills were not extraordinary. He claimed only that he was "passionately curious" (Hoffman, 1972, p. 7).

His curiosity was directed at what made things the way they were. For him, empirical observations were clues to an order, a unity creating and transcending all things. When he was four or five, sick and in bed, his father gave him a compass. He soon observed that the needle always pointed in the same direction and realized, with an overwhelming sense of awe, that it was subject to forces invisible to him. Biographer Banesh Hoffmann (1972, p. 9) writes:

> Here was a needle, isolated and unreachable, totally enclosed, yet caught in the grip of an invisible urge that made it strive determinedly toward the north. . . . To young Albert the magnetic needle came as a revelation. It did not fit. It mocked his early, simple picture of an orderly world.

While it is not clear how he attempted to discover the mysteries creating and transcending the world he perceived, it is clear that he did not form fixed concepts. His language was greatly delayed and he regarded his intellectual development as "retarded" (Clark, 1971, p. 10). Ironically, it was this very delay in creating concepts that he saw as allowing him to "wonder about space and time only when [he] had already grown up" (p. 10). Einstein did not spend his early years observing the world from a distance, filling reservoirs of facts, or cataloging his own observations as abstract principles or theories. He preferred cognitive exploration through action and through interaction with the environment in a formally unstructured context. His sister recalled, "He preferred games that required patience and perseverance, building complicated structures with building blocks and erecting houses of cards as high as fourteen stories high" (Hoffman, 1972, p. 18). As an adult, "He tried to describe his method of thought, saying that the essential part was a 'rather vague' nonlogical playing with 'visual' and 'muscular' signs, after which explanatory words had to be 'sought for laboriously'" (p. 255). (His use of the term "muscular" while undefined, suggests the kind of tactile, perhaps even proprioceptive experiences associated with childhood activity.) The fascinations and patterns of play in early life are manifest in Einstein's approach to science and in his discoveries.

When evaluating the worth of a scientific theory or proposition, he would ask himself "whether he would have created the universe in that way had he been God" (Hoffman, 1972, p. 18). He was not trying to understand the universe from the point of view of an objective observer viewing it from without, but from the originating imagination guiding the hand of its creator. An author of a modern-day "scientific Midrash," he thought of the laws of the universe as if in the first person—as one aesthetically applying them in the act of creation. The universe was not *out there*, but seamlessly connected to the creative within him and within us.

Frank Lloyd Wright (1867–1959), one of the most accomplished architects of the twentieth century, had an unparalleled capacity to integrate natural forms into his designs, and his designs into natural forms. He understood the rhythms, harmonies, and flowing proportions at work in nature and how to blend them into the functional aesthetic of architecture.

He experienced the formative shaping forms, the harmonious weaving harmonies, and the generative principles in the creations of nature. Wright, like Einstein, knew of the laws of nature in the first person working through him. The only essential difference between them was the language they spoke—one, physics, and the other, architecture.

Wright was a product of a Froebelian kindergarten, where he was given rich and varied opportunities to play with blocks and other simple toys as well as to work in gardens and other natural settings. In 1957, he wrote:

> Encouraged by my early training at the kindergarten table and subsequent work on the farm in the valley, I came to feel that in the nature of Nature—if from within outward—I would come upon nothing not sacred. Nature had become my Bible. (Brosterman, 1997, p. 145)

In 1932, he explained in more particular terms, "The smooth shapely maple blocks with which to build, the sense of which never afterward leaves the fingers: so form became feeling" (p. 139). Those maple blocks were fundamental to shaping the creative in him. "I soon became susceptible to the constructive pattern *evolving in everything I saw.* I learned to 'see' this way and when I did, I did not care to draw casual incidents in Nature, I wanted to *design*" (p. 138). The influence of these early experiences is evident in Wright's work. Consider the striking similarity between the creative efforts of young children in Froebelian kindergartens and some of Wright's mature architectural designs (see the folding of paper [Figure 1] and a wooden block construction [Figure 2]).

The creative in Wright was drawn forth by the creative in Nature. One wonders, had Einstein mentioned to him that he measured scientific theories by asking whether God would have so made the universe, if Wright might have responded that he used the very same standard to judge a work of architecture.

INDWELLING

These quick biographical sketches, while remarkable in their illustration of extraordinary genius, are intended to demonstrate that the

Figure 1
A comparison between paper folding by a student of the Froebelian kindergarten and an architectural design by Frank Lloyd Wright.

Left:
Unidentified kinder-
gartner. Beauty forms
made with the
eighteenth gift (paper
folding). United
States, c. 1880

Below:
Frank Lloyd Wright.
Price Tower—typical
floor plan. 1952. Ink,
35½ x 36". © 1996
The Frank Lloyd
Wright Foundation

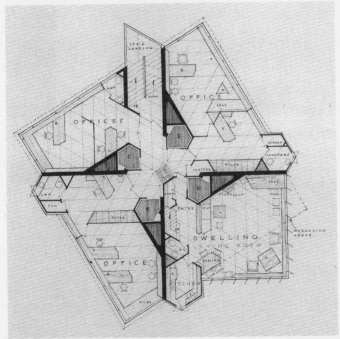

Opposite top:
Frank Lloyd Wright.
H. J. Ullman
residence—plan.
1904. Ink, 18 x 28⅛".
© 1996 The Frank
Lloyd Wright
Foundation

Wright utilized many
different square and
rectangular grids,
often combining sev-
eral on the same plan.

Opposite bottom:
Frank Lloyd Wright.
Roberts Quad
Housing—plan of
block development.
c. 1903. Ink, 15 x 27".
© 1996 The Frank
Lloyd Wright
Foundation

Courtesy of Frank Lloyd Wright Foundation.

unity of knowledge is not an abstraction, but grounded in the imme-
diacy of childhood. The intellectual and artistic achievements of these
three giants were rooted in and animated by their free-form imaginative encounters with the principles and forces at work in the world
when they were children. They are the exception for the magnitude of
their vision, not the manner and mode of their cognitive development.

Figure 2
A comparison between wooden block construction by a student of the Froebelian kindergarten and an architectural design by Frank Lloyd Wright.

Right: "House," nature form of the sixth gift. From *The Kindergarten Guide* by Maria Kraus-Boelte and John Kraus, New York, 1877

Below: Frank Lloyd Wright. Frederick C. Robie House. 1906. Sepia, 22 x 35″. © 1996 The Frank Lloyd Wright Foundation

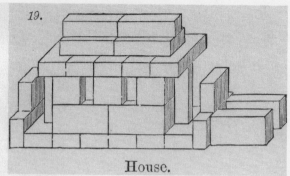

House.

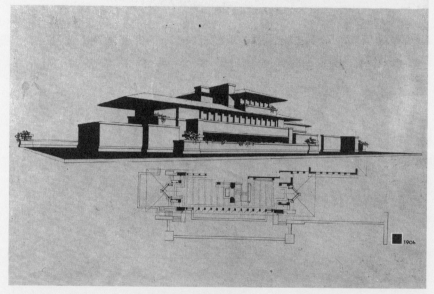

Courtesy of Frank Lloyd Wright Foundation.

In short, the structure of knowing was the same for them as it is for all of us. They were not early to form abstract concepts, but were given extended opportunity to dwell within phenomena in a way many of us, not having had similar time to develop such capacity, literally cannot imagine.

In the Newtonian universe, everything is either an object—such as a planet or an apple—or is subject to laws that are based on the interaction of these objects; for example, gravity is a function of the inter-action of masses. The problem here is that half of the equation is missing. There is no role for energy. Einstein's great insight, "$E = mc^2$," demonstrates that energy and matter are interchangeable, and that what we see is a function of patterns of energy as much as configurations of objects. The role of the imagination in the development of the human mind and the growth of knowledge are to apprehend, in a dynamic, fluid, and personal fashion, the flows of energy weaving through that which we see. The mode of cognition we develop, particularly as we receive formal education, has no place for the flow of cognitive energy to create knowledge. Knowledge is considered to be the possession of discrete objects called *facts* and the ability to apply them through the use of explicit skills. When the skills are not explicit, as is the case in all but the linguistic and mathematical intelligences identified by the eminent psychologist Howard Gardner, knowledge is not believed to be possible except as practical know-how. Consequently, we mistakenly separate the nonlinguistic, nonmathematical intelligences from the acquisition of knowledge even as we may celebrate them as a source of the arts.

The contemporary model of knowledge governing educational policy and practice, as well as public opinion, has no place for the flow of energy either in the world or within our minds. As we acquire knowledge and become adept in the ways of knowing which are currently given high value, the imagination becomes increasingly irrelevant. The earlier we receive formal education, the more likely we are to dwarf the imagination and our capacity for knowledge.

Every lesson we learn is at least as significant for its impact on the way we learn to cognize as for its content. We learn to read early, to break down language into bits of sound and reconstruct them into word sounds rather than to experience all that is around us through activity from which language may flow. We learn arithmetic as represented in numbers quite apart from the direct experience of the mathematical principles operating in the environment all around us, from the symmetries of our own bodies, to the balancing of the equations of block houses, and to the ratios of flour to water in the baking of bread. The imagination works formatively; it forms cognitive structures that only after the passage of time will break through the surface of consciousness to form concepts and ideas.

The imagination in cognition is not only a matter of expression, but of impression; it allows us to dwell within the formative, the generative, and in the world so that these energies shape and animate the prelinguistic cognitive structures of our minds. This "indwelling," as

philosopher scientist Michael Polanyi calls it, is a process of interacting
with phenomena (physically in childhood and cognitively through
ideas or the various media of the arts in adulthood) to explore the principles at work that generate what we perceive. The objectivity of our
thinking is measured not against what we see with our eyes or instruments, but by the consistency between the imaginative principles shaping our thinking and the principles shaping what we see. Polanyi
concludes, "In this wholly indeterminate scope of its true implications
lies the deepest sense in which objectivity is attributed to a scientific
theory" (Polanyi, 1964, p. 5).

The reason we trust our own thinking is based upon the belief that,
at least in some measure, we have been able to discern patterns in phenomena—whether in day-to-day social interactions or the properties
of variables in a laboratory—that allow us to anticipate what we will
encounter in new and unprecedented situations. Polanyi writes:

> Why do we entrust the life and guidance of our thoughts to our concep-
> tions? Because we believe that their manifest rationality is due to their
> being in contact with domains or reality, of which we have grasped one
> aspect. This is why the Pygmalion at work in us when we shape a con-
> ception is ever prepared to seek a guidance from his own creation.
> (Polanyi, 1964, p. 46)

The same is true when we learn from others, whether through books
or direct instruction. In order to transform the lessons they give us into
knowledge, it is essential that we learn to dwell in the principles that
underlie their thinking rather than to only study their ideas as objects
unto themselves. Their ideas are a viewing lens that amplifies or clari-
fies some aspect of the world that we hope to understand. They give
us a generative context to explore the world and anticipate new dimensions of it. Imagination is necessary to understand both the meaning
of their work and the natural phenomena we encounter.

It is possible to use formal mathematical formulae to apprehend the
principles at work in what we perceive, and it is possible to use formal rules to apply a theory to a data set. However, all such acts require
that we believe that the formalities we use will reveal what is truly at
work in the world, or some aspect of it. Logic and explicit forms of
reasoning cannot, however, move beyond the elaboration of what is
imagined; they cannot substitute for the imagination in opening new
areas and forms of inquiry.

Where there is little or no correspondence between what we anticipate and what we find, we may discover that our imaginative struc-

tures, or the refined imaginatively based formalisms of the theorists we choose to guide us, do not fully reveal the energies and laws operating in phenomena. We may also find that our data is wrong for any number of reasons we did not anticipate. This testing of correspondences is the primary function of experimental research. We anticipate what a theory will mean in new conditions, and we experiment in controlled ones to see if we have grasped principles that transcend anything we might have perceived before. Empirical research is, at its best, a process of affirmation—a demonstration—that what we understood through the imagination bears out consistently in new and unprecedented circumstances. It may also demonstrate that we had not apprehended the principle at work in what we perceived initially.

CHILD'S PLAY

How can the imagination take us to the other side of reality, to the formative in the formed, to the creative in the created, to the principles in the perceived?

The answer begins with Einstein. Recall his description of his own method of discovery. It was essentially a "'rather vague' nonlogical playing with 'visual' and 'muscular' signs, after which explanatory words had to be 'sought for laboriously'" (Hoffman, 1972, p. 255). Such "playing" is a process of direct engagement; it is not a standing back from the world or an act of abstraction. It is unstructured by formal concepts and rules other than those one chooses to apply; it is not bounded by specific practical objectives or goals beyond the activity itself.

Children explore the formative principles of the world through physical play. Their play with dolls or a pint-size kitchen stove making dinner is an exploration of social rules and roles from the perspective of a mother, a father, or a sibling. They place themselves in the position of *the other* and look out into the world. They will create patterns that may seem laughable, but with each new imaginary elaboration of social principles, they see the implications of their thinking. They discard some nascent understandings and create new ideas, all the while seeing how the patterns of social activity they create measure against those they see. In many circles, educators and developmental psychologists argue that young children learn through imitation. However, the key here is to suggest that imitation is not mimicry; it is a form of exploration, a building of the dynamic cognitive insights and understandings that will eventually flower as consistent, yet flexible, patterns of behavior. Imitation is a form of internalization, not of specific behaviors, but of the principles that generate them, and play is the elaboration of those principles in new and varied circumstances.

(These same patterns of cognitive development are active in forming insights and understandings of the physical world. Play in the sandbox, in the yard, or with the glasses of milk at the table that are forever a source of fascination until the inevitable spill, is a form of direct engagement with the principles at work in nature. Play enables them to see and explore the world from numerous angles and to form new imaginative patterns in phenomena that allow for coherence. Children will generate all sorts of mistakes and grapple with the implications of their errant, nascent ideas in the form of expectations that do not match what they find in other situations. They will imagine anew and start the process again, each time building a more comprehensive and refined cognitive foundation for expression, eventually in the form of concepts and other formal structures.

Abstraction, however, inhibits such play; it is the opposite of indwelling. It draws one out of the free-form exploration of principles; it fixes objects and ideas, and makes them static and isolated. When asked to work formally (with ideas that are explicitly formed) or to work in abstractions before the imagination has become a vital, fluid foundation for knowledge, the capacity for cognitive play that Einstein saw as the key to his method of discovery will not emerge fully. Neither will the full capacity to creatively adapt what one has experienced to drive artistic expression. When our imaginations are nourished in childhood, we are given the opportunity to know the world actively and to transform such personal insight into everything from scientific knowledge to artistic vision.

REFERENCES

Bateson, G. (1979). *Mind and nature.* New York: Bantam.

Bohm, D. (1980). *Wholeness and the implicate order.* London: Kegan Paul Ltd.

Brosterman, N. (1997). *Inventing kindergarten.* New York: Harry N. Abrams, Inc.

Clark, R.W. (1971). *Einstein: The life and times.* New York: The World Publishing Company.

Hartl, D.L. (2002). *McClintock, Barbara.* Retrieved from *World Book* [on-line]. Available: http://worldbook.bigchalk.com/350850.htm.

Hoffman, B. (1972). *Albert Einstein: Creator and rebel.* New York: The Viking Press.

Keller, E.F. (1983). *A feeling for the organism: The life and times of Barbara McClintock.* New York: W.H. Freeman and Company.

Polanyi, M. (1964). *Personal knowledge: Towards a post-critical philosophy.* New York: Harper & Row Publishers, Inc.

ABOUT THE CONTRIBUTORS

JEFFREY KANE, Ph.D., is a professor of education, and is the vice president for academic affairs at Long Island University. He is the former dean of the School of Education at C. W. Post, Long Island University, Brookville, New York, and was dean of the School of Education at Adelphi University, Garden City, New York. Dr. Kane has written essays and articles on existential issues in teaching and on educational policy. Most recently, he edited and contributed to the book *Education, Information and Transformation: Essays on Learning and Thinking,* published by Merrill/Prentice-Hall. He also served as editor of the journal *Encounter: Education for Meaning and Social Justice,* through August 2002. Earlier in his career, he was a classroom teacher in the Rudolf Steiner School in New York City. He lives on Long Island with his wife, Janet, and three children.

HEATHER CARPENTER, M.S., is a clinical psychology doctoral student at Long Island University/C. W. Post campus in New York. She received her undergraduate degree in psychobiology at Binghamton University.

7

The Vital Role of Emotion in Education

STUART SHANKER

PHILOSOPHY AND THE CHILD

What do the following great philosophers all have in common?

Antoine Arnaud
Francis Bacon
Isaiah Berlin
Thomas Carlyle
Auguste Comte
Abbé de Condillac
Thomas Hobbes
David Hume
Karl Jaspers
Immanuel Kant
Soren Kierkegaard
Godfried Wilhelm Leibniz
John Locke
John Stuart Mill
Isaac Newton
Blaise Pascal
Jean-Jacques Rousseau
Arthur Schopenhauer
Baruch Spinoza
François Voltaire
Ludwig Wittgenstein

The answer is that none of them had children. Admittedly, some of them may have fathered illegitimate children; but they took no part in their rearing. Rousseau actually had five children, all of whom he sent to an orphanage, on principle, on the grounds that they would receive a better upbringing there. No doubt if he felt this way, he was probably correct.

It is surprising to see how many of the great modern philosophers were confirmed bachelors, or had childless marriages. Or maybe it is not so surprising. For the fact is that modern philosophers have shown remarkably little interest in questions concerning the unique needs of children. One searches in vain for philosophical works on the nature of childhood, or the challenges involved in raising healthy and happy children. Nevertheless, many of the philosophers listed above wrote important books on child education. The central theme of these works is that the goal of education is to produce: "(a) disciplined thinking; (b) a cultivated outlook; and (c) a sense of moral rectitude" (Kanz, 1993). But the problem is, however noble their views on universal education may have been, the writings of Enlightenment philosophers all reflect the biases and limitations of someone who has absolutely no experience with children.

One of the first of these treatises, John Locke's *Some Thoughts Concerning Education*, marked an important advance over the miniaturist view of children that had predominated in the Middle Ages (Locke, 1693/1996). Locke stressed the importance of hygiene, physical exercise, and diet, for the key to producing a sound mind, he explains at the outset, is to produce a sound body. Hence, Locke advises "that children be not too warmly clad or cover'd, winter or summer," and warns that there is nothing "that more exposes to headaches, colds, catarrhs, coughs, and several other diseases, than keeping the head warm." This curious millinery obsession aside, Locke made the valuable—and at that time novel—suggestion that learning be made as enjoyable a process as possible for children, and that educators avoid trying to instill too much information into children before their reason is sufficiently developed. He eschewed corporal punishment and recommended in its stead that "Esteem and disgrace are the most powerful incentives to the mind, when once it is brought to relish them. If you can once get into children a love of credit, and an apprehension of shame and disgrace, you have put into 'em the true principle, which will constantly work and incline them to the right."

Locke's writings exercised a profound influence on philosophical thinking about education, not just in the eighteenth century, but in many ways right up to the behaviorists of the twentieth century. Perhaps the most famous of the eighteenth-century works on educational reform inspired by Locke was Rousseau's *Emile* (Rousseau, 1762). For Rousseau as well, the best way to ensure the development of a healthy mind was to attend to the needs of a healthy body. Mothers are told to feed their infants themselves, to get rid of their swaddling, and to bathe their young in cold water. Rousseau's vision of the ideal education is to raise a child in a state of nature. Thus, the young Emile spends all of his time running around outdoors in bare feet with hardly any clothing. Rousseau goes much further than Locke in his antipathy to formal education; for the young Emile receives no lessons whatsoever, and indeed, is spared that "curse of childhood"—book reading. Free to roam like a "noble savage," Emile develops his senses and learns whatever is worth learning by experience, never by instruction.

At the beginning of the nineteenth century, the philosophical pendulum swung sharply away from this Romantic view.[1] The great utilitarian, James Mill, wrote to Scottish historian John Miller that "when a man has risen to great intellectual or moral eminence, the process by which his mind was formed is one of the most instructive circumstances which can be unveiled to mankind" (Ryan, 1974). He would prove his point with his own son, John Stuart. In perhaps the first known example of the use of flash cards, Mill began showing his son, at the age of three, cards with Greek and English terms written on them that had to be matched to a card depicting the object named. No attention at all was paid to physical well-being; instead, the young boy was subjected to intense formal instruction in a number of advanced subjects (e.g., logic, political economy, calculus, Latin, and Greek). And to prevent his lessons from becoming merely rote learning, the young boy had to teach his sisters in turn the material he had mastered. One of the visitors to the house, Francis Place, reports that if one of the children made a slip in their lessons, they were sent to bed without supper. In Mill's case, at least, we know the effects of this great educational experiment: John Stuart Mill certainly did attain the great intellectual heights that his father desired, but he did so at the cost of suffering his first nervous breakdown at the age of twenty, and a lifetime thereafter of unremitting emotional turmoil.

The first—and perhaps only—philosopher to address directly the question of child development was Jean Piaget. This too may come as something of a surprise, insofar as Piaget is generally regarded as a psychologist—in fact, as one of the founders of developmental psychology. But Piaget always regarded himself as a philosopher, as what he called a "genetic epistemologist." In fact, Piaget only turned to psychology, for what initially he thought would be no longer than five

years, in order to answer the great epistemological questions that neither empiricists nor rationalists had been able to resolve over the past
three centuries. Thus, Piaget studied his own children closely in order
to answer such questions as whether knowledge is *constructed* by us
or *discovered*. And if it is the case that we construct knowledge, how
do we know that it conforms to reality? Is human knowledge built
upon basic concepts? What are the relative contributions made by innate ideas and environmental input to the growth of the mind? Is language necessary for logical thought?

Piaget's epistemological focus is very much the defining feature of
another of the twentieth century's most influential philosophers, Noam
Chomsky. To suggest that Chomsky be seen as a philosopher—and indeed, as one of the century's most influential philosophers—may perhaps seem not just surprising, but even outrageous. But then, such a
suggestion is not far removed from Chomsky's own perception of his
work, for Chomsky went to some pains to depict himself as Descartes's
intellectual heir. In fact, the philosopher to whom Chomsky bears an
even closer resemblance is Kant; for like Kant, Chomsky shuns empirical research and instead attempts to infer the structure of the mind
through transcendental deduction. And like Kant, Chomsky perceives
himself as involved in speculative metaphysics; the point of his theories about our innate knowledge of language is to stimulate research,
which, if productive, will constantly force us to revise our understanding of the nature of that innate knowledge. But most important of all
is the fact that, like Kant—and Piaget—Chomsky saw the problem of
language development as *epistemological*. The way he put this in his
Review of Skinner's Verbal Behavior was: "in principle it may be possible
to study the problem of determining what the built-in structure of an
information-processing (hypothesis-forming) system must be to enable
it to arrive at the grammar of a language from the available date in the
available time" (Chomsky, 1969, p. 58). In other words, Chomsky saw
the problem for developmental psycholinguists as that of figuring out
what sorts of built-in principles must guide a system—any system,
whether it is a computer program or the mind of a child—to work out
the formal properties of a natural language.

This has been the history of modern philosophy's view of children.
The "problems" that the child has been seen as solving are the abstract
epistemological problems that have long puzzled philosophers. When
philosophers talk about the "child," it is really just as a euphemism for
debating whether, for example, the particular type of knowledge that
the philosopher is concerned with could have been derived entirely

from experience or only acquired with the assistance of some internal constraint, or whether one domain of knowledge precedes and enables another or the two domains develop independently (Chomsky, 1969; Putnam, 1979; Quine, 1970; Shanker, 1996). The idea of actually studying children and learning from close observation what sorts of skills they are mastering, what sorts of problems they are trying to solve, and more to the point, what other sorts of factors are involved in the growth of the child's mind, is totally foreign to this epistemological point of view. Rather, the nature of child development is conceptualized as a matter that can be resolved by purely *a priori* reasoning, for example, by establishing what sorts of constraints must be built into a child's mind in order for her to be able to acquire higher reflective and communicative skills.

In short, the picture one gets of childhood from Western philosophers is precisely what one might expect from a group of isolated thinkers with no experience in child rearing, who are engaged in deep contemplation of abstract logical problems, and, like Mr. Casaubon in George Elliot's *Middlemarch*, in grand system building. The child is conceptualized as a nascent philosopher, struggling to impose order on the welter of sensations bombarding her senses by searching for patterns, and constantly constructing and revising concepts whereby she mentally records and classifies her experiences. Not until the great twentieth-century Russian psychologist Lev Vygotsky do we see any consideration of the integral role that a caregiver plays in the development of a child's mind. Rather, philosophers were intrigued by a rationalist picture, which they inherited from Descartes and Kant, of an isolated mind, equipped with "internal constraints" that enable the child to infer such things as what people are referring to when they make sounds, or that objects persist in space and time and that certain causes produce certain effects, or even that there is a difference between people and the other objects in her environment, and so on. But Descartes's influence extends still further, in a way that had the most unfortunate of consequences for Western attempts to realize the principles enshrined in the Enlightenment dream of universal education.

THE BIFURCATION BETWEEN REASON
AND THE EMOTIONS

In *Letter to Egmont*, dated August 14, 1649, Descartes wrote: "My purpose has not been to explain the Passions as an Orator, or even as a moral Philosopher, but only as a Physicist."

The fundamental principle of Descartes's view of the mind is that reason and the emotions belong to completely different levels of human functioning. Emotions represent the basest level of human behavior: the instincts, drives, and passions that we share with the animal kingdom. Pure reason, unaffected by emotional impulses, represents the highest level. The most advanced form of development based on this outlook is like the Vulcans in *Star Trek*, who, through centuries of mental discipline, have come to acquire complete control over their emotions.

Descartes's view that human nature is governed by these two opposing forces has dominated Western thinking about the mind for the past three and a half centuries. Emotions have been thought to constitute the mechanical side of human functioning—the innate feelings, moods, and mental states that are involuntary and automatic. Reason is thought to reside in a completely separate realm of the mind—the part that is independent from, and which, hopefully, comes to govern our emotions. To this day, cognitive scientists continue to study a child's emotional and intellectual development as if there were a bifurcation between these two elements of the human psyche, that is, as if a child's emotional development had no intrinsic bearing on her cognitive or linguistic development. The child's emotions are seen as a motivational factor that might facilitate or impede information processing, but the development and structure of our cognitive and linguistic faculties are seen as completely autonomous phenomena.

To make matters still worse, Descartes viewed emotions as *complex reflexes* that are triggered by internal and/or external stimuli, consist of distinctive bodily processes and sensations, and are associated with characteristic behaviors and stereotypical facial expressions (Descartes, 1637/1986). This is what he meant when he argued that emotions belong to the "animal" side of human nature, for, according to Descartes, what humans have in common with animals is the fact that the human body, like that of animals, is a machine that is governed by drives and emotions. But humans, unlike animals, are also endowed with the ability to reason and reflect, exercise moral choice, direct the actions of their bodies, be conscious of their mental states, speak a language, and live in a society. Thus, raw emotions, so to speak, may be a similar physiological phenomenon in both animals and humans, but through reason, humans, unlike animals, can come to understand, control, and even develop their emotions.

In exactly the same terms that he used to explain other biological processes, Descartes was attempting here to explain the fact that our emotional responses are often unconscious and instinctive. By construing emotion as a species of reflex, he sought to sunder the emotional from the rational causes of human behavior, placing them on either side of what he saw as the great involuntary/voluntary divide that separates humans from animals. The manner in which an individual makes sense of events in the world—both objective and subjective— is purely volitional and intentional. The mind infers what causes both objects and other agents to behave in such-and-such a manner. It is constantly framing and revising a store of physical and mental concepts that serve to identify and classify the various types of information that it receives.

Virtually by definition, therefore, education must be aimed at enhancing the child's rational processes and inhibiting her emotions. Anything that can facilitate the child's powers of induction is a worthy pursuit. All other activities should be limited, if not prohibited— especially those that might cater to the child's emotions. For the goal of education is to help a child realize her human birthright: to rise above the brutes by developing her capacity to think, to reason and solve problems and control her baser instincts. To be sure, such an approach to education could and did produce some extraordinary minds, capable of solving the most abstract of problems. But as the list at the start of this paper makes clear, these achievements seem to have come at a heavy cost in terms of the individual's capacity to engage in warm, nurturing relationships with others. Still more worrying are the consequences of attempting to base a system of universal education on such a foundation.

GREENSPAN'S "COPERNICAN REVOLUTION"

Stanley Greenspan has mounted an ambitious challenge to this bifurcationist paradigm, which dismisses the emotions as a species of reflex and focuses on cognitive development as if it were an isolated phenomenon. On the basis of more than twenty years of experience working with children who are faced with different kinds of biological deficits, Greenspan has articulated two fundamental principles that run completely contrary to this Cartesian view that has dominated Western thinking for the past three centuries. These two fundamental principles are that: "(1) a child develops her emotions through co-regulated nurturing interactions with her caregivers, and (2) these emotions play a critical role in the growth of the child's mind." These are complex principles and require careful exposition in order to be fully grasped (Greenspan & Shanker, in press), but for the purposes of this chapter, we can summarize their essence as follows.

An infant initially experiences a limited number of global states (e.g., calmness, excitement, and distress). As her nervous system develops, the infant begins, through interactive experiences with her caregivers, to associate subjective qualities with physical sensations. For example, the sweet taste of breast milk might be associated with pleasant or unpleasant feelings, depending on the physiological state that the infant is in and/or the emotional state that the caregiver is in. The child who associates pleasant feelings with the taste of breast milk will suck more vigorously and eagerly than the so-called fussy child, who associates unpleasant feelings with the taste of breast milk. For the same reason, a newborn may prefer the sound of her mother's voice or the smell of her breast milk to that of other female adults.

Every experience that a child undergoes involves this form of "dual coding" (Greenspan, 1997). Both these perceptions, the physical and the emotional, appear to be coded together. For example, a hug feels tight and secure or slack and unsettling; a father's voice sounds deep and comforting or harsh and alarming; a mobile looks colorful and interesting or chaotic and frightening. What is important here is that, as opposed to the Cartesian assumption that every infant responds in exactly the same way to the same stimuli, we see that, for both endogenous and exogenous reasons, infants' responses to physical sensations are infinitely variable. The same sound can be stimulating and pleasant for one child and piercing and shrill for another. The same fabric may feel soft and sensual for one and prickly and irritating for another.

The child's subjective world is thus formed over time through interactive experiences. The basic emotions emerge, at around six months, as a result of the organization of these experiences. These affects serve to categorize and, in this way, give meaning to subsequent interactive experiences. Affects become the complex mediators of experience and serve an internal organizing and differentiating role. What starts off as a physiological system receiving input from the senses becomes, through developmental experience, both a complex social tool and the vehicle for structuring internal mental life.

"Dual coding" therefore presents us with a fundamentally different picture of the growth of the child's mind from that which has dominated psychology since its inception. According to the Cartesian bifurcation of reason and emotion, the classification of sensory experience is strictly a rational phenomenon. According to modern philosophers, when a child encounters the exemplars of a category, her mind must abstract their common properties. The same sort of process must occur when she hears language speakers using a concept word. As opposed to this Cartesian view of the infant as a miniature scientist engaged in acts of induction and hypothesis testing, Greenspan's dual-coding view stresses the central role of emotions in the organization of the child's intellectual capacities.

During the formative years, there is a sensitive interaction between biological proclivities and environmental input. Experience appears to adapt the infant's biology to her environment, but not all experiences are the same in this process. Children seem to require certain types of experiences involving a series of specific types of emotional interactions that are geared to their particular developmental needs. In the first year, affects become more complex. There is a transition from simple affective states like hunger and arousal to, by eight months, complex affect states like surprise, fear and caution, joy and happiness, and enthusiasm and curiosity. As the child progresses, affects become more differentiated. Eventually, affects organize reciprocal interactions and problem solving. Then they become symbolized. Eventually, it becomes possible to reflect on them. Affect is thus responsible for helping a child go from simple interest in the world all the way up through social problem solving and procedural knowledge. It enables a child to progress through procedural knowledge up to symbolic knowledge. It gives meaning to what the child hears and how she processes visual-spatial information and sequences motor actions.

Emotions thus serve as the critical architect or mediator for higher-level mental functions. In *The Growth of the Mind* (1997), Greenspan showed how emotions create, organize, and orchestrate many of the mind's most important functions, including intelligence and emotional health. He further showed that intellect, academic abilities, sense of self, consciousness, and morality all have common origins in the child's earliest and ongoing emotional experiences, and that emotions serve as the architects of a vast array of cognitive operations throughout the life span. Therefore, this leaves us with the fundamental question: What are the implications of this fundamental paradigm shift for our views about the sorts of experiences that are critical for the growth of a healthy mind and a healthy society?

THE ACT OF WILL REQUIRED TO DISLODGE THE RATIONALIST MODEL OF EDUCATION

There are two reasons why I chose the title "Greenspan's 'Copernican Revolution'" for the previous section. The first was simply to dramatize the importance of Greenspan's functional/emotional theory of development, but there was another reason. What I am trying to

show in this chapter is that Greenspan's theory amounts to a fundamental *philosophical* revolution in our views about the factors that
promote a child's cognitive, communicative, social, and moral development. To embrace such a philosophical revolution involves far more,
however, than an act of logic.

It is precisely here where the comparison to the Copernican revolution is so fitting. It may seem today that the merits of the shift from
the geotropic to the heliotropic view of the universe would have been
obvious to everyone, but, in fact, Renaissance thinkers were able to
come up with all sorts of reasons to justify suppressing Copernicus's
ideas. For one thing, the Ptolemaic system still worked. To be sure, it
was a little cumbersome, for in order to make accurate predictions,
astronomers had to keep adding epicycles. (An epicycle is a circle
whose center is carried around the circumference of another circle; basically, it was just a contrivance to explain away anomalies.) In the fif-
teenth century, astronomers were working with eighty-seven such
epicycles—hardly an efficient tool, but then, it had the weight of tradition behind it. From the skeptic's point of view, the only advantage
to Copernicus's theory was that it was more economical insofar as it
only required seventeen epicycles. But weighing against this slight
improvement was the fact that Copernicus's ideas ran contrary to phe-
nomenal appearances. After all, didn't the horizon *look* flat? Didn't the
Sun rise in the east and set in the west (see Kuhn, 1959)?

Still more disturbing was the fact that Copernicus was challenging
the authority of the two great pillars of medieval thought: the Bible
and Aristotle. Not only was he insisting on the right of the individual
to think for herself, but still more heretical, he was also insisting that
science be based on induction, not deduction. Thus, as Bertolt Brecht
conveyed so movingly in his play *Galileo,* logic alone wasn't nearly
enough to bring about the demise of the Ptolemaic system; what was
needed were acts of heroic courage. It is hardly a surprise, then, that
it took a full century before philosophers were prepared to declare their
support for the Copernican revolution publicly, and even then, cau-
tiously and somewhat tepidly (Descartes, 1637/1986).

The analogy here to our attitudes toward education is disturbingly
apposite. The rationalist model of education is so entrenched in our
thinking that despite the legion of problems that we are witnessing
today, which get worse every year, we cannot conceive of any alternative to the current course we are on, except to pursue it even more
aggressively. Thus, if functional illiteracy; school performance; or
psychological and social, and for that matter, physical problems all

keep getting worse, then we have to respond in ever-more-extremist fashion. If the standardized testing and computer labs that were introduced for fifteen-year-olds haven't produced the results that were wanted, then we have to start earlier—with twelve-year-olds, eight-year-olds, even with six-year-olds. If students are performing poorly in the sciences and mathematics, we should adopt the types of rote-based learning systems developed in other cultures, even though it has been shown that such systems develop poor analytical skills and dull a child's creativity. Like James Mill, parents and educators are choosing to reduce still further the amount of time that children can spend just playing; and toys are now designed by teams of psychologists, armed with the latest findings on how best to stimulate a child's senses, but not how best to stimulate a child's imagination and curiosity. And since our children are not benefiting from the amount of contact time that they have with their teachers, we choose to reduce this contact time still further, with larger and larger classes and ever fewer extracurricular activities; for if the future lies in computers, then the child should spend as much time as possible on a computer, to the exclusion of all else. Why incur the costs of field trips when the same site can be viewed on the Internet? Indeed, this trend is being extended to prelinguistic children, despite the considerable evidence that the development of language skills, which are so critical for a child's cognitive as well as social and emotional development, depends on affective interactions with caregivers and peers. If the quality of our teachers is in serious decline because of the conditions they are forced to work in, we take away as much of the teacher's responsibility as possible with textbooks that script their every word. If young children are having trouble concentrating on their standardized tests, we seek to remove any and all possible distractions during the tests, even if this exacerbates the conditions that provoked their anxiety in the first place. And even though our children are developing poor social skills, we are choosing to restrict even further the amount and types of social contacts that they are allowed to have with their peers.

There is not a parent or a politician around who is not alarmed by this litany of woes. Yet the plea that the solution to many of the problems that we face lies in embracing a functional/emotional approach to education may sound like the utopian musings of just another philosopher who is divorced from the sociopolitical reality. But the point of Greenspan's theory is not that children can't learn unless they're happy and well adjusted. As it happens, this is likely true, but it is not the point of the theory. Rather, Greenspan's theory has to do with *the sorts of affective experiences that are critical for the growth of the mind.* And the primary problem with the rationalist course we are on is that it is leading us ever further away from those very sorts of emotional interactions that underpin cognitive development.

For example, in the very first stage of functional emotional development, a baby has to learn how to take in the world around her, and in order for this to happen, she has to *want* to engage with her caregivers and explore her surroundings. Caregivers have to work hard at promoting the development of their child's capacity to attend to the outer world and to regulate her sensations. Right from the start, caregivers and infants are engaged in rhythmic, co-regulated patterns that enable the infant to begin relating to and appreciating the outside world. As the baby becomes more interested in the world, she not only begins to discriminate what she sees, hears, smells, and touches, but as she progresses through the early stages of functional emotional development, she also becomes more and more interested in interaction. In particular, she starts to develop a strong attachment to her primary caregivers, which provides the foundation for the development of the child's capacity to engage in long chains of co-regulated affect signalling.

Engaging in long chains of co-regulated affective interactions is absolutely critical for the growth of the child's mind, for this enables her to recognize various patterns involved in satisfying her emotional needs: for example, what different kinds of affective gestures or facial expressions signify; the connection between certain kinds of facial expressions, tones of voice, or behavior with an individual's mood or intentions; or between certain kinds of vocalizations and actions; and so on. This capacity to recognize patterns is essential for a child to begin to have and to act upon her expectations. Now the child knows when to expect different kinds of responses from her caregiver, or what love, anger, respect, and shame all feel like. The capacity to recognize patterns also underpins the child's ability to use words in a meaningful manner. The key here is that the child must have had lots of affective interactions, for without a wealth of emotionally relevant experiences on which to draw, the child won't be capable of developing meaningful language, even though she might be neurologically capable of speaking. What we see in cases of emotional deprivation is that the child might be able to memorize words or label objects, but she can't explain what a story means or why the characters behave the way they do. It is only through co-regulated emotional interactions that words and images acquire meaning for a child. Only then can she use words to express her feelings, rather than acting them out. Only then can she use symbols to think and problem-solve creatively, and use words to convey differentiated, abstract feeling states.

As the child progresses through the various stages of functional emotional development, she learns how to connect symbols together and form larger categories. Through this process, she is able to begin to think causally and to figure out how one idea leads to another. This sets the stage for more advanced thinking, where the child becomes more reflective and forms a symbolic sense of "self" and "other" that provides the basis for reality testing. This ability to connect ideas and symbols together and construct a picture of reality establishes a foundation for more advanced levels of thinking and reasoning.

What is perhaps most profound about Greenspan's theory is that it is not limited to charting these functional/emotional stages of development for a young child; exactly the same model applies to the development of the older child's, the adolescent's, and indeed, the adult's capacity to develop higher-order reflective skills (Greenspan & Shanker, in press). That is, the capacities to engage in multicausal thinking, subtle gray-area thinking, to have an internal standard based on a stable sense of self that provides a basis to judge and further reflect on experiences, or to develop the highest levels of reflective thinking that involve comparing multiple frames of reference, are all just as dependent on ongoing emotional experiences as the young child's capacity to self-regulate and engage in warm, nurturing interactions with her caregivers. Thus, by reducing the student's opportunity to engage in such relationships with her teachers and peers, we are depriving the child of those very affective interactions that are vital for her cognitive, communicative, social, and moral development.

To be sure, the demands created by universal education are so onerous that it is difficult to conceive of embracing any approach that would involve vastly increasing the amount of contact time that children have with their teachers and their peers, not to mention the amount of time that children are involved in unscripted play activities and creative study exercises. And to make matters worse, we have the full weight of the rationalist tradition in education to overcome, even though it is clear that the system inspired by that philosophy has become not just unwieldy, but indeed, is in serious danger of collapse. But the thrust of this chapter is not that we must abandon the Enlightenment vision of universal education; rather, it is that those very goals that we have been pursuing for the past three and half centuries cannot be realized on the determinist model of the mind that Enlightenment thinkers embraced, which we continue to embrace to this day. That is, our goal remains that of enabling children to become reflective members of society, capable of nurturing their own families, and capable of dealing with the whole new set of problems that are being ushered in by the dawning age of global interdependency (Greenspan & Shanker, 2002). But in order for a child to develop the higher-level thinking skills that are necessary to function as a reflective problem solver and a reflective member of society, her education must be grounded in the affective experiences that underpin the growth of a healthy mind. Logic alone is clearly not enough to carry us through the necessary overhaul; what is needed now is a courageous act of will.

NOTE

1. At least it did among the English utilitarians. But, of course, Romantic ideas about education were being explored by Coleridge and Wordsworth, and Carlyle and even Mill himself, in papers that he wrote during the 1930s, tentatively embraced some of these Romantic ideals.

REFERENCES

Chomsky, N. (1969). Some empirical assumptions in modern philosophy of language. In S. Margenbaum, P. Suppes, & M. White (Eds.), *Philosophy, science, and method: Essays in honour of Ernest Nagel*. London: St. Martin's Press.

Descartes, R. (1986). Discourse on the Method. In J. Cottingham, R. Stoothoff, & D. Murdoch (Trans.), *Philosophical writings of Descartes*. Vol. I. Cambridge: Cambridge University Press. (Original work published 1637.)

Greenspan, S.I. (1997). *The growth of the mind*. New York: Addison-Wesley.

Greenspan, S.I., & Shanker, S.G. (2002). *Toward a psychology of global interdependency: A framework for international collaboration*. Washington, DC: ICDL Press.

Greenspan, S.I., & Shanker, S.G. (in press). Differences in affect cuing: A window for the identification of risk patterns for autism spectrum disorders in the first year of life. *Journal of Developmental and Learning Disorders*.

Greenspan, S.I., & Shanker, S.G. (1994). *The first idea: The evolution of symbols, logic and intelligence*. New York: Perseus Books.

Kanz, H. (1993). Immanuel Kant. *Prospects: The Quarterly Review of Comparative Education, 23*.

Kuhn, T. (1959). *The Copernican revolution: Planetary observation in the development of Western thought*. New York: Vintage Books.

Locke, J. (1996). *Some thoughts concerning education*. Indianapolis, IN: Hackett Publishing Co. (Original work published 1693.)

Putnam, H. (1979). What is innate and why: Comments on the debate. In M.

Piatelli Palmarini (Ed.), *Language and learning* (pp. 287–301). London: Routledge & Kegan Paul.

Quine, W.V.O. (1970). Philosophical progress in language theory. *Metaphilosophy, 1,* 2–19.

Rousseau, J.J. (1974). *Emile.* Translated by T. Foxley. New York: Dutton. (Original work published in 1762.)

Ryan, A. (1974). *J. S. Mill.* London: Routledge. (Original work published 1762.)

Shanker, S. (1996). Wittgenstein versus Quine on the nature of language and cognition. In R. L. Arrington & H. J. Glock (Eds.), *Wittgenstein and Quine.* London: Routledge.

ABOUT THE CONTRIBUTOR

STUART SHANKER, Ph.D. Oxon, is professor of philosophy and professor of psychology at York University in Toronto, Canada. He is codirector, with Stanley Greenspan, of the Council of Human Development and associate chair for Canada of the Interdisciplinary Council of Learning and Developmental Disorders. His recent publications include: *Wittgenstein's Remarks on the Foundations of AI* (1998); *Apes, Language and the Human Mind* (with Sue Savage-Rumbaugh and Talbot Taylor, 1998); *Towards a Psychology of Global Interdependency* (with Stanley Greenspan, 2002); "What a Child Knows When She Knows What a Name Is: The Non-Cartesian View of Language Acquisition," a target article in *Current Anthropology* (2001); and "The Emergence of a New Paradigm in Ape Language Research," a target article with Barbara King in *Brain and Behavioral Sciences* (2003). He is currently finishing a book with Stanley Greenspan on *The First Idea: The Evolution of Symbols, Language and Intelligence.* He has won numerous awards and currently holds grants from the Unicorn Foundation, the Templeton Foundation, and Cure Autism Now.

Part IV

A Mental Health Crisis among Our Children: The Rise of Technologies and Demise of Play

Photo courtesy of Tom Bell.

8

Attention Deficit Hyperactivity Disorder in Children: One Consequence of the Rise of Technologies and Demise of Play?

THOMAS ARMSTRONG

Over the past thirty years, Attention Deficit Hyperactivity Disorder (ADHD) has emerged from the obscurity of cognitive psychology research laboratories to become the leading psychiatric disorder of childhood in the United States. A recent study conducted at the Mayo Clinic stated that as many as 7.4 to 16 percent of all children and adolescents suffer from this disorder (Barbaresi et al., 2002). The American Psychiatric Association (1994) has established the following criteria for the ADHD diagnosis: The patient must exhibit behaviors related to *inattention* (e.g., "may fail to give close attention to details or may make careless mistakes in schoolwork or other tasks," p. 78) or *hyperactivity-impulsivity* (e.g., "they fidget with objects, tap their hands and shake their feet excessively," p. 79). In addition, symptoms must persist for at least six months, be maladaptive and inconsistent with developmental level, impair social or academic functioning, be present in the child before the age of seven, and have influenced behavior in two or more settings (e.g., school and home).

There is wide consensus among scientists, physicians, psychologists and educators that ADHD is a genetically influenced, neurologically based psychiatric disorder. Specific genes are believed to give rise to dysfunction in the frontal lobes of the cerebral cortex and their connections to subcortical structures in the limbic system and the cerebellum. The medical literature also earmarks disrupted dopaminergic pathways in the etiology of ADHD (Barkley, 1990, 2002; Giedd et al.,

1994; LaHoste et al., 1996). Despite the widely held belief that ADHD is a medical disorder, there are compelling reasons to question this assumption (see, for example, McGuinness, 1989; Reid, Maag, & Vasa, 1993; Armstrong, 1997, 1999; Nyland, 2002). First, there is not a single diagnostic test currently available that can definitively establish the presence of ADHD as a neurological disorder. As New York psychiatrist Esther Wender (2002, p. 210) states in her editorial on the Mayo Clinic study: "[ADHD] is identified by a cluster of typical behaviors and has no definitive biological marker. And because the condition cannot be objectively defined, the decision to treat will also be based on diagnostic uncertainties. The published diagnostic criteria lend an aura of objectivity to the diagnosis, but the application of these criteria is based on subjective judgments regarding the accuracy of information given by parents and teachers."

Second, many of the studies that have sought to establish a neurological basis for ADHD have used brain-scan technologies that are still in their infancy, such as Positron Emission Tomography (PET) and Functional Magnetic Resonance Imaging (MRI). Studies of childhood mental disorders that utilize these technologies are frequently riddled with methodological difficulties, such as relatively small subject populations, heterogeneous samples, and problems in measuring the neurological correlates of complex behaviors under highly controlled and artificial laboratory conditions. These factors should temper our ready acceptance of these results (Hendren, DeBacker, & Pandin, 2000).

Third, when brain-imaging results reveal differences in a child's brain functioning or structure, it is typically assumed that these differences are innate and immutable, rather than a response to environmental conditions. Brain-scan images are routinely interpreted as if they were neurological fingerprints: indelible and intractable. However, research on other psychiatric conditions such as Obsessive Compulsive Disorder (OCD) has demonstrated that psychotherapeutic interventions can significantly alter brain scan patterns (Schwartz, Stoessel, Baxter, Martin, & Phelps, 1996). Furthermore, there is compelling evidence that environmental factors such as stress and trauma may trigger neurochemical events in the brain that impair frontal lobe structure and functioning in children (Perry & Pollard, 1998; Arnsten, 1999). These findings suggest that nature and nurture work together in an intricate way to produce behaviors such as those seen in ADHD. Therefore, we must question whether ADHD is "in" the child as a fixed neurological disorder, or whether instead, ADHD symptoms reflect dysfunctional relationships between the child and the environment.

There are, in fact, a number of studies, discussed below, that support this premise.

ADHD AND ENVIRONMENTAL INFLUENCE

Research studies have demonstrated that children's ADHD symptoms decrease under a variety of environmental conditions, including when they are engaged in one-on-one learning experiences, when they're being paid to do tasks, when they have access to novel or highly stimulating activities, when they're in control of the pace of learning experiences, and when they're interacting with male authority figures (Barkley, 1990; McGuinness, 1985; Zentall, 1980; Sykes, Douglas, & Morgenstern, 1973; Sleator & Ullman, 1981). From this we can infer that symptoms of ADHD in children might increase when the opposite environmental conditions pertain, such as when they're performing in boring or low-stimulation environments, when they're not receiving a meaningful reward for their efforts, and when they're powerless to control the pace of learning tasks. Indeed, if these conditions are present in a child's home environment from birth, it is reasonable to suspect that they could lay the groundwork for the disorder itself.

In a survey of ADHD-diagnosed and "normal" children aged six to seventeen, the odds of a child being diagnosed with ADHD increased in proportion to the extent that they came from a family characterized by adversity, including severe marital discord, low social class, large family size, paternal criminality, maternal mental disorder, and foster care placement (Biederman et al., 1995). Other studies have demonstrated that the quality of caregiving in early childhood predicts distractibility (a key symptom of ADHD) better than early biological markers or temperament, and that a strong overlap exists between symptoms of ADHD and Post-Traumatic Stress Disorder (PTSD) in children, suggesting that early sexual, physical, and/or emotional abuse may play an important role in the origin of ADHD symptoms for some children (Carlson, Jacobvitz, & Sroufe, 1995; Weinstein, Staffelbach, & Biaggio, 2000).

THE SOCIOCULTURAL ORIGINS OF ADHD SYMPTOMS

If we expand our exploration of the role of the environment in creating ADHD symptoms to include broader sociocultural factors, we might consider the possibility that the disorder of ADHD is itself a cultural phenomenon that has been socially constructed as a "neurological disorder." There is compelling historical precedence for this type of construction. In the 1850s, for example, a Louisiana physician named Samuel A. Cartwright (1851) contributed a paper to the *New Orleans Medical and Surgical Journal*, in which he stated that he had discovered a new medical disorder that he named "drapetomania" (an obsession with fleeing). Dr. Cartwright believed that this "disorder" afflicted large numbers of runaway slaves, and that with proper identification and treatment, they could learn to live productive and successful lives back on the plantation (Cartwright, 1851). More recently (1973), the American Psychiatric Association (which played a leading role in defining and legitimizing the diagnosis of ADHD) rescinded its diagnosis of "homosexuality" as a pathological condition. Clearly, there is ample precedent for the influence of sociocultural context upon the thinking and discourse of mental health professionals in this country. As social values and norms change over time, so do the classifications of deviance. It has even been suggested, by the former president of the American Psychological Association, Nicholas Hobbs (1975), that society defines itself in part by the categories of deviance it assigns to its members, especially to its children.

In this spirit, a number of educators and mental health professionals have expressed concern that the diagnosis of ADHD in children is an attempt to medicalize behaviors that should more properly be seen as natural responses to the broader social and cultural environment. Thirty years ago, during the social upheavals of the 1960s and early 1970s, Harvard professor Lester Grinspoon observed that:

> Children growing up in the past decade have seen claims to authority and existing institutions questioned as an everyday occurrence . . . Teachers no longer have the unquestioned authority they once had in the classroom. . . . The child, on the other side, is no longer so intimidated by whatever authority the teacher has. . . . Hyperkinesis [a term used to describe ADHD symptoms in the 1960s and 1970s], whatever organic condition it may legitimately refer to, has become a convenient label with which to dismiss this phenomenon as a physical 'disease' rather than treating it as the social problem it is. (Grinspoon & Singer, 1973, pp. 546–547)

Since that time, the United States has seen even greater changes in its social makeup and values, with family upheaval on the rise, and individual time spent by working parents directly engaged with their children decreasing. One study suggested that fathers spend an average of only five minutes per day interacting with their adolescent children (Csikszentmihalyi, 2000). Additionally, children in contemporary society are subject to multiple stressors, including a faster pace of life, an increasingly regimented school system, neighborhood violence, and terrorist threats. As Antoinette Saunders and Bonnie Remsberg (1986, p. 25) point out in their book, *The Stress-Proof Child*: "Our children experience the stress of illness, divorce, financial problems, living with single parents, sex, drugs, sensory bombardment, violence, the threat of nuclear war—a long, long list. The effect can be overwhelming." Since symptoms of stress include restlessness, difficulty concentrating, and irritable behavior—in other words, the same behaviors characteristic of ADHD—it seems reasonable to suspect that a link may exist between these larger social forces and the increase in the number of children identified as ADHD over the past thirty years.

The Rise of Technologies and Demise of Play

Among the many social trends in our culture that may contribute to the ADHD behaviors of hyperactivity, distractibility, and impulsivity in children, I would like to focus on two developments in particular: the rise of technologies and the demise of play. These two events should be looked at in relation to each other, for as children spend more time watching television, playing video games, surfing on the Internet, manipulating toys run by computer chips, and engaging in other technologically based activities, there is less time available for them to engage in non-adult-supervised open-ended play situations such as pretense play (where children use their imaginations to make up and act out novel scenarios) and rough-and-tumble play (where children wrestle, fight, climb, run, build, and take part in other unstructured, whole-body activities). The link between the rise of technologies and the demise of play is well illustrated by University of Pennsylvania play expert Brian Sutton-Smith (in Hansen, 1998, p. 25), who writes: "American children's freedom for freewheeling play once took place in rural fields and city streets, using equipment of their own making. Today, play is increasingly confined to back yards, basements, playrooms and bedrooms, and derives much of its content from video games, television dramas, and Saturday morning cartoons."

The Crucial Role of Play for Healthy Brain Development. As noted earlier, ADHD is typically viewed by the scientific community as a neurological disorder resulting from dysfunction in the frontal lobes of the cerebral cortex and their connections to subcortical structures in the limbic system and the cerebellum (Barkley, 1990, 2002; Giedd et al., 1994; LaHoste et al., 1996). Thus, the executive functions of the frontal lobes are not able to properly regulate and inhibit the emotional and motor features of the limbic system and cerebellum. Put in the context of play, the limbic system enables the child's spontaneity and vitality of physical and emotional expression and the cerebellum enables a wide range of motor experiences in play, whereas the frontal cortex serves to inhibit or redirect those impulsive and motoric energies along socially appropriate channels through planning, empathy, focused attention, language, and reflection.

At first it may seem that free play is most obviously limbic system–driven, as children express their vitality and spontaneity in unpredictable and sometimes explosive ways. However, I was recently reminded of the role of inhibition, and the redirection of impulses in free play, after observing two primary-level boys engaged in a bit of rough-and-tumble play in a museum. The two were alternately thrusting their hands at each other and feigning to strike in an attempt to "fake out" the other person. Clearly in this aggressive play activity, there was plenty of inhibition involving suppressing the motor impulse to strike when it was strategically and/or socially appropriate to do so. If you observe any group of children engaged in healthy play, you will notice this element of inhibition being worked out, as they seek to adjust their own roles, postures, language, and imaginations to those of the other children in their play group. The more impulsive aspects of playfulness, which are directed by the limbic system (and come out as manic and unsocialized "play" in many children labeled ADHD), seem to be modulated and "civilized" by the more socialized and language-driven aspects of play that are directed by the frontal lobes.

There is evidence that the kinds of social adaptations and learning experiences that young children acquire through play actually modify brain structure and functioning by creating new synaptic connections in the neocortex (Diamond & Hopson, 1998). It has even been suggested by some researchers that the evolution of the frontal lobes in primates occurred in part as a result of the experience of play (Furlow, 2001). Neuroscientist Jaak Panksepp (1998, p. 96) writes: "Indeed, 'youth' may have evolved to give complex organisms time to play and thereby exercise the natural skills they will need as adults. We already know that as the frontal lobes mature, frequency of play goes down, and animals with damaged frontal lobes tend to be more playful . . . Might access to rough-and-tumble play promote frontal lobe maturation?" Panksepp suggests that "[t]he explosion of ADHD diagnoses may largely reflect the fact that more and more of our children no longer have adequate spaces and opportunities to express this natural biological need—to play with each other in vigorous rough-and-tumble ways, each and every day" (p. 91). If children don't have the opportunity to work out the relationship between limbic system explosiveness and frontal lobe appropriateness through normal play situations, this may indeed result in failure of the frontal lobes to fully mature, and set the neurological stage for the kinds of frontal lobe-limbic system dysfunctions described in the ADHD literature.

A recent report issued by the National Association for Sport and Physical Recreation recommended that children engage in one to two hours of physical activity every day, yet increasingly schools are cutting back on physical education programs and recess periods in order to dedicate more time to academic achievement (often spent in front of a computer), and to make matters worse, research suggests that children are not making up the physical activity they are losing in school by increasing their physical activities after school (Dale, Corbin, & Dale, 2000). Providing opportunities for physical release may be of critical importance for children with ADHD symptoms. A recent study has demonstrated that children identified as ADHD show improvement after participating in play activities in natural settings, and that the "greener" a child's play area (that is, the more it takes place outdoors), the less severe his or her attention-deficit symptoms (Taylor, Kuo, & Sulkivan, 2001).

The Rise of Technologies. Two years ago, while traveling in Asia, I had a layover at the Tokyo Narita Airport. While wandering around, I noticed that there was a "Children's Play Room" and went in to take a look. There were no play spaces, open spaces, gymnastic equipment, or other tools for pretense or rough-and-tumble play. The "play space" consisted solely of computer terminals. Every single child was sitting in front of an individual computer station utilizing a software program. (On a more recent trip, I noticed that a few Lego plastic building blocks had made their appearance in a back corner of the room.)

My visit to the "Children's Play Room" in Tokyo stunned me, and led me to realize how much the meaning of children's play has changed over the past several decades, from the kinds of open-ended active explorations described above, involving the broad use of imagination, physical expression, complex social interactions, and creative language, to "technological play," which is generally passive (children sitting in front of computer terminals making only occasional small motor movements with their fingers on the keyboard or joystick), close-ended (the software program structures the flow of play, even when it is highly interactive), unimaginative (the software images are the products not of the children's imagination but of Silicon Valley minds concerned with generating profit), and lacking in opportunities for language development and social interaction (children, even when playing together, do not face each other to relate, but rather are all turned toward the screen). There are virtually no opportunities in this kind of context for an active interplay between the child's spontaneous vitality—controlled by the limbic system—and the inhibition and redirection of impulses through social interaction, language expression, and reflection— mediated by the developing frontal lobes. Thus, one can hypothesize that such an environment could create the very dysfunction between the limbic system and the frontal lobe system that is hypothesized to cause or exacerbate the symptoms that compose the ADHD diagnosis.

The popular children's movie *Monsters, Inc.* illustrates how children have been influenced by our technologically sophisticated, violent media culture. *Monsters, Inc.* is a movie about a group of monsters that work for a utility company. The "affable" monsters make children scream by walking into their bedrooms at night, and then they bottle up the energy in the screams to use as an energy source in their subterranean monster world. A crisis erupts however, when it becomes apparent that children aren't screaming as much as they did before, and as a result the monsters' energy supply is becoming depleted. The problem is that "kids don't scare so easily anymore." As a result, the monsters need to up the ante by terrorizing the children even more than before (Mitchell, 2001).

The movie *Monsters, Inc.* highlights the fact that children are "harder to scare" in today's violent media culture, and thus require even higher doses of fright, or at least higher levels of stimulation, to get their attention. In my opinion, the real monsters in children's lives are the media advertisers and programmers who, over the past fifty years, have gradually perfected the art of grabbing people's attention to sell products and services that "fuel" the entertainment machines of America. To witness the magnitude of this change, one has only to view a television program from the early 1950s—let's say, *The Honeymooners*—and track the amount of time that the show stays fixed on a given scene with an unchanging camera view. In programs created a few decades ago, most of the camera shots stay fixed for several seconds on one scene. Contrast this with a current commercial or a program on MTV, and you will soon discover that contemporary scenes usually shift in increments of less than one second. In 1992, CBS News attempted a novel experiment in their political coverage of the presidential elections. They began using "30 second sound bites" in an attempt to provide greater "in-depth coverage" to the political candidates' views. This experiment was stopped after a short while because it was concluded that the average adult viewer was unable to sustain his attention for that long a period of time, and the network went back to the standard seven-second sound bite (Berke, 1992).

One of the reasons for the change from stationary camera shots to rapidly shifting ones in television programs is a concomitant change in our "orienting response," a mechanism first described by Russian physiologist Ivan Pavlov in 1927. The orienting response is our instinctive biological reaction to any sudden or novel stimulus, and includes dilation of the blood vessels to the brain and constriction of blood vessels to major muscle groups. Mental arousal becomes heightened (alpha waves in the brain are blocked for a few seconds) and visual and auditory perceptions are sharpened. The orienting response evolved to help protect Homo sapiens from sudden environmental changes, such as the threat of nearby predators. Television advertisers have discovered this powerful biological response and are using it to sell products. By using loud noises, sudden camera shifts, violent content, and other novel stimuli, they are manipulating these evolutionary structures in the service of non-life-threatening stimuli, for example, programming and commercials (Reeves & Thorson, 1986). However, like the story of "The Boy Who Cried Wolf," we eventually habituate to these attention-grabbing ploys as we learn that there is no real threat present. Viewers become "harder to scare," or at least harder to bring back to the screen. This necessitates even more novel stimuli, sudden shifts, explosions, and the like, to grab the attention of the viewer back again by activating their orienting response. Over a period of years, then, this process has gradually created faster, sharper, louder, and more violent stimuli in television, movies, and video games. And among consumers of media, it has behaviorally modified the orienting response so that much higher levels of stimulation are required to obtain the same biological effects that the 1950s sitcom *I Love Lucy* or the 1960s video game Pong used to produce. (It is interesting to note that the first movies of trains traveling toward the viewer in the early twentieth century sent audiences screaming out of the theaters.)

Thus, the rise of technologies and the needs of the market economy have apparently created a "short-attention-span" culture. A study conducted in the 1980s tracked the changes that occurred in a mountain community in Canada after it acquired access to television for the first time. Over a period of two years, the adults and children in that community became less able to persevere at tasks, less able to engage in creative problem solving, and less tolerant of unstructured time (Williams, 1986). It should hardly be surprising that today's media-fed children, growing up on MTV, video games, the Internet, and violent television, should have also developed short attention spans. Thirty-five years ago, Marshall McLuhan described the first wave of this trend when he spoke of a generation of kids whose worldview was no longer based on plodding, one-step-at-a-time thinking, but rather on instantaneous flashes of immediate sensory data (McLuhan & Fiore, 1967). Around the same time, media expert Tony Schwartz wrote: "Today's child is a scanner, his experience with electronic media has taught him to scan life the way his eye scans a television set or his ears scan auditory signals from a radio or stereo speaker" (1973, pp. 110–111). It may be no coincidence that Attention Deficit Hyperactivity Disorder was formulated as a disability category in the early 1970s, at the same time that McLuhan and Schwartz were making these observations.

The medical literature has targeted disrupted dopaminergic pathways as a key element in the etiology of ADHD. Dopamine plays a central role in the modulation of stimulus seeking or reward seeking. When dopamine transmission is interfered with, an individual can develop an insatiability for rewards, or a need for higher stimulation levels than normal. This, in fact, is what many researchers have typically seen in children identified as ADHD: they require higher levels of stimulation than the average person. Ritalin and other short-acting stimulants help to provide this missing stimulation in chemical form. Some researchers have found that nondrug forms of stimulation—such as music, color, and lights—also help to provide an optimal level of stimulation for these understimulated children and thereby calm them down (Zentall, 1975, 1993; Zentall & Zentall, 1983; Zentall, Hall, & Lee, 1998). These findings must be reexamined in light of the heightened media-fed orienting response described above, because it may be that the rising crescendo of media stimulation in children creates, or at the very least contributes, to the need for higher levels of stimulation at the dopaminergic level in children diagnosed as ADHD. Indeed, well over a thousand studies have demonstrated that exposure to violent programming among children and adolescents creates violent behavior (Johnson, 2002; Sappenfield, 2002). In addition, other physiological responses to high-stimulation television and video-game experiences have been documented in the literature, including "TV-induced fright," "video-game epilepsy," and the possibility of television addiction on a par with substance abuse

(Fylan, Harding, & Webb, 1999; Valkenburg, Cantor, & Peters, 2000; Kubey & Csikszentmihalyi, 2002).

CONCLUSION

In light of the above research on the impact of the demise of play and the rise of screen technologies on children's lives, we are compelled to ask what the consequences of these sociacultural developments could be for a child in today's world. What is likely to happen when a child is deprived of natural play experiences that facilitate the harmonious coordination of the limbic system and the frontal lobes of the brain, and instead is immobilized in front of a video game, computer, or television screen and exposed to violent or other high-stimulus material that activates his innate orienting response with no opportunity to respond motorically or emotionally to these stimuli except through a few twitches of a joystick, a keyboard, or a channel changer? It is hardly surprising that children might respond to the absence of a vital developmental force (play) and relentless exposure to devitalizing technological "mechanism manipulation" (TV, video games, computers) by becoming inattentive, hyperactive, and impulsive. Indeed, it is perhaps a very natural result of these very unnatural cultural developments.

Unfortunately, the ADHD community of researchers are for the most part ill-disposed toward investigating sociocultural influences on symptoms, and remain confident in the belief that ADHD is a culture-free neurological disorder of genetic origin. A recent consensus statement on ADHD signed by seventy-four international scientists working in the ADHD field assails those who suggest that "behavior problems associated with ADHD are merely the result of [among other things] excessive viewing of TV or playing of video games." It concludes: "To publish stories that ADHD is . . . merely a conflict between today's Huckleberry Finns and their caregivers is tantamount to declaring the earth flat, the laws of gravity debatable, and the periodic table in chemistry a fraud" (Barkley, 2002, p. 90). It remains to be seen whether thoughtful people will accept this highly positivist view of children and behavior, or will instead consider the possibility that historical events and cultural trends may also have powerful effects upon the brains and behaviors of our children.

REFERENCES

American Psychiatric Association. (1994). *Diagnostic and statistical manual of mental disorders* (4th ed.). Washington, DC: Author.

Armstrong, T. (1997). *The myth of the A.D.D. child: 50 ways to improve your child's behavior span without drugs and attention, labels, or coercion.* New York: Plume.

Armstrong, T. (1999). *ADD/ADHD alternatives in the classroom.* Alexandria, VA: Association of Supervision and Curriculum Development.

Arnsten, A.F.T. (1999). Development of the cerebral cortex: XIV. Stress impairs prefrontal cortical function. *Journal of the American Academy of Child & Adolescent Psychiatry, 38,* 220–222.

Barbaresi, W.J., et al. (2002, March). How common is Attention-Deficit-Hyperactivity Disorder? *Archives of Pediatric and Adolescent Medicine, 156,* 217–224.

Barkley, R.A. (1990). *Attention Deficit Hyperactivity Disorder: A handbook for diagnosis and treatment.* New York: Guilford Press.

Barkley, R.A. (2002, June). International consensus statement on ADHD. *Clinical Child and Family Psychology Review, 5(2),* 89–111.

Berke, R.L. (1992, July 11). Sound Bites Grow at CBS, Then Vanish. *New York Times,* p. L7.

Biederman, J., Milberger, S., Faranoe, S.V., Kiely, K., Guite, J., & Mick, J., et al. (1995, March). Family-environment risk factors for Attention-Deficit Hyperactivity Disorder. *Archives of General Psychiatry, 52,* 464–469.

Carlson, E.A., Jacobvitz, D., & Sroufe, L.A. (1995, February). A developmental investigation of inattentiveness and hyperactivity. *Child Development, 66(1),* 37–54.

Cartwright, S.A. (1851, May). Report on the diseases and physical peculiarities of the Negro race. *The New Orleans Medical and Surgical Journal, 7,* 691–716.

Csikszentmihalyi, M. (2000, April 19). Education for the 21st century. *Education Week, 46.*

Dale, D., Corbin, C.B., Dale, K.S. (2000, September). Restricting opportunities to be active during school time: Do children compensate by increasing physical activity levels after school? *Research Quarterly for Exercise and Sport, 71,* 240.

Diamond, M., & Hopson, J. (1998). *Magic trees of the mind: How to nurture your child's intelligence, creativity, and healthy emotions from birth through adolescence.* New York: Dutton.

Furlow, B. (2001, June 9). Kids need the playground just as much as the classroom: Having fun builds bigger, better brains. *New Scientist.*

Fylan, F., Harding, G.F., & Webb, R.M. (1999). Mechanisms of video-game epilepsy. *Epilepsia, 40,* 28–30.

Giedd, J.N., Castellanos, F.X., Casey, B.J., Kozuch, B.A., King, A.C., & Hamburger, S.D., et al. (1994, May). Quantitative morphology of the corpus callosum in Attention Deficit Hyperactivity Disorder. *American Journal of Psychiatry, 151,* 665–668.

Grinspoon L., & Singer, S.B. (1973, November). Amphetamines in the treatment of hyperkinetic children. *Harvard Educational Review, 43,* 546–547.

Hansen, L.A. (1998, March/April). Where we play and who we are. *Illinois Parks and Recreation, 29(2)*, 22–25.

Hendren, R.L., DeBacker, I., & Pandin, G.J. (2000, July). Review of neuroimaging studies of child and adolescent psychiatric disorders from the past 10 years. *Journal of the American Academy of Child & Adolescent Psychiatry, 39*, 815–828.

Hobbs, N. (1975). *The futures of children.* San Francisco, CA: Jossey-Bass.

Johnson. J.G., et al. (2002). Television viewing and aggressive behavior during adolescence and adulthood. *Science, 295*, 2468–2471.

Kubey, R., & Csikszentmihalyi, M. (2002, February). Television addiction is no mere metaphor. *Scientific American, 286(2)*, 64–80.

LaHoste, G.J., Swanson, J.M., Wigal, S.B., Glabe, C., Wigal T., & King, N., et al. (1996). Dopamine D4 receptor gene polymorphism is associated with Attention Deficit Hyperactivity Disorder. *Molecular Psychiatry, 1*, 121–124.

McGuinness, D. (1985). *When children don't learn.* New York: Basic Books.

McGuinness, D. (1989). Attention Deficit Disorder: The emperor's clothes, animal "pharm" and other fiction. In S. Fisher & R.P. Greenberg (eds.), *The limits of biological treatment for psychological distress* (pp. 151–183). Hillsdale, NJ: Lawrence Erlbaum.

McLuhan, M., & Fiore, Q. (1967). *The medium is the message.* New York: Bantam.

Mitchell, E. (2001, November 2). Monsters of childhood with feelings and agendas. *New York Times.*

Nyland, D. (2002). *Treating Huckleberry Finn: A new narrative approach to working with kids diagnosed SDD/ADHD.* New York: Jossey-Bass.

Panksepp, J. (1998). Attention Deficit Hyperactivity Disorders, psychostimulants, and intolerance of childhood playfulness: A tragedy in the making? *Current Directions in Psychological Science, 7*, 91–98.

Perry, B.D., & Pollard, R. (1998). Homeostasis, stress, and adaptation: A neurodevelopmental view of childhood trauma. *Child and Adolescent Psychiatric Clinics of North America, 7*, 33–51.

Reeves, B., & Thorson, E. (1986). Watching television: Experiments on the viewing process. *Communication Research, 13*, 343–361.

Reid, R., Maag, J.W., & Vasa, S.F. (1993). Attention Deficit Hyperactivity Disorder as a disability category: A critique. *Exceptional Children, 60*, 198–214.

Sappenfield, M. (2002, March 29). Mounting evidence links TV viewing to violence. *Christian Science Monitor.*

Saunders, A., & Remsberg, B. (1986). *The stress-proof child.* New York: Signet.

Schwartz, J.M., Stoessel, P.W., Baxter, L.R., Jr., Martin, K.N., & Phelps, M.E. (1996, February). Systematic changes in cerebral glucose metabolic rate after successful behavior modification treatment of obsessive-compulsive disorder. *Archives of General Psychiatry, 53*, 109–113.

Schwartz, T. (1973). *The responsive chord.* Garden City, NY: Doubleday.

174   ALL WORK AND NO PLAY . . .

Sleator, E.K., & Ullman, R.L. (1981, January). Can the physician diagnose hyperactivity in the office? *Pediatrics, 67,* 13–17.

Sykes, D.H., Douglas, V.I., & Morgenstern, G. (1973). Sustained attention in hyperactive children. *Journal of Child Psychology & Psychiatry & Allied Disciplines, 14,* 213–220.

Taylor, A.F., Kuo, F.E., & Sullivan, W.E. (2001, January). Coping with ADD: The surprising connection to green play settings. *Environment and Behavior 33(1),* 54–77.

Valkenburg, P.M., Cantor, J., & Peters, A.L. (2000, February). Fright reactions to television: A child survey. *Communication Research, 27(1),* 82–97.

Weinstein, D., Staffelbach, D., & Biaggio, M. (2000, April). Attention-Deficit Hyperactivity Disorder and Post-Traumatic Stress Disorder: Differential diagnosis in childhood sexual abuse. *Clinical Psychology Review, 20,* 359–378.

Wender, E.H. (2002, March). Editorial: Attention-Deficit/Hyperactivity Disorder: Is it common? Is it overtreated? *Archives of Pediatric and Adolescent Medicine, 156,* 209–210.

Williams, T. MacBeth. (1986). *The impact of television: A natural experiment in three communities.* Orlando, FL: Academic Press.

Zentall, S. (1975). Optimal stimulation as a theoretical basis for hyperactivity. *American Journal of Orthopsychiatry, 45,* 549–563.

Zentall, S. (1980). Behavioral comparisons of hyperactive and normally active children in natural settings. *Journal of Abnormal Child Psychology, 8,* 93–109.

Zentall, S.S. (1993). Research on the educational implications of Attention Deficit Hyperactivity Disorder. *Exceptional Children, 60,* 143–153.

Zentall, S.S., Hall, A.H., & Lee, D.L. (1998). Attentional focus of students with hyperactivity during a word-search task. *Journal of Abnormal Child Psychology, 26,* 335–343.

Zentall, S., & Zentall, T.R. (1983). Optimal stimulation: A model of disordered activity and performance in normal and deviant children. *Psychological Bulletin, 94,* 446–471.

ABOUT THE CONTRIBUTOR

THOMAS ARMSTRONG, Ph.D., is an award-winning author and speaker with twenty-eight years of teaching experience from the primary through the doctoral level. More than one million copies of his books are in print on issues related to learning and human development. He is the author of nine books, including *Multiple Intelligences in the Classroom, In Their Own Way, Awakening Your Child's Natural Genius, 7 Kinds of Smart, The Myth of the A.D.D. Child, ADD/ADHD Alternatives in the Classroom,* and *Awakening Genius in the Classroom.* His books have been translated into sixteen languages, including Spanish,

Chinese, Hebrew, Danish, and Russian. He has appeared on several national and international television and radio programs, including NBC's *The Today Show*, *CBS This Morning*, CNN, the BBC, and *The Voice of America*. Articles featuring his work have appeared in hundreds of newspapers and magazines around the country, including the *New York Times*, *Washington Post*, *Parenting*, and *Mothering*. His clients have included *Sesame Street*, the Bureau of Indian Affairs, the European Council of International Schools, the Republic of Singapore, and several State Departments of Education. He is currently writing a book on the stages of life.

9

Play and the Transformation of Feeling: Niki's Case

Eva-Maria Simms

States parties recognize the right of the child to rest and leisure,
to engage in play and recreational activities appropriate to the age
of the child, and to participate freely in cultural life and the arts.
—Article 31, Convention on the Rights of the Child,
United Nations

Traditionally, early childhood has been associated with play. From the
philosopher Rousseau's claim that play is the child's work, through the
poet Novalis's romantic view of the child's play world as the "golden
age," to the educator Froebel's kindergarten movement and the psychologist Erik Erikson's term "play age" for early childhood, the connection between early childhood and play seemed well established and
generally accepted by the end of the twentieth century. In 1990, the
United Nations ratified and legally protected child play in the International Convention on the Rights of the Child. It seems ironic that just
as child play has achieved internationally protected status, it begins
to vanish from American public life. Preschools and kindergartens are
trading in their play corners for worksheets and desks, elementary and
middle schools reduce leisure and playtime on the playgrounds, parents are too afraid of traffic and abductions to let their children play
in neighborhoods, and indoor play has been taken over by television

and computer games. To find time and space for free play, unregulated and unstructured by adults, has become difficult for most children, especially in our educational institutions. Indeed, play has become antithetical to the goals of Western education.

In this chapter, I will illustrate the critical role of play in children's affective and cognitive development through a *phenomenological-structural* analysis of play as it unfolds over the course of a play-therapy case. The case reveals many of the essential features of play and allows us to focus on the developmental trajectory from sensori-motor to symbolic play.

THE VITAL ROLE OF PLAY IN CHILDHOOD—
THE CASE OF NIKI

Psychotherapists who work with children understand the transformative power of play. Rather than enjoyment and leisure, which are the hallmarks of ordinary play, pain and pathology are the driving forces of therapeutic play. This kind of play has an existential urgency: it provides a lifeline back into a world shared with others. Therapeutic play is play with an edge, stripped of all but its essential features.

The following passages by therapist Eliana Gil (cited in James, 1994) introduce us to her work with a four-year-old child named Niki, who suffered from *failure to thrive* as a result of profound parental neglect. In witnessing Niki's courageous struggle to work through her abandonment issues through play therapy, we learn much about the vital role of play in children's lives.

In addition to malnutrition and untreated rashes and infections, Niki, at four years of age, could not walk, could barely talk, and was not toilet trained when she entered the foster care system:

> The foster mother reported that Niki was lethargic and passive. She did not cry, even when soiled or hungry. She preferred to stay in one spot, apparently uncomfortable with being out of her crib. She didn't seem interested in toys and usually clutched her blanket in her hands. Niki flinched when her foster mother came into the room in the morning. (Gil, in James, 1994, p. 142)

Her therapist found her to be passive and unresponsive for many months, unattached to anyone and uninterested in the activities of other people:

> Sitting next to her I would make sure she watched as I rolled a ball, cut a cardboard into shapes, played with water, built blocks, and built a

variety of other things. She usually sat staring, with fingers of both hands in her mouth. (p. 142)

In the absence of caring adults, the horizon of a child's world is severely restricted. Neglected, uncared-for children may not cry when hurt or upset because they do not expect a response from the world anymore. They do not call out in anticipation of a future gesture from their caregivers. Such children will restrict their engagement with the world to familiar experiences: the minute shadings of a white crib, a distance that spans a few feet, the touch of others that confines itself to the feeling of a spoon on one's lips or maybe the grasp of a hand under one's arms when placed on a potty chair. They will perfectly adapt their senses to this restricted world. As a result, their senses of hearing, sight, touch, and taste become atrophied. After their release from isolation and neglect, they will show autistic-like symptoms, and without intense therapeutic sensory work, their chances for succeeding in an ordinary family and school situation are not very good (Greenspan & Benderly, 1997).

Within this semiautistic world, play is replaced with repetitive, self-stimulating activities: rocking, head banging, flipping a light switch, or waving the fingers before the eyes. Unlike play, these activities are not modulated and varied, but are monotonously pursued without change in their structure. Normal play investigates the qualities of things as one encounters them, but autistic play limits the multiple possibilities inherent in a thing to action on just one exclusive feature. *Sensory defensiveness* implies that the horizon of possible modes of activity between self and world has been severely restricted. Play can arise only when children feel safe and cared for—when the halo of adult care lights up the world beyond the crib and makes it inviting instead of frightening.

Sensori-Motor Play

Sensory experience and interaction with water, sand, blocks, scissors, and other things affords the young child the opportunity of being shaped by and shaping her particular environment. But to do so requires the courage to be challenged: water slips away, sand runs to nothing between one's fingers, scissors cut, and things resist. This type of play, which Piaget (1929/1951) termed "sensori-motor," stimulates sensory and brain development. Rather than mere observation of the properties of objects, it entails direct experience, which in turn deepens the child's self-awareness. The child *discovers* her fingers as they try to contain the sand or stack the blocks, and she discovers their limitations when the sand is spilled or the tower of blocks collapses. The most fundamental requirement of any type of play is the experience that I can change the structure of the world through my own engagement with it—and that I am changed in turn.

Niki's therapist models simple forms of play, and tries to coax her out of the narrow circumference of her life in the crib by showing her that a playful engagement with things is safe. She opens up the possibilities inherent in the sand: it can be dug up or smoothed, hollowed or stacked, filtered or packed together. Experiencing the multiple possibilities inherent in objects is a precondition for play, and is one quality that sets it apart from other human activities, such as work or structured learning. When the sand responds to the touch of the hand, it makes suddenly visible the child's very own gesture. It becomes a possible location for self-expression and self-experience. It makes the child's intentionality visible: "Here *I want* to have a hollow in the sand . . . and there. . . . Do I want it to remain smooth?" Play becomes the location where *agency and selfhood are exercised without direct annunciation of the self* (Gadamer, 1996).

Initially, engaging in play is a big hurdle for Niki. For four months, she keeps her fingers to herself, as she learns how to participate in play by watching her therapist. The therapist is very aware that Niki needs the adult's constancy and the sameness of the small playroom. Niki first ventures into the world of play when she picks up two cups and pours sand from one into the other, a gesture that is followed by pouring water onto the sand. Filling and emptying, and giving and receiving are two primary forms of human experience. The satisfaction of sensory sand play, its visceral pleasure, is enhanced by this primary experience of emptiness and fullness that Niki herself can now create. The sand flowing from the cup is more than an object to Niki. The outpouring and receiving of the cups is emotionally satisfying because it makes visible a principle of human existence, one that Niki as the unfilled infant has experienced in her previous life. Interaction with objects condenses the complexity of human emotions into a simple form, which then can be re-created and reproduced in drawing, play, language, and other symbolic expressions (Langeveld, 1968). Symbols arise in childhood—not in the mind—but out of the *affective* encounter with the physical world.

Niki's initial inability to play despite being in the "play age" highlights a number of structural elements of play. Play is a bodily, emotional, and mental engagement with the *possibilities* inherent in the physical world. These possibilities can only be taken up and explored

when the child is *held* by a trusting and inviting relationship with
adults (Erikson, 1950/1963). Adult neglect leads to autistic-type narrowing of the horizon of engagement, as the child fearfully avoids
playing with the *possibilities of things*. Once the child takes up a playful relationship with the physical world, symbolism begins in the
sensory-affective realm, and only secondarily leads to cognitive
understanding. The self is displayed and affirmed without directly
announcing itself.

Symbolic Play

After playing with the sifting cups for quite a while, Niki achieves
a significant breakthrough: she brings a toy mother pig with seven
piglets into the sandbox. Out of the multiple forms that the sandbox
offers, she chooses a particular one: Niki creates a world by turning
the sandbox into a particular place, and establishing a meaningful
space for her piglets. In order to do this, she had to find the courage
to break out of the narrow, repetitive, sensory experience of the sand
and decide how to express herself. She tells us: "out of all possibilities, the piglets and their mother are the first to inhabit my world,
because their particular possibilities most closely mirror my need."
Niki is awakening to the potentialities of her environment, and she
steps into the clearing, allowing herself to be reflected back through
her toys. The curtain upon the unfolding drama of mothers and babies
has been opened, and the child cannot help but take up the narrative
in her particular way.

> From this time forward her play took on different characteristics, becom-
> ing repetitive and exact. At every session for about three months, she
> buried the mother pig in the left hand corner of the sand tray. The pig-
> lets were placed in the opposite corner, and they took turns trying to find
> the mother pig. The child said nothing during this play, yet appeared to
> be absorbed in what she was doing, frequently showing a low-range
> affective variance. The piglets would go looking for the mother and
> would alternately fall in water and drown, climb and fall off a tree, fall
> off a bridge, and be unable to climb fences, mountains, or other obstacles.
> (Gil, cited in James, 1994, pp. 142–143)

The endless journey of the piglets in search of their mother is deeply
tragic. Niki has stepped into the world of symbolic play, and its affective power carries her along. Despite its almost unbearable sadness,
Niki perseveres with her script over and over. The young in search of
mother fall and drown, get stopped by mountains, trees, fences, and

streams, and it seems as if the whole world prevents them from getting what they need. The exact repetition of this painful game points to one of the key elements of play: play is an emotional or *pathic* activity. Unlike cognitive or *Gnostic* activities that are articulate, process oriented, and focus on what we know about something, *pathic* activities are a feeling-toned communion with playthings. The pathic child experiences an immediate connection with her world (Buytendijk, 1976). Niki is not talking to her therapist to figure out how to live her life better (which would be a later, cognitive activity), but she is shaping the affective dimension of her life. Like a musician, she plays through the variations of her theme of "getting lost"; like a sculptor, she goes over and over the layers to peel away the emotional form that lies under the surface. Her play differentiates the affective domain, and her toys help her find containers or gestures for the pain in her life. Unhurried play makes it possible for the child to learn a silent symbolic language—prior to speech or even alongside the spoken word—which shapes and brings to visibility the affective threads that bind her, however tenuously, to things and people in her life.

"We play only with what is pathic in our presence" (Buytendijk, 1976, p. 129), with what addresses our feeling life. The primary motivation for play lies in its power to let the child move in an externalized feeling world. Play evokes a world that is ineffable and profound. The feeling world the child displays through her toys goes beyond articulation in its complexity and depth. Play displays the affective life of the child, but, as in theater, there are some scripts that are more differentiated and satisfactory than others. It takes Niki three months to perfect her "searching for mother" script. The first act, burying the mother, remains constant, but there are so many ways to get lost on the way to her!

> One day there was a major difference in Niki's repetitive scenario: None of the piglets drowned, fell down, or otherwise faced an overwhelming obstacle—they instead found and uncovered the mother pig! *Niki stopped abruptly, almost surprised by what she had done* and quickly moved away from the sand tray, indicating she was done for the day. (Gil, cited in James, 1994, p. 143, italics added)

One quality of play, which, once again, Buytendijk articulated beautifully, is that we continue to play with something only *if it plays with us*. The unpredictable response of the ball, the many responses of the other players collapsed in a heap at the end of ring-around-the-rosy, the piglets exploring possible paths through the sand tray, illustrate how playthings interact with the player and change the game. Niki is *surprised* when the piglets find and uncover their mother because the possibilities inherent in the sandbox go beyond the fixed game she has set up. At this juncture, the sand tray becomes uncanny because the new constellation of playthings implies affective possibilities that are overwhelming. She arrests her symbolic play because she does not know if it is safe to step into the new world that has opened up: piglets *with* mother. This is a fearful moment, an instant where the child gets a glimpse of the future: the piglets cannot go back now to getting lost. They must engage their mother. In her pathic world, the heroes find the grail, but they get more than they bargained for. Finding the mother is not the end, but just the beginning of another leg of the quest. It ushers in a new set of affective play gestures that symbolize the relationship between mother and child.

> During the following session one piglet began the "search for the mother" ritual and found and uncovered her quickly. This time the child put the piglet next to the mother, looked up at me, and said: "titty no milk." She seemed genuinely sad, and her eyes watered up. I said "No milk for the baby," and the child responded tearfully, "Baby sad." She held a big stuffed rabbit in her lap for the rest of the session and rocked it and fed it with a plastic bottle. From time to time a single tear would fall on her cheek. (Gil, cited in James, 1994. p. 143)

Niki's first verbal communicative act is the phrase: "titty no milk." It is the saddest and most hurtful insight of any abandoned child. Niki sums up what the mother's failure was: no milk signifies the absence of nourishment and intimacy, which in turn means the loss of the bond between mother and baby, thus threatening her development and even her very survival. This is the tragic disappointment at the core of Niki's life experience. "Titty no milk"—it seems that her play with the piglets from the beginning has been working toward finding this emotional expression.

By playing in the sandbox, she has elaborated the emotional ground in months of silent play, but finally words break through: "Baby sad." How skimpy these words seem compared to the full emotional impact of her play script! In response to these words, she picks up the stuffed rabbit and comforts it by *rocking and feeding* it. Taking up the maternal gestures herself, Niki changes perspective and supplies to another what the pig failed to give the piglets, what her mother failed to give to her. We see here, once again, an affective form as it changes location from one thing to the next. She retreats from the pigs into the sphere of the stuffed rabbit because it is more intimate and immediate: the cloth rabbit can be hugged and touched; it is closer to all the senses than the toys in the sand tray. Holding and feeding are sensuous experiences and more primary than symbolic play. Niki's play narrative is eclipsed at this point because she needs more than symbolism. Her regression to holding the rabbit is a regression to a familiar experience—her blanket. But as she hugs the soft toy, she also feeds it, and hence maintains the play space. She is not retreating into mute self-enclosedness as before. The sensuous and the symbolic come together and overlap without merging. Niki is comforted by the sensuousness of the rabbit's touch, as she herself symbolically comforts another infant.

Niki plays not merely with material objects, but with the affective dimension of the relationship between mother and infant as it reveals itself through the toys. In the world of play, she can assume the maternal gestures herself, while at the same time empathizing with the baby rabbit. The paradox of nurturing and abandonment is borne fully in Niki's pieta-like cradling of the rabbit, while "from time to time a single tear would fall on her cheek."

Language has great difficulty unraveling the complexity of Niki's affective gestures. Her therapist, in a very unadorned way, allows for an extremely simple language to describe the events that are visible. Her sentences, "The mother pig is buried. The baby pig fell from the tree," or "No milk for the baby," offer no other comfort but the communication that another human being is fully present and witnessing the drama unfold. Her language, which lifts into words the mute play of the child, is unobtrusive and lets the child's own intentionality unfold. It simply restates an unadorned reality, and by so doing respects the child's right to express her own suffering.

In the following therapy session, Niki repeats the same process a number of times: the piglet finds the mother, there is no milk, the rabbit is stroked and fed:

> When the piglet found no milk the third time Niki did this play, Niki reached over and placed a mother giraffe in the opposite corner of the tray. She then picked up the baby giraffe, and the baby giraffe and the piglet seemed to nestle together next to the mother giraffe. "This mommy gots milk!" the child exclaimed. She again held the rabbit and stroked its head, saying "There, there, . . . you awright." (Gil, cited in James, 1994, p. 143)

After this session, Niki's relationship with her therapist and foster mother became more engaged, and her play went beyond the piglets in the sand tray and included a whole variety of new forms. The narrative line of babies in search of mothers has come to its conclusion. The piglets, the baby rabbit, and Niki herself will be "awright."

Nikki's case powerfully highlights the potential of play to shift the feeling life of a child and to create a world that she understands and inhabits in a fuller way. Play is the creation of a symbolic world in all existential dimensions, and it allows for fluid experimentation with embodiment, coexistence, objects, spatiality, and temporality. The *body* can be young or old, do or pretend to do what is not yet or never possible. *Others* can be real people who are imitated, or they might be purely pathic figures who are given an anthropomorphic form. *Things* transform from one into the other in metaphoric splendor, pushing the edge of what a particular thing is. *Space* allows for an imaginary world to be created and enacted, and yet there is a faithfulness to the most essential spatial forms (corner, nest, miniature, etc.). *Time* curls in on itself: it is nonlinear, past and future weave together, it is intuitive and unfettered by the need for timed production. Play follows the spell of the sensuous; it is the lining, the curling over between natural and symbolic forms. It is essential for children at an age when they are not reflective, but learn by engagement.

EARLY CHILDHOOD AND THE STRUCTURES OF PLAY

Jean Piaget gave us a basic vocabulary for understanding childhood development that is still foundational to child psychology and education. I think one of his key insights about early childhood is that preschoolers are "egocentric," that is, they do not distinguish between themselves and the world and they are completely unreflective about themselves:

> Let us imagine a being, knowing nothing of the distinction between mind and body. Such a being would be aware of his desires and feelings but his notion of self would be undoubtedly much less clear than ours. Compared with us he would experience much less the sensation of the thinking self within him, the feeling of a being independent of the external world. The knowledge that we are thinking of things severs us in fact from the actual things. But above all the psychological perceptions of such a being would be entirely different from our own. Dreams, for example, would appear to him as a disturbance breaking in from without. Words would be bound up with things and to speak would mean to act

directly on these things. Inversely, external things would be less material and would be endowed with intentions and will. (Piaget, 1929/1951,
p. 37)

For Piaget, the young mind confuses itself with the universe and is unconscious of its own self. When the child, around the age of six, becomes more logical and reflective, the closeness to the world of things
dissolves slowly and a more distant and self-aware human being
emerges. Piaget thought that the child's entry into this new stage of
cognitive development, which he termed the "concrete operational
stage," was fixed according to a biological timetable, and that no
amount of hurrying could produce the loss of egocentrism and magical thinking without damaging the child. The experience of oneness
with the world is a fact of early human development that needs to be
respected.

Play, because of its affective, magical, prelogical relationship to
things and people is the perfect activity for a nondualistic, egocentric
mind. Piaget's insight that the young child does not separate self from
world and has very little understanding of an "inner" life has far-
reaching implications for how we deal with Niki and other young
children. For Niki, the world is not a panorama "out there," but its
openness and closedness, its invitation and repulsion are entwined
with who she is. Her egocentrism in Piaget's sense means that in the
beginning of her therapy, she has no distance from her environment,
and that the influence of the social world is immediate and profound.
We understand the smallness of her world as a direct reflection of the
smallness of her psychological life: no invitation from the world = no
person there to be invited.

Niki's case and its analysis underscore the following seven characteristic features of play:

1. *Play requires a safe, predictable, and caring adult presence in the background,*
   without which the child's horizon becomes constricted. Loving caregivers
   provide the sense of safety that emboldens the child to explore her environment, and to risk being changed or shaped by it.
2. *Play follows the invitation of the sensuous world.* We find here a reversal of
   our common dualistic attitude that sees things as distant objects out there,
   waiting to be manipulated by masterful adults. For the egocentric child,
   things have their own intentionality: *things play with the child.* Hence, it is
   important to think about the qualities of play materials and what kind of
   play they invite. Is their structure and texture pleasing or exciting to the
   senses? Do they call for narrowly defined play scripts, or are they gener-
   ous in what they allow the child to be?

3. *Play is an exercise in empathy.* Niki's exploration of the "lost piglet" script reveals the close attention she pays to her playthings. She explores the possibilities inherent in the sand and the piglet figures, and out of their imaginary interaction, new possibilities for action arise. Because young children do not have the preformed cultural explanations and concepts about the world that characterize adult thinking, their playful "magical" thinking is, in fact, a freer and unprejudiced investigation into the structure and symbolism of things. Play fosters an empathic relationship with things and people: the playing child allows herself to be touched by them. The child probes their being, which is also a probing of her own being. The piglets are like Niki, and their victory draws a possible horizon for her own future victory. Play fosters empathic observation, and it establishes an affective-ethical connection between the child and the physical/social world.

4. *Play explores and elaborates the affective dimension of the child's lived world.* For the young child, there is not a "physical world" out there, because her egocentrism does not see them as other, but as extensions of herself. When the child rearranges the visible world of things in her play, she is also rearranging her feeling life.

   The young child's egocentrism offers adults a wonderful opportunity: through the toys we offer, the stories we tell, the work we demonstrate, and the environments we create, we can influence our children's affective life immediately and profoundly. The young child absorbs what he sees without reflection, critique, or distance. Parents and teachers either issue the invitation to the child to step into a safe world and make something of it, or, in varying degrees, they foreclose the affective bond between the child and the world, as we saw in Niki's case.

5. *Symbols are discovered through the emotional/sensory contact with things and people before they become cognitive or linguistic.* Language is often insufficient to address the complexity of the affective domain, but play displays this complexity tangibly, over time and in all its paradoxical features. As Niki attaches her feelings to the piglet figures, her interaction with them changes her feeling life in particular ways. The lost piglets become a *symbolic affective form,* which is particularly suited to carry out Niki's emotional project. It allows her to explore the subtleties and range of possible feelings as they are narrated through the pigs' adventures. The imaginative manipulation of toys restructures the child's experience of her own emotions. The landscape of feelings that ties her to people and things becomes elaborated and refined through her play. It seems to me that this is one of the most profound functions of play: it differentiates and represents the child's evolving emotional life.

6. *Play involves the creation of a meaningful, coherent world with ordered locations and scripts.* The play scripts Niki developed, like those of kindergarten children playing prince and dragon, or mother cat and kittens, are of an archetypal nature. Mother/father-baby, venturing forth into a dangerous world, getting lost in the woods, rescuing people, fighting against evil—these are all typical plots for young children's play. By elaborating and

individualizing these scripts, the child traverses an emotional human landscape and in the process articulates her feeling and thinking life.
7. *Play is the locus of the child's developing capacity for intentionality. The self is
   revealed and affirmed in the play world without directly announcing itself.* Play
   thus honors the child's egocentrism by allowing awareness without self-
   awareness, self without self-reflection. We saw Niki display and affirm
   herself by developing and inhabiting a world of her own creation. She
   chose the mother pig and piglets, she made the trees, ditches, and walls.
   Play makes her emotional intentions visible. It allows for a symbolic space
   where the pre-reflective child can show her self *without directly announcing it.* The pleasure of play is driven by the satisfaction that the world I
   have created in my play reflects myself. Its failings in apathy and boredom, or in the extreme form of autistic repetition, are also a failing of the
   self. Play, to paraphrase Rousseau, is truly the child's work, because in
   play the child changes the world and herself. Play requires that adults give
   children the freedom to build their own imaginary worlds free from adult
   expectation and instruction, but never too far removed from a protective
   adult presence.

FROM PLAY TO LITERACY

The structural analysis of Niki's play has revealed that play has an
important function in educating the child's feeling life. Play in a preschool or kindergarten is not a waste of time in the antechambers of
literacy, but an activity appropriate for the egocentric, nondualistic
child. It teaches the child attention, observation, and empathy; it awak-
ens symbolic capacity and provides images for a varied emotional life;
and it strengthens the child's sense of agency, intentionality, and
selfhood.

The neglect of or even disdain for play in American education has
deep roots. Decades ago, Piaget was asked by American educators how
to speed up the developmental process in preoperational, young children. This has become known as the "American Question." Piaget's
reply was: "But why would you want to do that?" I share Piaget's
puzzlement, together with Spock, Brazelton, Elkind, and Greenspan.

Yet Piaget himself, despite his careful attention and understanding
of early childhood thought, often disparages young children's mental
activity. From the beginning of his research work, Piaget found children to exhibit forms of thinking that threatened adult logic. He evaluated the young child's egocentrism mostly in negative terms when
compared to adult cognition: it is an "absence of consciousness of the
self" and a "failure to differentiate between the self and the world"
(Piaget, 1929/1951, p. 35). The child's adherence to observation of the

physical world without distinguishing it from the self leads to a form of realism that, for Piaget, is an "anthropocentric illusion" and leads to "all those illusions which teem in the history of science" (p. 34). Even though Piaget showed much sensitivity to the texture of child thought, in the final analysis, he dismissed it as merely a step to a higher adult logic. As Johnson (1995, p. 47) so aptly summarizes: "For Piaget, the young child is a primitive *scientist*, with an immature set of hypotheses about the nature of reality." Piaget's dismissive attitude has clouded the minds of educators, who, against Piaget's own advice, try to hurry our children through this preoperational stage, which is merely a waiting room where one wastes time on the way to the good stuff.

Play is the first casualty in hurrying up our children because on the surface it seems to be unproductive and a waste of time. Would time not be better spent in adult structured, educational activities so that we can give our children a head start in the three R's?

Let us explore this premise by considering the precursors to literacy. Literacy is much more than the acquisition of a mechanical skill; indeed, it restructures the psychological life of young children. As Ong (1982) and Eisenstein (1979) in their social and historical studies have pointed out, the acquisition of writing technology transforms consciousness, and this is not only true in the cultural acquisition of print, but also in the lives of our young children. The cultural shift from orality to literacy is mirrored in each child's experience when he or she learns to read (Egan, 1998). A competent reader has to develop the following abilities: the capacity for physical, emotional, and mental self-restraint; a tolerance for delayed gratification; a sophisticated ability to think conceptually and sequentially; a preoccupation with both historical continuity and the future; and a high valuation of reason and hierarchical order (Postman, 1994). On a practical level, children who learn to read have to sit still and restrict physical and mental attention to a small space, memorize arbitrary symbols, stay focused on a purely mental activity, think and see sequentially, give up their social interactions, pay attention to their teacher, and enter a purely symbolic world that is not mediated by human voice or presence. In order to be a competent reader, the child has to restructure the way she lives in the world. With the shift from audible interactions to visual text come more subtle changes in the way reality is experienced. Walter Ong beautifully evokes the difference between a world shaped through the activities of either the ear or the eye, a shift that also applies to oral child culture:

In a primarily oral culture where the word has its existence only in sound, with no reference whatsoever to any visually perceptible text, and no awareness of even the possibility of such a text, the phenomenology of sound enters deeply into human being's feel for existence, as processed by the spoken word. For the way in which the world is experienced is always momentous in psychic life. The centering action of sound (the field of sound is not spread out before me but is all around me) affects man's sense of the cosmos. For oral cultures, the cosmos is an ongoing event with man at its center. Man is the *umbilicus mundi*, the navel of the world (Eliade 1958, pp. 231–5, etc.). Only after print and the extensive experience with maps that print implemented would human beings, when they thought about the cosmos or the universe or "world," think primarily of something laid out before their eyes, as in a modern printed atlas, a vast surface or assemblage of surfaces (vision presents surfaces) ready to be "explored." (Ong, 1982, p. 73)

The process of learning to read decenters the child from the "umbilicus mundi," the participatory, egocentric oneness with the world. Reading and the educational rituals that accompany it, send children on their way to becoming the rational, distanced, analytical observers that Piaget had in mind as the endpoint of development; the stage he labeled "formal operations."

Reading is an essential aspect of Western human development because it produces a particular self that functions relatively well in our technologically sophisticated societies and knows how to handle the vast array of symbolic material that characterizes a literate culture. But it is also clear that the qualities required of a good reader are in stark opposition to the egocentric nature of young children's thinking and experiencing. Our children need time in the oral world to develop the mental and emotional capacities that will turn them into creative, self-reflective, socially responsible adults who have the motivation and will to realize their projects. By pushing literacy into the kindergartens and preschools and by eliminating time and space for play, we prevent our children from developing emotional sophistication, an intelligence that relies on its own observation, an ethical bond with the people and things around them, and a faith in their own will and ability to create worlds—maybe with better scripts than the ones we provide them with today.

REFERENCES

Buytendijk, F.J.J. (1976). *Wesen und sinn des spiels*. New York: Arno Press.
Egan, K. (1998). *The educated mind: How cognitive tools shape our understanding*. Chicago: University of Chicago Press.

Eisenstein, E. (1979). *The printing press as an agent of change: Communications and cultural transformations in early-modern Europe*. New York: Cambridge University Press.

Eliade, M. (1958). *Patterns in comparative religion*. New York: Sheed & Ward.

Erikson, E.H. (1963). *Childhood and society*. New York: W. W. Norton & Co. (Original work published 1950.)

Gadamer, H.-G. (1996). *Truth and method* (2nd ed.). J. Weinsheimer & D.G. Marshall (Trans.). (2nd ed.). New York: Continuum.

Greenspan, S.I., & Benderly, B.L. (1997). *The growth of the mind: And the endangered origins of intelligence*. New York: Addison-Wesley Publishing Co.

James, B. (1994). *Handbook for treatment of attachment-trauma problems in children*. New York: Lexington Books.

Johnson, A. (1995). Constructing the child in psychology: The child as primitive in Hall and Piaget. *Journal of Phenomenological Psychology, 26(2)*, 35–57.

Langeveld, M.J. (1968). *Studien zur anthropologie des kindes*. Tuebingen, Germany: Max Niemeyer Verlag.

Ong, W.J. (1982). *Orality and Literacy. The technologizing of the word*. London and New York: Routledge.

Piaget, J. (1951). *The child's conception of the world*. J. Tomlinson & A. Tomlinson (Trans.). Savage, MD: Littlefield Adams. (Original work published 1929.)

Postman, N. (1994). *The disappearance of childhood*. New York: Vintage Books.

Simms, E.M. (2002). The child in the world of things. In D. J. Martino (Ed.), *The phenomenology of childhood*. Pittsburgh: Simon Silverman Phenomenology Center, Duquesne University.

ABOUT THE CONTRIBUTOR

EVA-MARIA SIMMS received her Ph.D. from the University of Dallas. She is currently associate professor of psychology at Duquesne University and director of the developmental psychology graduate program. She is interested in the historical study of childhood, as well as the phenomenology of children's experience. Her work includes publications on child development and phenomenology, as well as a number of papers on the German poet Rilke.

10

Pathogenic Trends in Early Childhood Education

SHARNA OLFMAN

In the past few decades, there has been a significant increase in the incidence and prevalence rates of child psychopathology across a wide range of diagnostic categories, including: Attention Deficit Hyperactivity Disorder (ADHD), Autistic Spectrum Disorders (Asperger's Disorder, in particular), Bipolar Disorder, depression, anxiety, and learning disabilities (Centers for Disease Control and Prevention, 2002; DeGrandpre, 1999; Fonbonne, 2001; Kluger, Song, Cray, & Ressner, 2002; Surgeon General, 2001). Advances in genetic research and brain-imaging techniques have led to a wealth of insights into the genetic and neurochemical substrates of a number of psychiatric illnesses, facilitating more precise interventions for scores of children who might otherwise have been misunderstood as lazy, moody, immature, unintelligent, or the victims of bad parenting.

While medical research has advanced our understanding of specific mental illnesses, it fails to explain the increase in the number of children being labeled as psychiatrically disturbed *across* diagnostic categories. Some researchers suggest that the percentage of children who suffer from psychiatric illness has not actually changed, but rather that increasingly sophisticated assessment tools enable us to identify more children who might not have been correctly diagnosed at an earlier time. However, given the sheer number of children who are purported to have gene- and brain-based psychiatric illnesses—and are ingesting daily doses of powerful psychotropic drugs (Kennedy, 2003)—and given the exquisite sensitivity of the brain and of gene activation to environmental influence during infancy and early childhood, we are compelled to consider the role of the environment.

Children in the United States are being challenged by a confluence of environmental factors that include widespread poverty, the disintegration of the family, inadequate access to medical care, unregulated and substandard day-care facilities, the pervasive presence of screen technologies, and trends in education that are profoundly insensitive to their developmental needs. Twenty percent of all children in the United States live in poverty and this number rises to 40 percent among children of single mothers (McLeod & Shanahan, 1996; National Center for Children in Poverty, 2000; Zigler & Hall, 2000). We have the highest divorce rate in the world (*twice* as high as Sweden, which has the second highest), and children compose the largest group without health insurance (Children's Defense Fund, 2000; Hetherington, Bridges, & Insabella, 1998; U.S. Bureau of the Census, 2000; Vandell, Dadisman, & Gallagher, 2000). Overcrowded classrooms increasingly serve as prep schools for standardized testing and the tech industry, and uncensored information garnered from the World Wide Web is taking precedence over social and emotional growth (Cordes & Miller, 2000; Greenspan, 1997; Healy, 1998; Sacks, 1999). Many vulnerable children may be succumbing to psychiatric illnesses that they might have avoided in healthier and more supportive environments. In addition, as caregivers and teachers become more stressed, they may be quicker to label children under their care as disturbed whose personalities, profile of talents, or developmental timetables are not an ideal fit with the environment. In the following sections, we take a close look at the role of school, work, and home environments in creating, exacerbating, and perpetuating children's mental illness.

TRENDS IN EARLY CHILDHOOD EDUCATION

No Time for Play

Politicians, parents, and educators alike are dismayed by the poverty of American children's academic skills. As a consequence, play is being sidelined in preschools and kindergartens in favor of early academics, computer-based learning, and "scripted" teaching. While this might appear to be a viable solution, it actually compounds the problem because it ignores established principles of child development. As Jean Piaget (1950) demonstrated, children's cognitive skills develop according to a biologically primed timetable. A young child's worldview and intellect is *qualitatively* rather than quantitatively different from that of an older child. While we can teach three-year-olds to count and memorize text, if they don't understand what numbers and letters symbolize, the lasting value of these exercises is questionable.

More to the point, according to Erik Erikson's (1985) path-breaking theory of psychosocial stages, the central challenge for young children is the development of *initiative* through fantasy play. Children the world over engage in vivid fantasy play between the ages of three and five. These activities are not mere diversions, but vital exercises that spark creative potential. In the words of Lev Vygotsky, "children stand a head taller when they play," as they learn to symbolize objects and events, delay gratification, practice self-regulation, assimilate adult roles, exercise imagination, practice motor skills, and develop emotional, social, and verbal literacy (Klugman & Smilansky, 1990; Roskos & Christie, 2000; Saracho & Spodek, 1998; Vygotsky, 1978). When we force children to foreclose on the stage of *initiative*, and then prematurely push them into the stage of *industry*, we may indeed succeed in getting some children to read, write, and complete math equations precociously. But we may also be creating a cohort of children who lack spontaneity, creativity, and a love of learning.

As Stanley Greenspan's (1997) compelling research demonstrates, emotional awareness is not merely a form of intelligence, but rather the cornerstone of *all* aspects of intellectual development (see chapter 7). Children cannot grow intellectually if they are not emotionally engaged with the material they are learning and by the teachers who instruct them. Teachers who facilitate healthy play provide an ideal means of integrating social, emotional, and intellectual growth in a stage-appropriate way.

Standardized Education

Standardized Testing. "Standards-Based Education" was a cornerstone of President George W. Bush's election campaign, and it has received near unanimous bipartisan support at the federal, state, and local levels of government. It goes without saying that preschool education should be required to meet the highest standards. However, assertions concerning what these standards should be, and how they should be assessed, raise profound philosophical, psychological, pedagogical, and ethical issues, which should not be left to politicians or the business community, as has largely been the case. Furthermore, initial efforts to create and assess standards have punished the very school districts in need of the greatest support. In a tragic irony, schools that don't perform well *because* they lack resources and *because* they are teaching children with multiple needs are frequently denied aid because of their students' poor test scores, thus deepening existing inequities. In many instances, teachers' job security and salaries are also tied to test scores. As a result, many teachers feel pressured to get results by *teaching to the test,* even though the tests themselves are insensitive barometers of what and how children should be learning. No amount of testing will address the root causes of the inequities in public education. We will not level the playing field until every child has access to medical care, safe housing, nourishing food, after-school programs, small class sizes, and quality education.

We are now seeing the mind-set of high-stakes testing filtering down to preschools, as their test scores also become tied to funding. It is painful to even contemplate three- and four-year-olds being prepped for tests and having to feel anxious about their performance. Children as young as two years old are now being diagnosed with attention deficit disorders and treated with Ritalin. We can't help but feel that the pathology resides not within the child, but within the culture that demands sustained attention and regimentation from children barely out of diapers.

Standardized Minds. Advances in computer technology in the 1960s were the catalyst for the creation of the *information-processing* model of thinking. This model, with the computer as its guiding metaphor, has become the backbone of American educational philosophy (see chapter 6; Kane, 1999). The goals of education are thus construed as giving children the skills to *process information* and solve problems in much the same fashion as a computer. Some of our leading cognitive neuroscientists are taking this metaphor one step further and conceptualizing the human brain as an organic computer (Kane, 1999).

So enamored are we of our machines that we have narrowed our definition of intelligence to that which most computers can do faster and better than we, and in so doing, lose sight of the qualities that enable us to weave the vibrant tapestry of human potential. These include: emotion, intuition, spirituality, creativity, artistry, morality, and the ability not just to solve a problem, but to recognize in the first instance that a problem exists and is worthy of our attention. Given the leading role that the information-processing model plays in American education, it comes as no surprise that computer software, scripted teaching, and standardized tests now rule the classroom, in our efforts to make our children as clever as our machines. It also follows that the

visual and performing arts, humanities, mentoring, experiential learning, and opportunities to create meaning out of experience (as opposed
to gathering facts) are increasingly viewed as expendable. Thus, for
many children, education has become a sterile affair, which will not
enable them to acquire or value the full palette of human abilities.

"Standardized" Children. It seems that the divide between established
and incontrovertible principles of child development on the one hand, and
educational practice on the other, is widening. While the theories of Piaget
(1950), Vygotsky (1978), Erikson (1985), Gardner (1993), and Greenspan
(1997), among others, have taught us to be aware of children's developmental timetables and individual learning styles, as well as the need for
sensitive scaffolding, experience-based learning, and an emotional connection to the material being taught, we are moving in the diametrically
opposite direction. Ever-larger class sizes and standardized testing demand standardized methodologies, and human mentors are being replaced by machines. But children are not turned out of cookie cutters; they
enter the school system with a unique mix of temperamental, learning,
and intellectual profiles. And they should not be expected to cope with a
uniform approach to learning any more than adults would be expected
to enter a single career track. (How easily, for example, could an accoun-
tant and a sculptor change roles?)

Alexander Thomas and Stella Chess (1977) discovered that children
typically inherit one of three enduring temperaments or genetically
primed clusters of traits, which they named "easy," "slow-to-warm-
up," and "difficult." Although Western cultures favor so-called "easy"
children, who are habitually cheerful, quick to establish routines in
infancy, and capable of adapting readily to new experiences, only 40
percent of their sample fell into this category, but *all* of the children
were regarded as normal. Follow-up research reveals that these temperamental categories exist in many different cultures, and that it is
not always the *easy* children who make the best adjustment to their
environment. Evolutionary pressures spanning millions of years selected not one but several temperamental styles, each of which is optimal in specific environments. Psychiatrist Stanley Turecki (cited in
Armstrong, 1997) estimates that as many as 20 percent of American
children fit into the "difficult" category, and that these children have
some or all of the characteristics typically associated with ADHD. He
emphasizes, as did Thomas and Chess, that these are *normal* children.
We used to have many names for these children; they were bullheaded,
stubborn, a handful, mischievous, daredevils, bundles of energy, or
dreamers. Increasingly, however, we have diagnostic categories. Recent

cultural trends have lessened our tolerance for children who do not fit the "easy" profile. This is particularly worrisome because creative or precocious children have notoriously difficult times fitting into mainstream settings and are becoming increasingly at risk for diagnosis and medication which may ease their adjustment but undermine the very qualities that make them unique.

Recent research supports the concept of learning styles—the idea that people learn optimally in different ways (Kleinfeld, 1994). For example, we may be visual versus auditory learners, or "central-task" as opposed to "incidental" learners (Armstrong, 1997). At the same time, Gardner's (1993) theory of multiple intelligences has been widely heralded and firmly establishes that intelligence wears many cloaks. However, the American school system continues to favor children who are visual, central-task learners and whose intellectual strengths lie in the arena of language and mathematics. Our growing knowledge about temperament, learning styles, and intelligences should be mirrored in educational reform. Unfortunately, the converse is true as the "standards" movement gains momentum.

Prior to the institution of compulsory education, children who did not do well in school had other viable options, including working alongside their parents or caring for younger siblings. Today, all children, regardless of temperament or talents, must succeed in a school system that is making ever-greater demands. Children are expected to function in crowded classrooms, with many distractions, to work for long periods of time without supervision, to succeed or fail according to narrow parameters, and to begin to manage these demands at increasingly younger ages. Preschool and kindergarten children also have to cope with extended days created not for their intellectual or social benefit, but to accommodate the needs of working parents. Is it any wonder that increasing numbers of children are exhibiting difficulties with attention, impulse control, anxiety, and depression? The changes that are taking place in public education today born of budget cuts and the desire to position our children competitively in the world market are not good for children. They are *disastrous* for children whose talents and temperaments are a poor fit for the average classroom. While we may be successful in achieving higher average test scores, some of our most talented and creative children are being sidelined by repeated experiences of failure, emotional strain, and diagnoses that may lead to drugs or placement in "special" classrooms. Charles Darwin and Albert Einstein were notoriously poor students. What would our world be like today if they had been diagnosed with

ADHD and given Ritalin so that they too could sit quietly and copy their letters?

Wired Classrooms

Computer- and Internet-based learning has become *de rigueur* in the kindergarten. This trend has become so pervasive and reflexive that educators do not trouble to ask *whether* computer and Internet technologies enhance learning, but rather *which* technologies and programs should be purchased and how to fund these purchases. Tragically, the wiring of American schools is being funded by slashing budgets, space, and time for creative play, the visual and performing arts, music, field trips, and physical education. Even library budgets are being eliminated in support of the purchase of technologies (Cordes & Miller, 2000). Apparently, in our "race to read," books need no longer apply!

Despite the fantastic sums of money spent on classroom technologies by all levels of government, private industry, and parents, the quality of research on the benefits of computers in the early childhood classroom has been scant and of low quality, with results that are inconclusive at best. In contrast, there is considerable research to support the educational value of play, the arts and humanities, physical education, and small classroom size (Cordes & Miller, 2000; Klugman & Smilansky, 1990). What then, we are compelled to ask, is driving the push to wire the classroom? As Cordes and Miller document in *Fool's Gold* (2000), the immediate catalysts for these trends stem from (1) the technology industry, for which children form an inordinately profitable market, and (2) politicians; in part because of campaign pledges from the technology industry and in part because of the desire to train children to be competitive in the technologically driven global economy.

We have come to accept the sound bite that "computers and the Internet are the great levelers that will give children from all walks of life access to excellence in education and the good life." Many parents, even those with very limited resources, believe that if they don't provide their children with access to computers at home and at school, they are disadvantaging them. They feel that their children are making productive use of their time when they are using educational software, surfing the Net, or even playing computer games as opposed to watching television. Whereas a decade or so ago, it was rare to see a toddler sitting in front of a computer screen, today, software designed specifically for toddlers and even infants has become a successful market niche (Healy, 1998).

We can only imagine the impact on a child's developing nervous system of being exposed to hours of screen time and virtual reality each day beginning in infancy. What is the effect of being bombarded on the one hand with rapid-fire images, and starved on the other for sensory experience in the three-dimensional world, the human touch, and interpersonal connection? We can *only* imagine, because as Jane Healy (1998) informs us, no one is doing the research. Nonetheless, based on a thorough analysis of the literature on brain development during early childhood, and her own clinical observations, Healy concludes that heavy computer use prior to the age of seven years may generate a range of emotional, social, and intellectual deficits. It is intriguing to note that many of these symptoms dovetail with key features of Autistic Spectrum Disorders. These include: (1) diminished language skills, (2) interpersonal difficulties, (3) an inability to play symbolically, (4) difficulty integrating multimodal sensory experiences, (5) impoverished affective capacity, and (6) a poorly developed theory of mind (see chapter 4 for further discussion).

Temple Grandin, a professor who suffers from autism, and is an acclaimed author on the subject of autism, states that she finds an analogue of her own wiring in the computer. "I use Internet talk because there is nothing closer to how I think" (*New York Times*, cited in Healy, 1998, p. 173). What is the effect of imposing on children a cyber world that recreates a "best-fit" environment for autistic individuals?

TRENDS IN AMERICAN SOCIETY

Thus far, I have suggested that certain trends in education are insensitive to children's psychological needs, and may be contributing to the recent upsurge of psychiatric disturbance. This begs the question: What underlying currents in American culture are fomenting these changes? Why have so many policymakers, parents, and educators become obsessed with teaching three-year-olds—barely out of diapers—to read, in increasingly uniform, high-tech settings? We will now examine features of American life that are directly or indirectly influencing what is happening in the classroom.

Trends in the Workplace

Throughout most of human history, women have worked and raised children. Until the time of the industrial revolution in the early to mid–nineteenth century, work took place predominantly in the home or in the community. Work was visible and meaningful to children (e.g., baking, farming, gathering), who worked and played alongside their elders and peers (Westcott, 1986). As paid work became increasingly removed from the home, requiring specialized training, women were initially limited to the domestic sphere and were denied access to higher education. Those who were not suited to their narrowly prescribed lives sometimes went mad in their efforts to adapt to untenable conditions or welcomed the numbing effects of alcohol and, more recently, Valium (Olfman, 1994). In the first decades of the twentieth century, children's well-being was at times purchased with their mothers' sanity. With the exception of a few "glass ceilings," women are now free to work at virtually any profession. While these changes are essential and only for the good, concomitant changes to ensure the integrity of family life did not occur. Today, it is children whose psychological well-being is compromised. Tragically, we have traded one untenable set of expectations in family life for another (Elkind, 1988).

The Cult of Individualism. The quintessentially American valorization of rugged *individualism* has served American pioneers and successive waves of immigrants fleeing oppression very well. In the 1960s and 1970s, the lure of self-actualization led feminists in North America to pursue *individual* rights for women as exemplified by the Equal Rights Amendment, while their sisters in Europe focused on *family* rights. As a consequence, many Western European nations have established exemplary systems of universal health care, regulated and subsidized day care, parental and child sick leave, family-friendly work policies, and a living wage. The social policies of these countries (Sweden is an excellent example) loudly proclaim that women's contributions to the workforce are valued, and that children are their nations' treasure (Scarr, 1996).

In stark contrast, the structure of the workforce in the United States is still designed for the (now mythical) middle-class male in a traditional marriage with a stay-at-home wife to maintain his home, cook his meals, and see to the needs of the children. In consequence, many working mothers find themselves working long hours in order to keep their jobs or advance to more challenging ones, and then coming home to do a second full-time shift with their children. Without the protection of a living wage or a welfare system, many parents are forced to cobble together two or three full-time jobs, and to leave their children in unregulated and unsafe care (Hewlett & West, 1998).

Contrary to predictions that technology would create a leisure society, we are actually working longer hours and earning less than our parents or grandparents. With our cell phones, e-mail, and fax machines, we are never more than a click away from the office, and so for many, the workday has become a multitasking juggling act that never really ends. Rather than leveling the playing field, it seems that the divide between rich and poor in the postindustrial world is becoming a yawning chasm and the gap between the middle class and the poor is narrowing. As television and the Internet continue to promote relentless consumerism and immediate gratification, and successive administrations continue to impoverish aid to struggling families, parents are increasingly less able or willing to take responsibility for their children. And so, without the safety net of community or family, many children are fending for themselves—they are becoming miniature adults, and adults are becoming more childlike (Postman, 2000).

Women's liberation and the technological revolution were meant to improve the quality of life. Instead, many of us are working more and feeling increasingly time-pressured and unhappy. If anything speaks to our current malaise, it is the fact that Americans consume "nearly as many psychotropic drugs as does the rest of the world combined, including about 80 to [90] percent of all the Ritalin in the world . . . and a majority of all the Prozac" (DeGrandpre, 1999, p. 174). It seems that increasingly we rely on drugs to cope with the stress of living.

How do parents resolve the cognitive dissonance imposed by the desire to be successful in their work and responsible parents when the structure of the workplace makes it so difficult? One increasingly visible response is to deny that childhood is a distinct developmental phase and that children have special needs. When we deny the existence of childhood, it also becomes easier to configure the preschool as a form of job training and to allow educational software and the Internet to take our place as sources of mentoring and wisdom in our children's lives. The recent spate of books that privilege the importance of peer over parental influence, children's fashions, music, makeup, and uncensored access to information through the Internet both reflect and hasten the disappearance of childhood (Postman, 2000).

The waning belief in childhood as a distinct phase of life helps us to make sense of two seemingly contradictory trends. Many parents working long hours may (1) enroll their children in a host of structured and competitive after-school programs—witness the "hurried-child syndrome" (Elkind, 1988)—or (2) they may render their children silent and invisible by offering them a variety of screens (television, computer, etc.). On the one hand, we have the child who, like the winning racehorse, spends every waking hour perfecting her skills (Damon, 1995). On the other hand, we have the child who is immersed in a world of virtual reality or a sea of information that she is not equipped to process. In either case, the child's developmental imperatives are not being respected.

In fairness to hard-working parents, our postindustrial society provides them with few, if any, guidelines. Rapid technological advances that radically alter our lifestyles, combined with the advent of the nuclear (as opposed to the extended) family, often leave us devoid of role models. The highly technical and abstract nature of most labor renders it incomprehensible to children who consequently cannot readily participate in work that is deemed valuable or essential to the well-being of the family or community. Instead, we create work for children in the form of skills development, be it dance classes or foreign language study, and we provide them with endless entertainments. This creates a culture of egocentrism in which children are groomed to be the best at several activities to further their own sense of worth, but that have no immediate bearing on the welfare of society (Damon, 1995).

While we as a society are denying childhood, children are informing us that their developmental needs are being ignored at our peril. The increasing number of children who are diagnosed and drugged for an ever-widening spectrum of pathologies (Surgeon General, 2001) tell us that we must examine the values that inform the choices we are making for our children.

Screen Nation

Our cultural love affair with technology has rapidly transformed children's environments into ones that are dominated by screens. We use screens to baby-sit, educate, mentor, and silence our children. As a parent, I am struck that there is virtually no public place that I can take my children that does not offer them some form of screen entertainment, whether it be the department store, shoe store, furniture store, hair salon, grocery store, or museum. Even our local library—the last bastion of literacy—has banks of computers designated for children. Inevitably, gaudy cartoon images and electronic voices permeate the children's section, and all of the children who are old enough to leave their mothers' laps are staring at computer screens.

Rapid-Fire Culture. Richard DeGrandpre (1999) coined the phrase "rapid-fire culture" to describe our exponentially accelerating pace of life. Technologies allow us instant global communication and information, to reach any destination in the world within a day, or to be dazzled by increasingly complex computer-generated virtual realities, providing intense levels of stimulation to the relatively passive consumer. DeGrandpre reminds us that our brains are wired to respond to novelty and to tune out steady sources of stimulation. Thus, for example, we might stop "hearing" the steady noise of traffic or "seeing" a light that has been flickering in the background. In the past, there were natural brakes on how much we could consume or how fast we could pace ourselves. But today's technology gives us unlimited access to speed and novelty. Thus, DeGrandpre (1999) suggests that "[r]apid-fire culture has transformed the American mind . . . by promoting sensory adaptation in a world of constant sensory consumption" (p. 204). The increased use of stimulants in our society including coffee (note the proliferation of coffee bars) and recreational drugs like cocaine, crack, hallucinogens with stimulant properties like ecstasy, and the methamphetamine epidemic in the southwestern United States support DeGrandpre's theory.

Preschoolers compose the single largest TV audience, watching an average of fifty-four hours per week (TV-Free America, cited in Jenkinson, 2000). When we add to this figure the time spent playing computer games, the implications are staggering. This could indeed explain why some children may lack the patience or discipline for the slow pace of the classroom and come to rely on Ritalin to provide the level of stimulation that their brains have grown to crave.

Screen Rage. Psychiatrist Marilyn Benoit (2000) is struck by the poor frustration tolerance that many youngsters have today. She believes that it is directly related to their high-tech lifestyles:

> [c]hildren now live in an ecology of technology . . . as [p]arents provide more elaborate video games, TVs and entertainment centers in their children's rooms, where the kids can cocoon themselves in their multimedia environment. Those same kids go to the ATM with the parent and see real money emerge from a machine with the use of a plastic card and the touch of some buttons. . . . Many children are now on the internet receiving almost instant responses to queries. Groups can form instant "chat rooms," creating rapid virtual social gatherings. A recent cartoon by Mike Twohy in the *Washington Post* (1/11/00) depicted a young boy leaving the family dinner table in anger while shouting "Fine—I'll go talk to my chat room family!" The instant solution is available through the capability of technology to readily substitute a new social entity and gratify his perceived needs. The emerging mantra of this technological era is *"wait no more."*

Benoit is deeply concerned about the potential link between "technology, instant gratification, poor frustration tolerance, lack of empathy, and aggression." She notes a troubling increase in the diagnosis of *explosive children* who are "unable to cope with the slightest of frustrations, and lash out aggressively. They are entitled, demanding, impatient, disrespectful of authority, often contemptuous of their peers, unempathic and easily 'wounded.'"

While Benoit remains circumspect about the relationship between screen technologies and the recent spate of school shootings, Lt. Col. Dave Grossman (2000) is not:

> Michael Carneal, the 14-year old killer in the Paducah, Kentucky, school shootings, had never fired a real pistol in his life. He stole a .22 pistol, fired a few practice shots, and took it to school. He fired 8 shots at a high school prayer group. He hit 8 different kids with eight shots, five of them head shots and the other three upper torso. I train numerous elite military and law enforcement organizations around the world. When I tell them of this achievement they are stunned. Nowhere in the annals of military or law enforcement history can I find an equivalent "achievement." Where does a 14-year-old boy who never fired a gun before get the skill and the will to kill? Video games and media violence.

While some people take comfort in a reported decline in the murder rate in recent years, Grossman points out that fewer deaths are occurring due to more sophisticated life-saving techniques, but, in fact, *attempted* murder has gone up from around 60 per 100,000 in 1957, to more than 440 per 100,000 by the mid-1990s, and these same increases are occurring in Canada, South America, Japan, and several European nations. Grossman, a psychology professor at West Point who has done extensive research on "how we enable people to kill," points out that:

> most healthy members of most species have a powerful, natural resistance to killing their own kind. . . . [Even when we] are overwhelmed with anger and fear . . . we slam head on into that hard-wired resistance against killing. During World War II, we discovered that only 15–20 percent of the individual riflemen would fire at an exposed enemy soldier. . . . When the military became aware of this, they systematically went about the process of "fixing" this "problem." And fix it they did. By the Korean War around 55 percent of the soldiers were willing to fire to kill. And by Vietnam the rate rose to over 90 percent. (Grossman, 2000)

Grossman points out that all of the elements used in desensitizing soldiers so that they can kill on the battlefield—*brutalization, classical conditioning,* and *operant conditioning*—exist in children's lives through media exposure, "but without the safeguards." *Brutalization* refers to the process of breaking down existing mores and norms to accept new values. According to Grossman, we achieve this with our children through massive exposure to violence. The average American child witnesses 200,000 acts of screen violence—including being shot, stabbed, raped, brutalized, and degraded—and 16,000 murders by the time they are eighteen (TV-Free America, cited in Jenkinson, 2000). This process begins in the early years, before a child is able to "discern the difference between fantasy and reality." The American Medical Association (cited in Grossman, 2000) has published definitive research on the relationship between TV violence and murder rates: "In nations, regions or cities where television appears there is an immediate explosion of violence on the playground, and within 15 years there is a doubling of the murder rate. Why 15 years? That's how long it takes for a brutalized two year-old to reach the 'prime crime' years."

The second technique for desensitizing soldiers to murder is *classical conditioning*, in which violence comes to be associated with pleasure. Our children "watch vivid images of human death and suffering and they learn to associate it with: laughter, cheers, popcorn, soda." The third technique used by the military is *operant conditioning* or stimulus-response training. When World War II soldiers learned to fire at a bull's-eye target, they were often unable to perform on the battlefield.

> Now soldiers learn to fire at realistic man-shaped silhouettes that pop up in their field of view hundreds of times, so that they will reflexively shoot to kill . . . when they are in combat and somebody pops up with a gun[.] . . . [E]very time a child plays an interactive point-and-shoot video game, they are learning the exact same conditioned reflex and motor skills. (Grossman, 2000)

Add to this the celebrity status that high school shooters are achieving, and we put gasoline on the fire.

A Socially Patterned Defect. Erich Fromm coined the phrase "socially patterned defect," a pathogenic belief system that becomes normative and sets the stage for behaviors and lifestyles among the majority that impair our capacity for reason and love, but receive such intense and widespread social validation that they do not give rise to inner conflict (cited in Burston & Olfman, 1996). Nazi Germany and the Apartheid regime in South Africa are recent examples. In every society that embraces socially patterned defects, the overwhelming majority internalize the belief system and live relatively unconflicted lives. A few heroic individuals actively rebel against the social norms, but others become symptomatic because they are unable to conform or to rebel without suffering inner turmoil.

I suggest that there is a socially patterned defect in contemporary American culture—our *uncritical* embrace of new technologies. Admittedly, there are parents who are very wary of their children's exposure to the media and the Internet and actively try to limit it. Meanwhile, however, our children are falling ill. Many become dispirited, anxious, hyperactive, or simply unable to relate to others in reaction to hours of exposure to screens and the burgeoning constraints of the classroom. In other cases, perfectly healthy children are being diagnosed because their spontaneous inclinations to play render them unable or unwilling to conform to their environments (e.g., the four-year-old who won't sit still and do desk work, who is given Ritalin to be less disruptive).

Whereas socially patterned defects such as sexism and racism encountered growing opposition in the twentieth century, our immersion in screens may not be as tractable in the twenty-first. First, very few individuals actually experience it as a problem and therefore screen culture is growing, not receding. Second, as Healy (1998) suggests, screen immersion may be hard-wiring our children's brains, creating an addiction to screens. Finally, many scientists now predict that there will come a time in the not-too-distant future when we no longer have control over our technologies as the fields of genetic engineering, robotics, and nanotechnologies merge and "evolve" independently of our efforts and intentions.

Scientists from leading universities including Carnegie Mellon, MIT, Harvard, and Princeton, among others, are predicting a time within this century when our machines will

> become knowledgeable enough to handle their own maintenance, reproduction, and self-improvement without help. When this happens, the new genetic takeover will be complete. Our culture will then be able to evolve independently of human biology and its limitations, passing instead directly from generation to generation of ever more capable intelligent machinery. (Moravec, 1988, in Bowers, 1999, p. 25)

It is chilling to realize that our species may soon be replaced by machinery, and that this is greeted as a *positive* development in some quarters. How is it that a scenario that passed for macabre science fiction a few decades ago is being heralded as the ultimate in progress and emancipation? How have we come to so devalue our humanity? One piece of the puzzle can be found in our cultural adoption of computer-based models of intelligence as the standard to which we aspire. In so doing, we neglect our capacities for feeling, intuiting, spirituality, and morality, and we stop cultivating our ability to express ourselves and be transformed by our active participation in music, dance, visual arts, theatre, poetry, and prose.

As we continue to redesign our children's home and school environments to reflect this bloodless definition of "human" potential, with multiple-screen entertainments, and the use of the Internet and educational software as surrogate parents and teachers; as we slash the arts, humanities, field trips, and physical education from the curriculum, we may indeed be setting the stage in the not-too-distant future for a generation of children who don't privilege reality over virtual reality, human intelligence over machine intelligence. We may be creating a cohort of children for whom merging with their machines may feel less foreign and frightening than a stroll on a nature trail with all of its messy unpredictability.

In a recent article for *Wired* magazine, Bill Joy (in Cordes & Miller, 2000), cofounder and chief scientist for Sun Microsystems and the co-chair of President Clinton's 1998 blue-ribbon panel on the future of information-technology research, reiterated the prediction that we are only decades away from designing artificial life forms that may overtake our species. In addition, he cautioned that we will also have the capacity to produce self-replicating knowledge-enabled weapons of mass destruction. Our desire and capacity for invention is a defining quality of human nature. But it is not our only defining quality. We also have the capacity for journeys of equal depth and complexity in the realms of spirituality, community building, artistry, and communion with nature. Our privileging of scientific discovery over these other modes of development is threatening our very survival. Future generations will need more than ever to redress this imbalance if they are to possess the creative, ethical, and spiritual vision necessary to develop a guiding set of values on which the wise and humane use of technologies is predicated.

CONCLUSION

It is a striking paradox that as adults feel increasingly entitled to place their individual needs first, we are creating educational environments that do not respect children's individuality or their special status as children. We introduce complex concepts long before they are ready to master them, deny their need for play, subject them to uniform curricula and assessment, and transform their world from one that is three-dimensional and experiential to one that is dominated by two-dimensional virtual reality. Then we label and drug the children who do not fit in. Our preoccupation with the genetic and neurological explanations of mental illness, and corresponding indifference to the impact of the environment, speaks to our increasingly mechanized conceptualization of human nature.

If we value our humanity, and wish to avoid the nightmarish scenarios that many scientists are marketing as utopias, we must engage in some collective soul searching to decide what type of world we want our children to inhabit. We must humanize our classrooms and curricula, and stop diagnosing and drugging the very children whose creativity, energy, and budding intellect render them incapable of adjusting well to the narrow constraints of a technological society. It is these very children who might grow up to provide us with the vision and wisdom that future generations will require.

REFERENCES

American Psychiatric Association. (1994). *Diagnostic and statistical manual of mental disorders* (4th ed.). Washington, DC: Author.

Armstrong, T. (1997). *The myth of the A.D.D. child*. New York: Plume.

Benoit, M. (2000). The dot.com kids and the demise of frustration tolerance. In C.

Bowers, C.A. (1999). Why culture rather than data should be understood as the basis of intelligence. In J. Kane (Ed.), *Education, information, and transformation: Essays on learning and thinking* (pp. 23–40). Upper Saddle River, NJ: Prentice-Hall.

Burston, D., & Olfman, S. (1996). Freud, Fromm and the pathology of normalcy: Clinical, social and historical perspectives. In M. Cortina & M. Maccoby (Eds.), *A prophetic analyst: Reclaiming Fromm's legacy* (pp. 301–324). Northvale, NJ: Jason Aronson.

Centers for Disease Control and Prevention (2002). http://www.cdc.gov/ncbddd/dd/ddautism.htm and http://www.cdc.gov/ncbddd/adhd/dadphra.htm.

Children's Defense Fund. (2000). *The state of America's children: Yearbook 2000*. Washington, DC: Author.

Clouder, S. Jenkinson, & M. Large (Eds.), *The future of childhood*. London: Alliance for Childhood.

Cordes, C., & Miller, E. (eds.). (2000). *Fool's gold: A critical look at computers in childhood*. College Park, MD: Alliance for Childhood.

Damon, W. (1995). *Greater expectations: Overcoming the culture of indulgence in America's homes and schools*. New York: The Free Press.

DeGrandpre, R. (1999). *Ritalin nation: Rapid-fire culture and the transformation of human consciousness*. New York: W. W. Norton.

Elkind, D. (1988). *The hurried child: Growing up too fast too soon*. Reading, MA: Addison-Wesley.

Erikson, E. (1985). *Childhood and society*. New York: W. W. Norton.

Fonbonne, E. (2001). Is there an epidemic of autism? *Pediatrics, 107*, 411–413.

Gardner, H. (1993). *Multiple intelligences: The theory in practice.* New York: Basic Books.

Greenspan, S.I. (1997). *The growth of the mind: And the endangered origins of intelligence.* Cambridge, MA: Perseus Books.

Grossman, D. (2000). Teaching kids to kill. In C. Clouder, S. Jenkinson, & M. Large (Eds.), *The future of childhood.* London: Alliance for Childhood.

Healy, J.M. (1998). *Failure to connect: How computers affect our children's mind—and what we can do about it.* New York: Simon & Schuster.

Hetherington, E.M., Bridges, M., & Insabella, G.M. (1998). What matters? What does not? Five perspectives on the association between marital transitions and children's adjustment. *American Psychologist, 53*, 167–184.

Hewlett, S.A., & West, C. (1998). *The War Against Parents.* Boston: Houghton Mifflin Company.

Hoyenga, K.B., & Hoyenga, K.T. (1993). *Gender-related differences: Origins and outcomes.* Boston: Allyn and Bacon.

Jenkinson, S. (2000). Childhood matters: The present future—a Steiner Waldorf perspective. In C. Clouder, S. Jenkinson, & M. Large (Eds.), *The future of childhood.* London: Alliance for Childhood.

Kane, J. (Ed.). (1999). *Education, information and transformation: Essays on learning and thinking.* Upper Saddle River, NJ: Prentice-Hall.

Kennedy, J (2003). Psychotropic drug use in young patients is rising. *Monitor on Psychology, 34*, p. 13.

Kleinfeld, J. (1994). Learning styles and culture. In W. J. Lonner & R. S. Malpass (Eds.), *Psychology and culture* (pp. 151–156). Boston: Allyn and Bacon.

Kluger, J., Song, S., Cray, D., & Ressner, J. (2002, August 19). Young and bi-polar. *Time, 32*, 42.

Klugman, E., & Smilansky, S. (Eds.). (1990). *Children's play and learning.* New York: Teacher's College Press.

McLeod, J.D., & Shanahan, M.J. (1996). Trajectories of poverty and children's mental health. *Journal of Health and Social Behavior, 37*, 207–220.

National Center for Children in Poverty. (2000). *Child poverty in the United States.* New York: Author.

Olfman, S. (1994). Gender, patriarchy and women's mental health: Psycho-analytic perspectives. *Journal of the American Academy of Psychoanalysis, 22(2).*

Piaget, J. (1950). *The psychology of intelligence.* New York: International Universities Press.

Postman, N. (2000). *Building a bridge to the eighteenth century.* New York: Alfred A. Knopf.

Roskos, K.A., & Christie, J.F. (Eds.). (2000). *Play and literacy in early childhood: Research from multiple perspectives.* Mahwah, NJ: Lawrence Erlbaum.

Sacks, P. (1999). *Standardized minds: The high price of America's testing culture and what we can do to change it.* Cambridge, MA: Perseus.

Saracho, O.N., & Spodek, B. (Eds.). (1998). *Multiple perspectives on play in early childhood education*. Albany: State University of New York Press.

Scarr, S. (1996). Individuality and community: The contrasting role of the state in family life in the United States and Sweden. *Scandinavian Journal of Psychology, 37*, 93–102.

Snowdon, D. (2001). *Aging with grace*. New York: Bantam.

Surgeon General. (2001). *Summary of conference on children's mental health*. Department of Health and Human Services [on-line]. Available: http://www.surgeongeneral.gov/topics/cmhchildreport.htm# sum.

Thomas, A., & Chess, S. (1977). *Temperament and development*. New York: Brunner/Mazel.

U.S. Bureau of the Census. (2000). *Statistical abstract of the United States* (120th ed.). Washington, DC: U.S. Government Printing Office.

Vandell, D.L., Dadisman, K., & Gallagher, K. (2000). Another look at the elephant: Child care in the nineties. In R.D. Taylor & M.C. Wang (Eds.), *Resilience across contexts: Family, work, culture, and community* (pp. 91–120). Mahwah, NJ: Lawrence Erlbaum.

Vygotsky, L. (1978). Play and its role in the mental development of the child. In J. Bruner, J. Jolly, & K. Sylva (Eds.), *Play: Its role in development and evolution* (pp. 537-554). New York: Basic Books.

Westcott, M. (1986). *The feminist legacy of Karen Horney*. New Haven: Yale University Press.

Zigler, E.F., & Hall., N.W. (2000). *Child development and social policy: Theory and applications*. New York: McGraw-Hill.

ABOUT THE CONTRIBUTOR

SHARNA OLFMAN, Ph.D., is a clinical psychologist and an associate professor of psychology in the Department of Humanities and Human Sciences at Point Park College, Pittsburgh, where she teaches child development and directs the Childhood and Society Symposium series. Dr. Olfman has published and presented papers on the subjects of gender development, women's mental health, infant care, and child psychopathology. She is the editor of a book series entitled "Childhood in America" for Praeger Publishers, and a partner in the Alliance for Childhood.

Index